ESSAYS ON LOGIC AND LANGUAGE

LOGIC AND LANGUAGE

(FIRST SERIES)

Essays by

PROFESSOR GILBERT RYLE
PROFESSOR J. N. FINDLAY
PAUL EDWARDS
MARGARET MACDONALD
G. A. PAUL
DR. F. WAISMANN
H. L. A. HART
JOHN WISDOM

EDITED WITH AN INTRODUCTION BY
ANTONY FLEW

BASIL BLACKWELL
OXFORD
1968

631 03420 X

First printed 1951
Sixth impression, 1968

Printed in Great Britain by Alden & Mowbray Ltd
at the Alden Press, Oxford
and bound at the Kemp Hall Bindery

Perhaps if ideas and words were distinctly weighed and duly considered, they would afford us another sort of logic and critic than what we have hitherto been acquainted with.

JOHN LOCKE, *An Essay concerning Human Understanding.*

CONTENTS

ESSAYS ON LOGIC AND LANGUAGE

CHAPTER I

INTRODUCTION

By A. G. N. Flew

'PERHAPS if ideas and words were distinctly weighed and duly considered, they would afford us another sort of logic and critic than what we have hitherto been acquainted with' (John Locke, *An Essay concerning Human Understanding*, Bk. IV, chap. 21, § 4). It is this new sort of 'logic and critic', foreseen over two centuries ago by John Locke, which philosophers of the movement represented in this collection of essays have been working to produce. This movement of philosophic opinion has been taking shape and growing in influence in the universities of the British Isles since the beginning of this century. It has gained momentum until now it dominates the philosophy faculties of Oxford, Cambridge, and London, is powerfully represented elsewhere in the United Kingdom, and even has outposts overseas, especially in Australasia and the United States. But in spite of this steady progress inside the philosophic world, almost nothing is known of these developments by that general educated and interested public which has no direct contact with academic philosophy. This isolation is certainly the responsibility, though not perhaps the fault, of the professional philosophers. For those of them who have been in touch with the new developments have been so engrossed in the exciting work of following up their fresh insights that they have for the most part written little or even nothing at all: and what has been written has been in the form of articles which have been published only in technical journals which are not read, and are usually not even accessible, outside professional philosophic circles.

In compiling this collection of articles we had two purposes in view: first, we wanted to do something to end this isolation by making some of these articles available in book form to the lay public, so that they could examine examples of this new kind of philosophizing; second, we wanted to make it possible for people studying philosophy to buy and to own some of the important articles which previously they could only borrow from those few libraries which take the journals in which they originally appeared. In the attempt to achieve these two purposes simultaneously we have had to apply complex multiple principles of selection. In one way this has made the job of selection easier. For, since to choose is always to exclude, the more necessary criteria there are which have to be satisfied by any candidate, the more possible grounds are there upon which otherwise eligible candidates may be reasonably excluded. But in another way the demands of this dual purpose have made the job of selection harder. For articles which would have been ideal for one purpose have had to be excluded because their inclusion would have obstructed the other purpose. Inevitably any editor who has had reluctantly to omit so many first-rate articles must hope that the reception of the present volume will make it possible to produce further similar collections in the near future. Equally inevitably no one other than he will be satisfied with the selection finally made. Perhaps some of the unavoidable regrets over the omission of favourite articles may be softened if we say something more about the criteria of selection which we have tried to apply. And then perhaps something needs also to be said about the origins and character of the philosophic movement from the work of which these essays have been selected.

We have tried to compile a collection of articles which would as far as possible satisfy a multiple set of criteria. Firstly, they had to be immediately readable by and intelligible to the layman. All symbolism was therefore excluded. This was easily achieved, for the protagonists of this movement in England, unlike those of the similar and parallel philosophic tendencies of Logical Positivism and Semanticism on the Continent and in the United States, strive to write in plain untechnical and unsymbolic English. And in this they stand squarely in the British tradition of Thomas Hobbes and John Locke, of Bishop Berkeley and

David Hume. It was Berkeley who proclaimed in the first draft of the Introduction to his *Principles of Human Knowledge* that 'I shall throughout endeavour to express myself in the clearest, plainest, and most familiar manner, abstaining from all hard and unusual terms which are pretended by those that use them to cover a sense abstracted and sublime'. Secondly, the collection had to contain the maximum number of those articles which are most constantly recommended by tutors to their pupils: and thus the claims of Mr. Paul's contribution were irresistible, even in spite of his own protests that, taken out of its context, it might give a wrong impression of the discussions from which it emerged. Thirdly, the essays selected had preferably to be ones which were not, and were not likely to become, available elsewhere in book form. But the claims of Mr. Wisdom's 'Gods' were too strong to be passed over, even though this article should shortly appear again in a volume of his collected papers. Fourthly, an effort was made to select articles representative of as many as possible of the major problems and branches of philosophy. Mr. Edwards, Professor Findlay, and Miss Macdonald deal with aspects of the complexes of problems which are loosely and confusingly dubbed the problems of Induction, Time, and Substance; articles by Mr. Hart, Miss Macdonald, and Mr. Wisdom represent moral philosophy, political philosophy, and the philosophy of religion, respectively. Fifthly, the articles included had to contain patterns of argument which would be stimulating, and suggestive of further developments and applications in other parts of philosophy. Dr. Waismann's conception of 'open texture', for example, could be used to illuminate those fascinating and perplexing legal and quasi-legal dilemmas in which a grammatically interrogative sentence is used to express something which is logically not so much a question asking for an answer as a demand requiring a decision. When we raise the problem 'Is a flying-boat a ship?' we may not be asking for information about flying-boats or ships nor yet even for linguistic information about the present and proper use of the words 'ship' and 'flying-boat'. The problem arises just because the concept of 'ship' does have this 'open texture', and just because we are here faced with one of the situations in which there is no established correct usage. We have no linguistic rules ready to tell us whether a flying-boat is or is not properly describable as a ship. And so the problem has to be taken to the courts for decision. It was so taken by the case of *Polpen Shipping Co.* v. *Commercial Union Assurance Co.*, [1943] K.B.161, and the court decided that the answer was to be in the negative. But this solution to the problem was, of course, not an answer to a question as to what proper usage was, for there was no pre-existing proper usage to be discovered, but a decision as to what proper usage was to be, for now in law at least proper usage is usage which accords with this decision.

Similarly, again, Mr. Wisdom's parable of the dispute about the interventions of a hypothetical gardener, which he offers in order to illuminate problems of the philosophy of religion, might also be exploited as a paradigm of the scientific debates about animal spirits or the ether. For in these debates claims which started their careers as genuine and respectable hypotheses, risking falsification in the hope of achieving verification, degenerated through successive stages of qualification until they were abandoned as idle and scientifically worthless. Like Mr. Wisdom's gardener hypothesis, they were never strictly speaking disproved. They were never disproved because, whenever counter evidence was produced, their protagonists added further qualifications: if the entities could never be seen, that was because they were invisible; if they could never be touched that was because they were intangible; if they could never be weighed that was because they had the unusual property of having no weight; and so on. And there came a time when the scientists abandoned the search for the unfindable animal spirits and the forever elusive ether: not because they had proved that there were no such things but because it had become clear that they never could prove this. These sometime hypotheses had thus degenerated into what was, scientifically considered, mere idle talk. A scientific hypothesis is only valuable so long as it is not in fact proved to be false, but it is only a scientific hypothesis at all so long as it is in principle falsifiable.

It would be possible to go on for a long time pointing out possible developments and applications of things said by the authors of these articles, but this is all that is necessary to illustrate our fifth principle of selection. Perhaps it would be as well to stress here both that the authors are responsible solely for their own contributions and that many of these were first written several years ago: it must not be assumed that any author necessarily agrees with anything written by any other contributor or by the Editor; nor yet that all the contributors would still wish to stand by everything they said when they originally wrote these articles. The final main principle of selection was that the collection taken together had to present a picture of this modern movement in British philosophy which should be as far as possible self-explanatory. It therefore opens with Professor Gilbert Ryle's first powerful plain manifesto, 'Systematically Misleading Expressions'. These six are not all the principles of selection which were employed, and the reasons given are by no means the only reasons for the inclusion of each of the articles mentioned. But enough may have been said to explain, if not perhaps to excuse, the most flagrant omissions.

Perhaps something needs to be said about the nature and the history of the philosophic developments which this volume tries to represent. A few remarks on this subject might help to initiate the uninitiated: though this is neither the time nor the place to write the history of these developments, and actual examples of this sort of philosophizing will show its nature better than any description could hope to do. We have already shown by quotations that these developments are in the main British philosophic tradition: Berkeley was expressing a traditional aspiration when he claimed credit for his good, plain, untechnical English; John Locke was expressing what has been an almost traditional insight when he foresaw that a new sort of logic and critic might arise from the study of ideas and words. Before either Locke or Berkeley wrote, Thomas Hobbes in his *Leviathan* had combined these two aspects of the tradition in his protest that 'the Writings of Schoole-Divines, are nothing else for the most part, but insignificant Traines of strange and barbarous words, or words otherwise used, than in the common use of the Latine tongue; such as would pose Cicero, and Varro, and all the Grammarians of ancient Rome. Which if any man would see proved, let him (as I have said once before) see whether he can translate any Schoole-Divine into any of the Modern tongues, as French, English, or any other copious language: for that which cannot in most of these be made Intelligible, is not Intelligible in the Latine. Which Insignificancy of language, though I cannot note it for false Philosophy; yet it hath a quality, not only to hide the Truth, but also to make men think they have it, and desist from further search.' (This passage comes in Chapter 46 which, like the similar Chapters 1–12, seems to have been almost entirely neglected: Hobbes is still generally supposed to be a political philosopher only.) Passages such as these occur again and again, notably in Book III of Locke's *Essay concerning Human Understanding* and in Berkeley's attacks on the doctrine of abstract ideas, in *The Principles of Human Knowledge* and in Book VII of *Alciphron, or the Minute Philosopher*. But though the classical British philosophers realized that the distortion of and departure from plain, common English was a prime source of philosophical befuddlement and nonsensical construction, and sometimes even, like Locke in the passage quoted at the beginning of this Introduction, foresaw that a new sort of 'logic and critic' might be evoked from the study of ideas and words, they never realized quite how important these insights were, and they consequently failed to follow them up by developing this new sort of 'logic and critic'. This task was left for the philosophers of this and future centuries.

It is almost twenty years since Gilbert Ryle, now Waynflete Professor of Metaphysical Philosophy in the University of Oxford, first proclaimed to the Aristotelian Society his reluctant conversion to the view that the main if not the only proper business of philosophy is 'the detection of the sources in linguistic idioms of recurrent misconstructions and absurd theories'. This proclamation was made at the end of the paper which is reprinted as the first item in this collection. Ten years earlier, Dr. Ludwig Wittgenstein, who was later to become Professor of Philosophy in the University of Cambridge, had claimed in his apocalyptic *Tractatus Logico-Philosophicus* (Kegan Paul, 1922) that 'Most propositions and questions, that have been written about philosophical matters, are not false but senseless. We cannot, therefore, answer questions of this kind at all, but only state their senselessness. Most questions and propositions of the philosophers result from the fact that we do not understand the logic of our language'. And he went on to assert that 'All philosophy is "Critique of language" . . . Russell's merit is to have shown that the apparent logical form of the proposition need not be its real form'. (These sentences come in theses 4.003 and 4.0031.) It is this discovery, which Professor Wittgenstein here credits to his teacher, Bertrand Russell, which is most central and most fundamental to modern British philosophy, or rather to the dominant tendency in modern British philosophizing. Professor Wittgenstein and Professor Ryle were both expressing in their very different ways what was substantially the same insight. To-day they would no doubt wish to put it all very differently, not placing the stress in the same places. But nevertheless it remains true that it is from this and upon this central and fundamental discovery that all the other characteristic doctrines and assumptions of modern British philosophy have been developed and founded. It has been realized that expressions may be grammatically similar and yet logically different. We might say that 'This is past' and 'This is red', 'It goes on to London' and 'It goes on to Infinity', and 'Nobody came' and 'Somebody came' are pairs of grammatically similar expressions. But the members of all these pairs of grammatically similar expressions are logically very different. That is to say that nothing but nonsense and paradox will result if we ask questions about one assertion which are only appropriate and significant when asked about the other. It would be absurd, but it would also be easy, to be misled by the grammatical similarity of 'It goes on to London' to 'It goes on to Infinity' into the misconception that 'Infinity' like 'London' refers to a place, albeit a very queer and very inaccessible place. It is absurd, but to some people it is also easy, to be misled by the grammatical similarity of 'Somebody came' to 'Nobody came' into the misconception that 'Nobody' refers to a person just as does 'Somebody'. It was this misconception of the logic of the word 'Nobody' which Lewis Carroll exploited in *Through the Looking Glass*:

' "I see nobody on the road," said Alice.

' "I only wish *I* had such eyes," the King remarked in a fretful tone. "To be able to see Nobody! And at that distance too! Why, it's as much as *I* can do to see real people, by this light!" '

These are very simple and rather hackneyed examples of the sort of thing which philosophers have been pointing out when they have distinguished between logical and grammatical form, between logical and grammatical resemblance. And when they have talked of misunderstanding the logic of our language they have been alluding to the mistakes made by people who are misled by grammatical similarities or dissimilarities into overlooking logical dissimilarities or similarities. Such is the mistake of the King who treats 'Nobody' as if it had the logic of 'Somebody', as if 'Nobody' referred to somebody, albeit a rather insubstantial somebody. Such, in a slightly more subtle form, is the mistake of the person who fails to appreciate the fact, which we pointed out earlier, that the grammatically interrogative sentence 'Is a flying-boat a ship?' may be used to express something which is not logically interrogative at all. It may be used not as, or to express, a question asking for information but rather to raise a dilemma demanding a decision. Such in ever more subtle forms are the mistakes about the logic of 'defeasible' concepts which Mr. Hart exposes in his paper on 'The Ascription of Responsibility and Rights', the mistakes and perplexities arising from the question 'What is Time?' which Professor Findlay disentangles in his 'Time: a Treatment of some Puzzles'. Such in an even more subtle form still is the mistake about the logic of 'invisible and intangible gardeners', which Mr. Wisdom suggests in the parable of the gardener in his 'Gods': though 'invisible and intangible gardener' is grammatically very similar to 'irritable and irascible gardener', it seems that logically the two expressions are very different indeed; while the latter refers to a particular and not uncommon kind of gardener, the former expression seems logically to be embarrassingly similar to 'no gardener at all'.

It is from this first fundamental insight, that grammatical resemblances and dissimilarities may be logically misleading, that the new sort of logical criticism of language represented in this volume has been developed. It was this discovery that led on to the realization that grammatically respectable sentences might be logically disreputable, that sentences which appear to be good English, which contain no grammatical errors, may logically speaking be nonsense, but specious just because they do resemble grammatically other sentences which are logically quite in order.

And this realization made it easier to appreciate the point and the necessity of the contribution of that apostle of common-sense and linguistic propriety, Professor G. E. Moore. For it has been Professor Moore who has made philosophers see how easy it is to slip into nonsense by even apparently trivial deviations from standard English, how easy it is to use sentences which look all right, which have a close grammatical resemblance to sentences which are indeed proper, but which are nevertheless logically disreputable, which are deviations from standard English to which no sense has been attached.

As such discoveries have been developed and applied in field after field, enterprises of metaphysical construction have seemed less and less practicable, less and less respectable. For anyone who has seen how much muddle and perplexity, how much paradox and absurdity, has already been traced back to its tainted sources in misleading idiom, or in unexplained and unnoticed distortions of standard English, must suspect that any further metaphysical construction which he might be tempted to erect would soon meet with a similar humiliating and embarrassing débacle under the assaults of the new 'logic and critic'.

We have already said enough to suggest that this new sort of 'logic and critic' has strong, deep, traditional roots. Locke foresaw that it was possible to develop it. Hobbes realized how much philosophic absurdity might be dissolved by translating or trying to translate into plain English. Hobbes, Locke, Berkeley, and Hume all realized how too easy it was to be misled by words. Others before Professor G. E. Moore had seen, though unsteadily, how philosophic error could arise from unnoticed distortions of proper language: Locke for instance (in the *Essay* Bk. II, Chap. 21, § 21) wrote 'I think the question is not proper, *whether the will be free*, but *whether a man be free*'. Others before Bertrand Russell had seen, though dimly, that grammatical similarity might conceal logical dissimilarity: Plato for instance pointed out that 'barbarian', though it looked like a positive term such as 'Persian', was logically a negative term, that is to say that barbarians were so called not in virtue of some positive common quality they shared, but in virtue of the fact that none of them possessed the positive quality of being Greek. (The modern English parallel would be the mistake of thinking that foreigners must have something positive, and perhaps positively perverse, in common in virtue of which they are all properly called foreigners.) These and innumerable other points made by previous philosophers will be brought into attention when the history of this modern movement in British philosophy comes to be written. But however much may have been seen by predecessors it remains true that it was left to our contemporaries to develop these flashes of foresight and insight into the new logical criticism of language represented in this volume.[1]

We should like here to thank the authors of the various papers both for giving their consent to the reproduction of their work and for the encouragement they have offered to the whole project. We should also like to thank the Editors of the various journals in which these articles were first published for granting permission for them to be reprinted here. Nos. II, V, VIII, IX and X originally appeared in the *Proceedings of the Aristotelian Society* for 1931–2, 1937–8, 1948–9, 1940–41, and 1944–5, respectively. Nos. VI and VII were first included in Supplementary Volumes XV and XIX of the same *Proceedings*. And Nos. III and IV were published in the *Australasian Journal of Psychology and Philosophy* for 1941 and in *Mind* for 1949, respectively.

Finally we think that all who have been associated with this book and with the philosophic developments which it tries to represent would wish to acknowledge their debt to the genius of one man above all. Though his name is almost unknown outside the world of academic philosophy, everyone who belongs to that world will see throughout this volume marks of the enormous influence, direct and indirect, of the oral teachings of Professor Wittgenstein.

Christ Church,
Oxford.

March 1950.

[1] When I wrote this Introduction I had not yet read Frege's *Foundations of Arithmetic* (Breslau, 1884; and recently reprinted with an English translation, Blackwell, 1950.) I should now be more hesitant about the attribution of the distinction between logical and grammatical form to Russell, especially in view of Frege's remarks about the difference between 'wise' and 'one' (pp. 39–40 of the new edition); and should therefore write this paragraph differently.

CHAPTER II

SYSTEMATICALLY MISLEADING EXPRESSIONS

By Professor Gilbert Ryle

PHILOSOPHICAL arguments have always largely, if not entirely, consisted in attempts to thrash out 'what it means to say so and so'. It is observed that men in their ordinary discourse, the discourse, that is, that they employ when they are not philosophizing, use certain expressions, and philosophers fasten on to certain more or less radical types or classes of such expressions and raise their question about all expressions of a certain type and ask what they really mean.

Sometimes philosophers say that they are analysing or clarifying the 'concepts' which are embodied in the 'judgements' of the plain man or of the scientist, historian, artist, or who-not. But this seems to be only a gaseous way of saying that they are trying to discover what is meant by the general terms contained in the sentences which they pronounce or write. For, as we shall see, '*x* is a concept' and '*y* is a judgement' are themselves systematically misleading expressions.

But the whole procedure is very odd. For, if the expressions under consideration are intelligently used, their employers must already know what they mean and do not need the aid or admonition of philosophers before they can understand what they are saying. And if their hearers understand what they are being told, they too are in no such perplexity that they need to have this meaning philosophically 'analysed' or 'clarified' for them. And, at least, the philosopher himself must know what the expressions mean, since otherwise he could not know what it was that he was analysing.

Certainly it is often the case that expressions are not being intelligently used and to that extent their authors are just gabbling parrot-wise. But then it is obviously fruitless to ask what the expressions really mean. For there is no reason to suppose that they mean anything. It would not be mere gabbling if there was any such reason. And if the philosopher cares to ask what these expressions *would* mean *if* a rational man were using them, the only answer would be that they would mean what they would then mean. Understanding them would be enough, and that could be done by any reasonable listener. Philosophizing could not help him, and, in fact, the philosopher himself would not be able to begin unless he simply understood them in the ordinary way.

It seems, then, that if an expression can be understood, then it is already known in that understanding what the expression means. So there is no darkness present and no illumination required or possible.

And if it is suggested that the non-philosophical author of an expression (be he plain man, scientist, preacher, or artist) does know but only knows dimly or foggily or confusedly what his expression means, but that the philosopher at the end of his exploration knows clearly, distinctly, and definitely what it means, a two-fold answer seems inevitable. First, that if a speaker only knows confusedly what his expression means, then he is in that respect and to that extent just gabbling. And it is not the rôle—nor the achievement—of the philosopher to provide a medicine against that form of flux. And next, the philosopher is not *ex officio* concerned with ravings and ramblings: he studies expressions for what they mean when intelligently and intelligibly employed, and not as noises emitted by this idiot or that parrot.

Certainly expressions do occur for which better substitutes could be found and should be or should have been employed. (1) An expression may be a breach of, e.g., English or Latin grammar. (2) A word may be a foreign word, or a rare word or a technical or trade term for which there exists a familiar synonym. (3) A phrase or sentence may be clumsy or unfamiliar in its structure. (4) A word or phrase may be equivocal and so be an instrument of possible puns. (5) A word or phrase may be ill-chosen as being general where it should be specific, or allusive where the allusion is not known or not obvious. (6) Or a word may be a malapropism or a misnomer. But the search for paraphrases which shall be more swiftly intelligible to a given audience or more idiomatic or stylish or more grammatically or etymologically correct is merely applied lexicography or philology—it is not philosophy.

We ought then to face the question: Is there such a thing as analysing or clarifying the meaning of the expressions which people use, except in the sense of substituting philologically better expressions for philologically worse ones? (We might have put the problem in the more misleading terminology of 'concepts' and asked: How can philosophizing so operate by analysis and clarification, upon the concepts used by the plain man, the scientist, or the artist, that after this operation the concepts are illumined where before they were dark? The same difficulties arise. For there can be no such thing as a confused concept, since either a man is conceiving, i.e. knowing the nature of his subject-matter, or he is failing to do so. If he is succeeding, no clarification is required or possible; and if he is failing, he must find out more or think more about the subject-matter, the apprehension of the nature of which we call his 'concept'. But this will not be philosophizing about the concept, but exploring further the nature of the thing, and so will be economics, perhaps, or astronomy or history. But as I think that it can be shown that it is not true in any natural sense that 'there are concepts', I shall adhere to the other method of stating the problem.)

The object of this paper is not to show what philosophy in general is investigating, but to show that there remains an important sense in which philosophers can and must discover and state what is really meant by expressions of this or that radical type, and none the less that these discoveries do not in the least imply that the naïve users of such expressions are in any doubt or confusion about what their expressions mean or in any way need the results of the philosophical analysis for them to continue to use intelligently their ordinary modes of expression or to use them so that they are intelligible to others.

The gist of what I want to establish is this. There are many expressions which occur in non-philosophical discourse which, though they are perfectly clearly understood by those who use them and those who hear or read them, are nevertheless couched in grammatical or syntactical forms which are in a demonstrable way *improper* to the states of affairs which they record (or the alleged states of affairs which they profess to record). Such expressions can be reformulated and for philosophy but *not* for non-philosophical discourse must be reformulated into expressions of which the syntactical form is proper to the facts recorded (or the alleged facts alleged to be recorded).

I use 'expression' to cover single words, phrases, and sentences. By 'statement' I mean a sentence in the indicative. When a statement is true, I say it 'records' a fact or state of affairs. False statements do not record. To know that a statement is true is to know that something is the case and that the statement records it. When I barely understand a statement I do not know that it records a fact, nor need I know the fact that it records, if it records one. But I know what state of affairs *would* obtain, if the statement recorded a state of affairs.

Every significant statement is a quasi-record, for it has both the requisite structure and constituents to be a record. But knowing these, we don't yet know that it is a record of a fact. False statements are pesudo-records and are no more records than pseudo-antiquities are antiquities. So the question, What do false statements state? is meaningless if 'state' means 'record'. If it means, What *would* they record if they recorded something being the case? the question contains its own answer.

When an expression is of such a syntactical form that it is improper to the fact recorded, it is systematically misleading in that it naturally suggests to some people—though not to 'ordinary' people—that the state of affairs recorded is quite a different sort of state of affairs from that which it in fact is.

I shall try to show what I am driving at by examples. I shall begin by considering a whole class of expressions of one type which occur and occur perfectly satisfactorily in ordinary discourse, but which are, I argue, *systematically misleading*, that is to say, that they are couched in a syntactical form improper to the facts recorded and proper to facts of quite another logical form than the facts recorded. (For simplicity's sake, I shall speak as if all the statements adduced as examples are true. For false statements are not formally different from true ones. Otherwise grammarians could become omniscient. And when I call a statement 'systematically misleading' I shall not mean that it is false, and certainly not that it is senseless. By 'systematically' I mean that all expressions of that grammatical form would be misleading in the same way and for the same reason.)

I. Quasi-ontological Statements

Since Kant, we have, most of us, paid lip service to the doctrine that 'existence is not a quality' and so we have rejected the pseudo-implication of the ontological argument; 'God is perfect, being perfect entails being existent, ... God exists'. For if existence is not a quality, it is not the sort of thing that can be entailed by a quality.

But until fairly recently it was not noticed that if in 'God exists' 'exists' is not a predicate (save in grammar), then in the same statement 'God' cannot be (save in grammar) the subject of predication. The realization of this came from examining negative existential propositions like 'Satan does not exist' or 'unicorns are non-existent'. If there is no Satan, then the statement 'Satan does not exist' cannot be about Satan in the way in which 'I am sleepy' is about me. Despite appearances the word 'Satan' cannot be signifying a subject of attributes.

Philosophers have toyed with theories which would enable them to continue to say that 'Satan does not exist' is none the less still somehow about Satan, and that 'exists' still signifies some sort of attribute or character, although not a quality.

So some argued that the statement was about something described as 'the idea of Satan', others that it was about a subsistent but non-actual entity called 'Satan'. Both theories in effect try to show that something may *be* (whether as being 'merely mental' or as being in 'the realm of subsistents'), but not be in existence. But as we can say 'round squares do not exist', and 'real nonentities do not exist', this sort of interpretation of negative existentials is bound to fill either the realm of subsistents or the realm of ideas with walking self-contradictions. So the theories had to be dropped and a new analysis of existential propositions had to begin.

Suppose I assert of (apparently) the general subject 'carnivorous cows' that they 'do not exist', and my assertion is true, I cannot really be talking about carnivorous cows, for there are none. So it follows that the expression 'carnivorous cows' is not really being used, though the grammatical appearances are to the contrary, to denote the thing or things of which the predicate is being asserted. And in the same way as the verb 'exists' is not signifying the character asserted, although grammatically it looks as if it was, the real predicate must be looked for elsewhere.

So the clue of the grammar has to be rejected and the analysis has been suggested that 'carnivorous cows do not exist' means what is meant by 'no cows are carnivorous' or 'no carnivorous beasts are cows'. But a further improvement seems to be required.

'Unicorns do not exist' seems to mean what is meant by 'nothing is *both* a quadruped *and* herbivorous *and* the wearer of one horn' (or whatever the marks of being an unicorn are). And this does not seem to imply that there are some quadrupeds or herbivorous animals.

So 'carnivorous cows do not exist' ought to be rendered 'nothing is both a cow and carnivorous', which does not as it stands imply that anything is either.

Take now an apparently singular subject as in 'God exists' or 'Satan does not exist'. If the former analysis was right, then here too 'God' and 'Satan' are in fact, despite grammatical appearance, predicative expressions. That is to say, they are that element in the assertion that something has a specified character, which signifies the character by which the subject is being asserted to be characterized. 'God exists' must mean what is meant by 'Something, and one thing only, is omniscient, omnipotent, and infinitely good' (or whatever else are the characters summed in the compound character of being a god and the only god). And 'Satan does not exist' must mean what is meant by 'nothing is both devilish and alone in being devilish', or perhaps 'nothing is both devilish and called "Satan" ', or even ' "Satan" is not the proper name of anything'. To put it roughly, '*x* exists' and '*x* does not exist' do not assert or deny that a given subject of attributes *x* has the attribute of existing, but assert or deny the attribute of being *x*-ish or being an *x* of something not named in the statement.

Now I can show my hand. I say that expressions such as 'carnivorous cows do not exist' are systematically misleading and that the expressions by which we paraphrased them are not or are not in the same way or to the same extent systematically misleading. But they are not false, nor are they senseless. They are true, and they really do mean what their less systematically misleading paraphrases mean. Nor (save in a special class of cases) is the non-philosophical author of such expressions ignorant or doubtful of the nature of the state of affairs which his expression records. He is not a whit misled. There is a trap, however, in the form of his expression, but a trap which only threatens the man who has begun to generalize about sorts or types of states of affairs and assumes that every statement gives in its syntax a clue to the logical form of the fact that it records. I refer here not merely nor even primarily to the philosopher, but to any man who embarks on abstraction.

But before developing this theme I want to generalize the results of our examination of what we must now describe as 'so-called existential statements'. It is the more necessary in that, while most philosophers are now forewarned by Kant against the systematic misleadingness of 'God exists', few of them have observed that the same taint infects a whole host of other expressions.

If 'God exists' means what we have said it means, then patently 'God is an existent', 'God is an entity', 'God has being', or 'existence' require the same analysis. So '... is an existent', '... is an entity' are only bogus predicates, and that of which (in grammar) they are asserted is only a bogus subject.

And the same will be true of all the items in the following pair of lists.

Mr. Baldwin—	Mr. Pickwick—
is a being.	is a nonentity.
is real, or a reality.	is unreal or an unreality, or an appearance.
is a genuine entity.	is a bogus or sham entity.
is a substance.	is not a substance.
is an actual object or entity.	is an unreal object or entity.
is objective.	is not objective or is subjective.
is a concrete reality.	is a fiction or figment.
is an object.	is an imaginary object.
is.	is not.
	is a mere idea.
	is an abstraction.
	is a logical construction.

None of these statements is really about Mr. Pickwick. For if they are true, there is no such person for them to be about. Nor is any of them about Mr. Baldwin. For if they were false, there would be no one for them to be about. Nor in any of them is the grammatical predicate that element in the statement which signifies the character that is being asserted to be characterizing or not to be characterizing something.

I formulate the conclusion in this rather clumsy way. There is a class of statements of which the grammatical predicate *appears* to signify not the having of a specified character but the having (or not having) of a specified *status*. But in all such statements the appearance is a purely grammatical one, and what the statements really record can be stated in statements embodying no such quasi-ontological predicates.

And, again, in all such quasi-ontological statements the grammatical subject-word or phrase *appears* to denote or refer to something as that of which the quasi-ontological predicate is being predicated; but in fact the apparent subject term is a concealed predicative expression, and what is really recorded in such statements can be re-stated in statements no part of which even appears to refer to any such subject.

In a word, all quasi-ontological statements are systematically misleading. (If I am right in this, then the conclusion follows, which I accept, that those metaphysical philosophers are the greatest sinners, who, as if they were saying something of importance, make 'Reality' or 'Being' the subject of their propositions, or 'real' the predicate. For at best what they say is systematically misleading, which is the one thing which a philosopher's propositions have no right to be; and at worst it is meaningless.)

I must give warning again, that the naïve employer of such quasi-ontological expressions is not necessarily and not even probably misled. He has said what he wanted to say, and anyone who knew English would understand what he was saying. Moreover, I would add, in the cases that I have listed, the statements are not merely significant but true. Each of them records a real state of affairs. Nor *need* they mislead the philosopher. We, for instance, I hope are not misled. But the point is that anyone, the philosopher included, who abstracts and generalizes and so tries to consider what different facts of the same type (i.e.

facts of the same type about different things) have in common, is compelled to use the common grammatical form of the statements of those facts as handles with which to grasp the common logical form of the facts themselves. For (what we shall see later) as the way in which a fact *ought* to be recorded in expressions *would* be a clue to the form of that fact, we jump to the assumption that the way in which a fact *is* recorded *is* such a clue. And very often the clue is misleading and suggests that the fact is of a different form from what really is its form. 'Satan is not a reality' from its grammatical form looks as if it recorded the same sort of fact as 'Capone is not a philosopher', and so was just as much denying a character of a somebody called 'Satan' as the latter does deny a character of a somebody called 'Capone'. But it turns out that the suggestion is a fraud; for the fact recorded would have been properly or less improperly recorded in the statement ' "Satan" is not a proper name' or 'No one is called "Satan" ' or 'No one is both called "Satan" and is infinitely malevolent, etc.', or perhaps 'Some people believe that someone is both called "Satan" and infinitely malevolent, but their belief is false'. And none of these statements even pretend to be 'about Satan'. Instead, they are and are patently about the noise 'Satan' or else about people who misuse it.

In the same way, while it is significant, true, and directly intelligible to say 'Mr. Pickwick is a fiction', it is a systematically misleading expression (i.e. an expression misleading in virtue of a formal property which it does or might share with other expressions); for it does not really record, as it appears to record, a fact of the same sort as is recorded in 'Mr. Baldwin is a statesman'. The world does not contain fictions in the way in which it contains statesmen. There is no subject of attributes of which we can say '*there* is a fiction'. What we can do is to say of Dickens '*there* is a story-teller', or of Pickwick Papers '*there* is a pack of lies'; or of a sentence in that novel, which contains the pseudo-name 'Mr. Pickwick' '*there* is a fable'. And when we say things of this sort we are recording just what we recorded when we said 'Mr. Pickwick is a fiction', only our new expressions do not suggest what our old one did that some subject of attributes has the two attributes of being called 'Mr. Pickwick' and of being a fiction, but instead that some subject of attributes has the attributes of being called Dickens and being a coiner of false propositions and pseudo-proper names, or, on the other analysis, of being a book or a sentence which could only be true or false *if* someone was called 'Mr. Pickwick'. The proposition 'Mr. Pickwick is a fiction' is really, despite its *prima facies*, about Dickens or else about Pickwick Papers. But the fact that it is so is concealed and not exhibited by the form of the expression in which it is said.

It must be noted that the sense in which such quasi-ontological statements are misleading is not that they are false and not even that any word in them is equivocal or vague, but only that they are formally improper to facts of the logical form which they are employed to record and proper to facts of quite another logical form. What the implications are of these notions of formal propriety or formal impropriety we shall see later on.

II. Statements seemingly about Universals, or Quasi-Platonic Statements

We often and with great convenience use expressions such as 'Unpunctuality is reprehensible' and 'Virtue is its own reward'. And at first sight these seem to be on all fours with 'Jones merits reproof' and 'Smith has given himself the prize'. So philosophers, taking it that what is meant by such statements as the former is precisely analogous to what is meant by such statements as the latter, have accepted the consequence that the world contains at least two sorts of objects, namely, particulars like Jones and Smith, and 'universals' like Unpunctuality and Virtue.

But absurdities soon crop up. It is obviously silly to speak of an universal meriting reproof. You can no more praise or blame an 'universal' than you can make holes in the Equator.

Nor when we say 'unpunctuality is reprehensible' do we really suppose that unpunctuality ought to be ashamed of itself.

What we do mean is what is also meant but better expressed by 'Whoever is unpunctual deserves that other people should reprove him for being unpunctual'. For it is unpunctual men and not unpunctuality who can and should be blamed, since they are, what it is not, moral agents. Now in the new expression 'whoever is unpunctual merits reproof' the word 'unpunctuality' has vanished in favour of the predicative expression '. . . is unpunctual'. So that while in the original expression 'unpunctuality' seemed to denote the subject of which an attribute was being asserted, it now turns out to signify the having of an attribute. And we are really saying that anyone who has that attribute, has the other.

Again, it is not literally true that Virtue is a recipient of rewards. What is true is that anyone who is virtuous is benefited thereby. Whoever is good, gains something by being good. So the original statement was not 'about Virtue' but about good men, and the grammatical subject-word 'Virtue' meant what is meant by '. . . is virtuous' and so was, what it pretended not to be, a predicative expression.

I need not amplify this much. It is not literally true that 'honesty compels me to state so and so', for 'honesty' is not the name of a coercive agency. What is true is more properly put 'because I am honest, or wish to be honest, I am bound to state so and so'. 'Colour involves extension' means what is meant by 'Whatever is coloured is extended'; 'hope deferred maketh the heart sick' means what is meant by 'whoever for a long time hopes for something without getting it becomes sick at heart'.

It is my own view that all statements which seem to be 'about universals' are analysable in the same way, and consequently that general terms are never really the names of subjects of attributes. So 'universals' are not objects in the way in which Mt. Everest is one, and therefore the age-old question what *sort* of objects they are is a bogus question. For general nouns, adjectives, etc., are not proper names, so we cannot speak of 'the objects called "equality", "justice", and "progress"'.

Platonic and anti-Platonic assertions, such as that 'equality is, or is not, a real entity', are, accordingly, alike misleading, and misleading in two ways at once; for they are both quasi-ontological statements and quasi-Platonic ones.

However, I do not wish to defend this general position here, but only to show that in *some* cases statements which from their grammatical form seem to be saying that 'honesty does so and so' or 'equality is such and such', are really saying in a formally improper way (though one which is readily understandable and idiomatically correct) 'anything which is equal to *x* is such and such' or 'whoever is honest, is so and so'. These statements state overtly, what the others stated covertly, that something's having one attribute necessitates its having the other.

Of course, the plain man who uses such quasi-Platonic expressions is not making a philosophical mistake. He is not philosophizing at all. He is not misled by and does not even notice the fraudulent pretence contained in such propositions that they are 'about Honesty' or 'about Progress'. He knows what he means and will, very likely, accept our more formally proper restatement of what he means as a fair paraphrase, but he will not have any motive for desiring the more proper form of expression, nor even any grounds for holding that it is more proper. For he is not attending to the form of the fact in abstraction from the special subject-matter that the fact is about. So for him the best way of expressing something is the way which is the most brief, the most elegant, or the most emphatic, whereas those who, like philosophers, must generalize about the *sorts* of statements that have to be made of *sorts* of facts about *sorts* of topics, cannot help treating as clues to the logical structures for which they are looking the grammatical forms of the common types of expressions in which these structures are recorded. And these clues are often misleading.

III. Descriptive Expressions and Quasi-descriptions

We all constantly use expressions of the form 'the so and so' as 'the Vice-Chancellor of Oxford University'. Very often we refer by means of such expressions to some one uniquely described individual. The phrases 'the present Vice-Chancellor of Oxford University' and 'the highest mountain in the world' have such a reference in such propositions as 'the present Vice-Chancellor of Oxford University is a tall man' and 'I have not seen the highest mountain in the world'.

There is nothing intrinsically misleading in the use of 'the'-phrases as unique descriptions, though there is a sense in which they are highly condensed or abbreviated. And philosophers can and do make mistakes in the accounts they give of what such descriptive phrases mean. What are misleading are, as we shall see, 'the'-phrases which behave grammatically as if they were unique descriptions referring to individuals, when in fact they are not referential phrases at all. But this class of systematically misleading expressions cannot be examined until we have considered how genuine unique descriptions do refer.

A descriptive phrase is not a proper name, and the way in which the subject of attributes which it denotes is denoted by it is not in that subject's being *called* 'the so and so', but in its possessing and being *ipso facto* the sole possessor of the idiosyncratic attribute which is what the descriptive phrase signifies. If Tommy is the eldest son of Jones, then 'the eldest son of Jones' denotes Tommy, not because someone or other *calls* him 'the eldest son of Jones', but because he is and no one else can be both a son of Jones and older than all the other sons of Jones. The descriptive phrase, that is, is not a proper name but a predicative expression signifying the joint characters of being a son of Jones and older than the other sons of Jones. And it refers to Tommy only in the sense that Tommy and Tommy alone has those characters.

The phrase does not in any sense *mean* Tommy. Such a view would be, as we shall see, nonsensical. It means what is meant by the predicative expression, '. . . is both a son of Jones and older than his other sons', and so it is itself only a predicative expression. By a 'predicative expression' I mean that fragment of a statement in virtue of which the having of a certain character or characters is expressed. And the having a certain character is not a subject of attributes but, so to speak, the tail end of the facts that some subject of attributes has it and some others lack it. By itself it neither names the subject which has the character nor records the fact that any subject has it. It cannot indeed occur by itself, but only as an element, namely, a predicative element in a full statement.

So the full statement 'the eldest son of Jones was married to-day' means what is meant by 'someone (namely, Tommy) (1) is a son of Jones, (2) is older than the other sons of Jones [this could be unpacked further] and (3) was married to-day'.

The whole statement could not be true unless the three or more component statements were true. But *that* there is someone of whom both (1) and (2) are true is not guaranteed by their being stated. (No statement can guarantee its own truth.) Consequently the characterizing expression '. . . is the eldest son of Jones' does not *mean* Tommy either in the sense of being his proper name or in the sense of being an expression the understanding of which involves the knowledge that Tommy has this idiosyncratic character. It only *refers* to Tommy in the sense that well-informed listeners will know already, that Tommy and Tommy only has in fact this idiosyncratic character. But this knowledge is not part of what must be known in order to understand the statement, 'Jones' eldest son was married to-day'. For we could know what it meant without knowing that Tommy was that eldest son or was married to-day. All we must know is that someone or other must be so characterized for the whole statement to be true.

For understanding a statement or apprehending what a statement means is not knowing that this statement records this fact, but knowing what *would* be the case if the statement *were* a record of fact.

There is no understanding or apprehending the meaning of an isolated proper name or of an isolated unique description. For *either* we know that someone in particular is called by that name by certain persons or else has the idiosyncratic characters signified by the descriptive phrase, which requires that we are acquainted both with the name or description and with the person named or described. *Or* we do not know these things, in which case we don't know that the quasi-name is a name at all or that the quasi-unique description describes anyone. But we can understand statements in which quasi-names or quasi-unique descriptions occur; for we can know what would be the case if someone were so called or so describable, and also had the other characters predicated in the predicates of the statements.

We see, then, that descriptive phrases are condensed predicative expressions, and so that their function is to be that element or (more often) one of those elements in statements (which as a whole record that something has a certain character or characters) in which the having of this or that character is expressed.

And this can easily be seen by another approach.

Take any 'the'-phrase which is naturally used referentially as the grammatical subject of a sentence, as 'The Vice-Chancellor of Oxford University' in 'The Vice-Chancellor of Oxford University is busy'. We can now take the descriptive phrase, lock, stock, and barrel, and use it non-referentially as the grammatical predicate in a series of statements and expressions, 'Who is the present Vice-Chancellor of Oxford University?' 'Mr. So-and-So is the present Vice-Chancellor of Oxford University', 'Georges Carpentier is not the present Vice-Chancellor of Oxford University', 'Mr. Such-and-Such is either the Vice-Chancellor of Oxford University or Senior Proctor', 'Whoever is Vice-Chancellor of Oxford University is overworked', etc. It is clear, anyhow, in the cases of the negative, hypothetical, and disjunctive statements containing this common predicative expression that it is not implied or even suggested that anyone does hold the office of Vice-Chancellor. So the 'the'-phrase is here quite non-referential, and does not even pretend to denote someone. It signifies an idiosyncratic character, but does not involve that anyone has it. This leads us back to our original conclusion that a descriptive phrase does not in any sense *mean* this person or that thing; or, to put it in another way, that we can understand a statement containing a descriptive phrase and still not know of this subject of attributes or of that one that the description fits it. (Indeed, we hardly need to argue the position. For no one with a respect for sense would dream of pointing to someone or something and saying 'that is the meaning of such and such an expression' or 'the meaning of yonder phrase is suffering from influenza'. 'Socrates is a meaning' is a nonsensical sentence. The whole pother about denoting seems to arise from the supposition that we could significantly describe an object as 'the meaning of the expression "*x*" ' or 'what the expression "*x*" means'. Certainly a descriptive phrase can be said to *refer* to or *fit* this man or that mountain, and this man or that mountain can be described as that to which the expression '*x*' refers. But this is only to say that this man or that mountain has and is alone in having the characters the having of which is expressed in the predicative sentence-fragment '. . . is the so-and-so'.)

All this is only leading up to another class of systematically misleading expressions. But the 'the'-phrases which we have been studying, whether occurring as grammatical subjects or as predicates in statements, were not formally fraudulent. There was nothing in the grammatical form of the sentences adduced

C

to suggest that the facts recorded were of a different logical form from that which they really had.

The previous argument was intended to be critical of certain actual or possible philosophical errors, but they were errors about descriptive expressions and not errors *due* to a trickiness in descriptive expressions as such. Roughly, the errors that I have been trying to dispel are the views (1) that descriptive phrases are proper names and (2) that the thing which a description describes is what the description means. I want now to come to my long-delayed muttons and discuss a farther class of systematically misleading expressions.

Systematically Misleading Quasi-referential 'The'-phrases

1. There frequently occur in ordinary discourse expressions which, though 'the'-phrases, are not unique descriptions at all, although from their grammatical form they look as if they are. The man who does not go in for abstraction and generalization uses them without peril or perplexity and knows quite well what he means by the sentences containing them. But the philosopher has to re-state them in a different and formally more proper arrangement of words if he is not to be trapped.

When a descriptive phrase is used as the grammatical subject of a sentence in a formally non-misleading way, as in 'the King went shooting to-day', we know that if the statement as a whole is true (or even false) then there must be in the world someone in particular to whom the description 'the King' refers or applies. And we could significantly ask 'Who is the King?' and 'Are the father of the Prince of Wales and the King one and the same person?'

But we shall see that there are in common use quasi-descriptive phrases of the form 'the so-and-so', in the cases of which there is in the world no one and nothing that could be described as that to which the phrase refers or applies, and thus that there is nothing and nobody about which or whom we could even ask 'Is it the so-and-so?' or 'Are he and the so-and-so one and the same person?'

It can happen in several ways. Take first the statement, which is true and clearly intelligible, 'Poincaré is not the King of France'. This at first sight looks formally analogous to 'Tommy Jones is not (i.e. is not identical with) the King of England'. But the difference soon shows itself. For whereas if the latter is true then its converse 'the King of England is not Tommy Jones' is true, it is neither true nor false to say 'The King of France is not Poincaré'. For there is no King of France and the phrase 'the King of France' does not fit anybody—nor did the plain man who said 'Poincaré is not the King of France' suppose the contrary. So 'the King of France' in this statement is not analogous to 'the King of England' in the others. It is not really being used referentially or as a unique description of somebody at all.

We can now redraft the contrasted propositions in forms of words which shall advertise the difference which the original propositions concealed between the forms of the facts recorded.

'Tommy Jones is not the same person as the King of England' means what is meant by '(1) Somebody and—of an unspecified circle—one person only is called Tommy Jones; (2) Somebody, and one person only has royal power in England; and (3) No one both is called Tommy Jones and is King of England'. The original statement could not be true unless (1) and (2) were true.

Take now 'Poincaré is not the King of France'. This means what is meant by '(1) Someone is called "Poincaré" and (2) Poincaré has not got the rank, being King of France'. And this does not imply that anyone has that rank.

Sometimes this twofold use, namely the referential and the non-referential use of 'the'-phrases, troubles us in the mere practice of ordinary discourse. 'Smith is not the only man who has ever climbed Mont Blanc' might easily be taken by some people to mean what is meant by 'One man and one man only has climbed Mont Blanc, but Smith is not he', and by others, 'Smith has climbed Mont Blanc but at least one other man has done so too'. But I am not interested in the occasional ambiguity of such expressions, but in the fact that an expression of this sort which is really being used in the non-referential way is apt to be construed as if it *must* be referentially used, or as if any 'the'-phrase was referentially used. Philosophers and others who have to abstract and generalize tend to be misled by the verbal similarity of 'the'-phrases of the one sort with 'the'-phrases of the other into 'coining entities' in order to be able to show to what a given 'the'-phrase refers.

Let us first consider the phrase 'the top of that tree' or 'the centre of that bush' as they occur in such statements as 'an owl is perched on the top of that tree', 'my arrow flew through the centre of the bush'. These statements are quite unambiguous, and convey clearly and correctly what they are intended to convey.

But as they are in syntax analogous to 'a man is sitting next to the Vice-Chancellor' and 'my arrow flew through the curtain', and as further an indefinite list could be drawn up of different statements having in common the 'the'-phrases, 'the top of that tree' and 'the centre of that bush', it is hard for people who generalize to escape the temptation of supposing or even believing that these 'the'-phrases refer to objects in the way in which 'the Vice-Chancellor' and 'the curtain' refer to objects. And this is to suppose or believe that the top of that tree is a genuine subject of attributes in just the same way as the Vice-Chancellor is.

But (save in the case where the expression is being misused for the expression 'the topmost branch' or 'the topmost leaf of the tree') 'the top of the tree' at once turns out not to be referring to any object. There is nothing in the world of which it is true (or even false) to say 'That is the top of such and such a tree'. It does not, for instance, refer to a bit of the tree, or it could be cut down and burned or put in a vase. 'The top of the tree' does not refer to anything, but it signifies an attribute, namely, the having of a relative position, when it occurs in statements of the form '*x* is at or near or above or below the top of the tree'. To put it crudely, it does not refer to a thing but signifies a thing's being in a certain place, or else signifies not a thing but the site or locus of a thing such as of the bough or leaf which is higher than any of the other boughs or leaves on the tree. Accordingly it makes sense to say that now one bough and now another is at the top of the tree. But 'at the top of the tree' means no more than what is meant by 'higher than any other part of the tree', which latter phrase no one could take for a referential phrase like 'the present Vice-Chancellor'.

The place of a thing, or the whereabouts of a thing is not a thing but the tail end of the fact that something is there. 'Where the bee sucks, there suck I', but it is the clover flower that is there which holds the honey, and not the whereabouts of the flower. All that this amounts to is that though we can use quasi-descriptive phrases to enable us to state where something is, that the thing is there is a relational character of the thing and not itself a subject of characters.

I suspect that a lot of Cartesian and perhaps Newtonian blunders about Space and Time originate from the systematically misleading character of the 'the'-phrases which we use to date and locate things, such as 'the region occupied by *x*', 'the path followed by *y*', 'the moment or date at which *z* happened'. It was not seen that these are but hamstrung predicative expressions and are not and are not even ordinarily taken to be referentially used descriptive expressions, any more than 'the King of France' in 'Poincaré is not the King of France' is ordinarily treated as if it was a referentially used 'the'-phrase.

Take another case. 'Jones hates the thought of going to hospital', 'the idea of having a holiday has just occurred to me'. These quasi-descriptive phrases suggest that there is one object in the world which is what is referred to by the phrase 'the thought of going to hospital' and another which is what is referred to by 'the idea of having a holiday'. And anyhow partly through accepting the grammatical *prima facies* of such expressions, philosophers have believed as devoutly in the existence of 'ideas', 'conceptions' and 'thoughts' or 'judgements' as their predecessors did (from similar causes) in that of substantial forms or as children do (from similar causes) in that of the Equator, the sky, and the North Pole.

But if we re-state them, the expressions turn out to be no evidence whatsoever in favour of the Lockean demonology. For 'Jones hates the thought of going to hospital' only means what is meant by 'Jones feels distressed when he thinks of what he will undergo if he goes to hospital'. The phrase 'the thought of...' is transmuted into 'whenever he thinks of...', which does not even seem to contain a reference to any other entity than Jones and, perhaps, the hospital. For it to be true, the world must contain a Jones who is sometimes thinking and sometimes, say, sleeping; but it need no more contain both Jones and 'the thought or idea of so and so' than it need contain both someone called 'Jones' and something called 'Sleep'.

Similarly, the statement 'the idea of taking a holiday has just occurred to me' seems grammatically to be analogous to 'that dog has just bitten me'. And as, if the latter is true, the world must contain both me and the dog, so it would seem, if the former is true, the world must contain both me and the idea of taking a holiday. But the appearance is a delusion. For while I could not re-state my complaint against the dog in any sentence not containing a descriptive phrase referring to it, I can easily do so with the statement about 'the idea of taking a holiday', e.g. in the statement 'I have just been thinking that I might take a holiday'.

A host of errors of the same sort has been generated in logic itself and epistemology by the omission to analyse the quasi-descriptive phrase 'the meaning of the expression "*x*" '. I suspect that all the mistaken doctrines of concepts, ideas, terms, judgements, objective propositions, contents, objectives and the like derive from the same fallacy, namely, that there must be *something* referred to by such expressions as 'the meaning of the word (phrase or sentence) "*x*" ', on all fours with the policeman who really is referred to by the descriptive phrase in 'our village policeman is fond of football'. And the way out of the confusion is to see that some 'the'-phrases are only similar in grammar and not similar in function to referentially-used descriptive phrases, e.g. in the case in point, 'the meaning of "*x*" ' is like 'the King of France' in 'Poincaré is not the King of France', a predicative expression used non-referentially.

And, of course, the ordinary man does not pretend to himself or anyone else that when he makes statements containing such expressions as 'the meaning of "*x*" ', he is referring to a queer new object: it does not cross his mind that his phrase might be misconstrued as a referentially used descriptive phrase. So he is not guilty of philosophical error or clumsiness. None the less, his form of words is systematically misleading. For an important difference of logical form is disguised by the complete similarity of grammatical form between 'the village policeman is reliable' and 'the meaning of "*x*" is doubtful' or again between 'I have just met the village policeman' and 'I have just grasped the meaning of "*x*" '.

(Consequently, as there is no object describable as that which is referred to by the expression 'the meaning of "*x*" ', questions about the status of such objects are meaningless. It is as pointless to discuss whether word-meanings (i.e. 'concepts' or 'universals') are subjective or objective, or whether sentence-meanings (i.e. 'judgements' or 'objectives') are subjective or objective, as it would be to discuss whether the Equator or the sky is subjective or objective. For the questions themselves are not about anything.)

All this does not, of course, in the least prevent us from using intelligently and intelligibly sentences containing the expression 'the meaning of "*x*"' where this can be re-drafted as 'what "*x*" means'. For here the 'the'-phrase is being predicatively used and not as an unique description. 'The meaning of "*x*" is the same as the meaning of "*y*"' is equivalent to '"*x*" means what "*y*" means', and that can be understood without any temptation to multiply entities.

But this argument is, after all, only about a very special case of the systematic misleadingness of quasi-descriptions.

2. There is another class of uses of 'the'-phrases which is also liable to engender philosophical misconstructions, though I am not sure that I can recall any good instances of actual mistakes which have occurred from this source.

Suppose I say, 'the defeat of the Labour Party has surprised me', what I say could be correctly paraphrased by 'the fact that the Labour Party was defeated, was a surprise to me' or 'the Labour Party has been defeated and I am surprised that it has been defeated'. Here the 'the'-phrase does not refer to a thing but is a condensed record of something's being the case. And this is a common and handy idiom. We can always say instead of 'because A is B, therefore C is D' 'the D-ness of C is due to the B-ness of A'. 'The severity of the winter is responsible for the high price of cabbages' means what is meant by 'Cabbages are expensive because the winter was severe'.

But if I say 'the defeat of the Labour Party occurred in 1931', my 'the'-phrase is referentially used to describe an event and not as a condensed record of a fact. For events have dates, but facts do not. So the facts recorded in the grammatically similar statements 'the defeat of the Labour Party has surprised me' and 'the defeat of the Labour Party occurred in 1931' are in logical form quite different. And both sorts of facts are formally quite different from this third fact which is recorded in 'the victory of the

Labour Party would have surprised me'. For this neither refers to an event, nor records the fact that the Labour Party was victorious, but says 'if the Labour Party had won, I should have been surprised'. So here the 'the'-phrase is a protasis. And, once more, all these three uses of 'the'-phrases are different in their sort of significance from 'the defeat of the Conservative Party at the next election is probable', or 'possible', or 'impossible'. For these mean 'the available relevant data are in favour of' or 'not incompatible with' or 'incompatible with the Conservative Party being defeated at the next election'.

So there are at least these four different types of facts which can be and, in ordinary discourse, are conveniently and intelligibly recorded in statements containing grammatically indistinguishable 'the'-phrases. But they can be restated in forms of words which do exhibit in virtue of their special grammatical forms the several logical structures of the different sorts of facts recorded.

3. Lastly, I must just mention one further class of systematically misleading 'the'-phrase. 'The whale is not a fish but a mammal' and 'the true Englishman detests foul play' record facts, we may take it. But they are not about this whale or that Englishman, and they might be true even if there were no whales or no true Englishmen. These are, probably, disguised hypothetical statements. But all I wish to point out is that they are obviously disguised.

I have chosen these three main types of systematically misleading expressions because all alike are misleading in a certain direction. They all suggest the existence of new sorts of objects, or, to put it in another way, they are all temptations to us to 'multiply entities'. In each of them, the quasi-ontological, the quasi-Platonic and the quasi-descriptive expressions, an expression is misconstrued as a denoting expression which in fact does not denote, but only looks grammatically like expressions which are used to denote. Occam's prescription was, therefore, in my view, 'Do not treat all expressions which are grammatically like proper names or referentially used "the"-phrases, as if they were therefore proper names or referentially used "the"-phrases'.

But there are other types of systematically misleading expressions, of which I shall just mention a few that occur to me.

'Jones is an alleged murderer', or 'a suspected murderer',

'Smith is a possible or probable Lord Mayor', 'Robinson is an ostensible, or seeming or mock or sham or bogus hero', 'Brown is a future or a past Member of Parliament', etc. These suggest what they do not mean, that the subjects named are of a special kind of murderer, or Lord Mayor, or hero, or Member of Parliament. But being an alleged murderer does not entail being a murderer, nor does being a likely Lord Mayor entail being a Lord Mayor.

'Jones is popular' suggests that being popular is like being wise, a quality; but in fact it is a relational character, and one which does not directly characterize Jones, but the people who are fond of Jones, and so 'Jones is popular' means what is meant by 'Many people like Jones, and many more like him than either dislike him or are indifferent to him', or something of the sort.

But I have, I think, given enough instances to show in what sense expressions may seem to mean something quite different from what they are in fact used to mean; and therefore I have shown in what sense some expressions are systematically misleading.

So I am taking it as established (1) that what is expressed in one expression can often be expressed in expressions of quite different grammatical forms, and (2) that of two expressions, each meaning what the other means, which are of different grammatical forms, one is often more systematically misleading than the other.

And this means that while a fact or state of affairs *can* be recorded in an indefinite number of statements of widely differing grammatical forms, it is stated better in some than in others. The ideal, which may never be realized, is that it should be stated in a completely non-misleading form of words.

Now, when we call one form of expression better than another, we do not mean that it is more elegant or brief or familiar or more swiftly intelligible to the ordinary listener, but that in virtue of its grammatical form it exhibits, in a way in which the others fail to exhibit, the logical form of the state of affairs or fact that is being recorded. But this interest in the best way of exhibiting the logical form of facts is not for every man, but only for the philosopher.

I wish now to raise, but not to solve, some consequential problems which arise.

1. Given that an expression of a certain grammatical form is proper (or anyhow approximates to being proper) to facts of a certain logical form and to those facts only, is this relation of propriety of grammatical to logical form *natural* or *conventional*?

I cannot myself credit what seems to be the doctrine of Wittgenstein and the school of logical grammarians who owe allegiance to him, that what makes an expression formally proper to a fact is some real and non-conventional one-one picturing relation between the composition of the expression and that of the fact. For I do not see how, save in a small class of specially-chosen cases, a fact or state of affairs can be deemed like or even unlike in structure a sentence, gesture or diagram. For a fact is not a collection—even an arranged collection—of bits in the way in which a sentence is an arranged collection of noises or a map an arranged collection of scratches. A fact is not a thing and so is not even an arranged thing. Certainly a map may be like a country or a railway system, and in a more general, or looser, sense a sentence, as an ordered series of noises, might be a similar sort of series to a series of vehicles in a stream of traffic or the series of days in the week.

But in Socrates being angry or in the fact that either Socrates was wise or Plato was dishonest, I can see no concatenation of bits such that a concatenation of parts of speech could be held to be of the same general architectural plan as it. But this difficulty may be just denseness on my part.

On the other hand, it is not easy to accept what seems to be the alternative that it is just by convention that a given grammatical form is specially dedicated to facts of a given logical form. For, in fact, customary usage is perfectly tolerant of systematically misleading expressions. And, moreover, it is hard to explain how in the genesis of languages our presumably non-philosophical forbears could have decided on or happened on the dedication of a given grammatical form to facts of a given logical form. For presumably the study of abstract logical form is later than the entry into common use of syntactical idioms.

It is, however, my present view that the propriety of grammatical to logical forms is more nearly conventional than natural: though I do not suppose it to be the effect of whim or of deliberate plan.

2. The next question is: How are we to discover in particular cases whether an expression is systematically misleading or not? I suspect that the answer to this will be of this sort. We meet with and understand and even believe a certain expression such as 'Mr. Pickwick is a fictitious person' and 'the Equator encircles the globe'. And we know that if these expressions are saying what they seem to be saying, certain other propositions will follow. But it turns out that the naturally consequential propositions 'Mr. Pickwick was born in such and such a year' and 'the Equator is of such and such a thickness' are not merely false but, on analysis, in contradiction with something in that from which they seemed to be logical consequences. The only solution is to see that being a fictitious person is not to be a person of a certain sort, and that the sense in which the Equator girdles the earth is not that of being any sort of a ring or ribbon enveloping the earth. And this is to see that the original propositions were not saying what they seemed on first analysis to be saying. Paralogisms and antinomies are the evidence that an expression is systematically misleading.

None the less, the systematically misleading expressions as intended and as understood contain no contradictions. People do not really talk philosophical nonsense—unless they are philosophizing or, what is quite a different thing, unless they are being sententious. What they do is to use expressions which, from whatever cause—generally the desire for brevity and simplicity of discourse—disguise instead of exhibiting the forms of the facts recorded. And it is to reveal these forms that we abstract and generalize. These processes of abstraction and generalization occur before philosophical analysis begins. It seems indeed that their results are the subject matter of philosophy. Pre-philosophical abstract thinking is always misled by systematically misleading expressions, and even philosophical abstract thinking, the proper function of which is to cure this disease, is actually one of its worst victims.

3. I do not know any way of classifying or giving an exhaustive list of the possible types of systematically misleading expressions. I fancy that the number is in principle unlimited, but that the number of prevalent and obsessing types is fairly small.

4. I do not know any way of proving that an expression

contains no systematic misleadingness at all. The fact that antinomies have not yet been shown to arise is no proof that they never will arise. We can know that of two expressions '*x*' and '*y*' which record the same fact, '*x*' is less misleading than '*y*'; but not that '*x*' cannot itself be improved upon.

5. Philosophy must then involve the exercise of systematic restatement. But this does not mean that it is a department of philology or literary criticism.

Its restatement is not the substitution of one noun for another or one verb for another. That is what lexicographers and translators excel in. Its restatements are transmutations of syntax, and transmutations of syntax controlled not by desire for elegance or stylistic correctness but by desire to exhibit the forms of the facts into which philosophy is the inquiry.

I conclude, then, that there is, after all, a sense in which we can properly inquire and even say 'what it really means to say so and so'. For we can ask what is the real form of the fact recorded when this is concealed or disguised and not duly exhibited by the expression in question. And we can often succeed in stating this fact in a new form of words which does exhibit what the other failed to exhibit. And I am for the present inclined to believe that this is what philosophical analysis is, and that this is the sole and whole function of philosophy. But I do not want to argue this point now.

But, as confession is good for the soul, I must admit that I do not very much relish the conclusions towards which these conclusions point. I would rather allot to philosophy a sublimer task than the detection of the sources in linguistic idioms of recurrent misconstructions and absurd theories. But that it is at least this I cannot feel any serious doubt.

CHAPTER III

TIME: A TREATMENT OF SOME PUZZLES

By Professor J. N. Findlay

(This article was written in 1941. Though I still agree with its general approach, I am now inclined to attach rather more positive value and importance to the metaphysical perplexities and positions it deals with. It will be obvious that the basic ideas of this paper derive from Wittgenstein.)

THE aim of this paper is to inquire into the causes of some of our persistent perplexities with regard to time and change. We do not propose to offer a solution for these difficulties, but rather to make clear how they have come to worry us. For we shall suggest that they have their origin, not in any genuine obscurity in our experience, but in our ways of thinking and talking, and we shall also suggest that the clear consciousness of this origin is the only way to cure them. It is plain that we do not, in any ordinary frame of mind, find time so hard to understand: we are in fact always competently dealing with what we may describe as 'temporal situations'. We are dealing with such situations whenever we say, without hesitation or confusion, that this lasted longer than that, that this took place at the same time as that, that this has just happened or that that will happen soon. We have no difficulty in showing other people what we mean by such forms of statement, nor in getting them to agree that we have used them truly and appropriately. Yet all these forms of statement, and the situations to which they refer, seem capable of creating the most intense perplexity in some people: people are led to say that time is 'paradoxical', 'contradictory', 'mysterious', and to ask how certain things are 'possible' whose actuality seems obvious. Thus it has been asked how it is 'possible' for anything to reach the end of a phase of continuous change, or how it is 'possible' for that which *is* the case ever to cease being the case, or how it is 'possible' for the duration of any happening to have a length and a measure. In all such cases it seems reasonable to say that the burden of proof that there *is* a genuine problem or difficulty is on the person who feels it, and not on the person who refuses to depart from ordinary ways of speaking. And it certainly does seem odd that people who have always had to deal with changing objects and situations, and whose whole language is perfectly adapted to dealing with them, should suddenly profess to find time so very strange. If time is so odd, we may very well ask, in terms of what things more familiar and understandable shall we proceed to explain it or to throw light on its possibility? We may indeed regard it as a strange disorder that people who have spent all their days 'in time', should suddenly elect to speak as if they were casual visitors from 'eternity'. And it must be our business to cure them of this disorder through a clear awareness of its causes. There is indeed 'a short way with puzzlers' who inquire into the 'possibility' of perfectly familiar and understandable situations: we may simply point to some instance of the kind that perplexes them and say: 'That's how it is possible for so-and-so to be the case'. Thus if a man were to ask me 'How is it possible that that which *is* the case should cease to be the case?', I might simply crook my finger and say 'Now my finger is crooked', then straighten it and say 'Now it has ceased to be crooked. And that's how it's possible for that which *is* the case to cease being the case.'[1] But such an expedient, though perfectly proper in itself, and more than a man has a right to ask for in most cases, would not suffice to allay our questioner's perplexity, since he, presumably, is quite as familiar with ordinary usage as we are.

A treatment of the puzzles of time will also serve to illustrate a treatment which might be applied to many other questions and difficulties. For some people quite readily fall into a mood in which they feel that there is something mysterious and doubtful about things that they would normally regard as elementary and obvious. They are then led to ask questions which seem queer, because it is not in the least plain how one should set about answering them. Thus a man may wonder how it is possible for a number of distinct things to share in the same quality, or whether

[1] The example given and the general method indicated was suggested by Professor Moore's proof that external objects exist. He proves that there are such objects by proving that there are two human hands, the latter being proved 'by holding up his two hands, and saying as he makes a certain gesture with the right hand, "Here is one hand", and adding, as he makes a certain gesture with the left, "and here is another"' (*Proof of an External World*, p. 25). [Reprinted in *British Academy Proceedings*, Vol. 25, 1939).—Editor.]

he really is the same person from year to year, or why *this* world exists rather than any other. Now in ordinary unreflective moods we should regard these questions as either unanswerable or not worth answering, but our questioner plainly wants an answer and he doesn't want an obvious answer. It is plain, in particular, that we couldn't remove our questioner's perplexity by 'appealing to experience', by pointing to anything that both he and we could observe. For he *has* all the kinds of experience that could throw light on his problem, and yet he is puzzled. It seems clear that, where the simplest and most familiar instances of something occasion profound perplexity, we cannot hope to remove such perplexity, or even to allay it, by indefinitely accumulating other instances of the same kind, some of which would be strange and others highly complex. We are accordingly brought back to our supposition that there are some questions which beset us, not because there is anything genuinely problematic in our experience, but because the ways in which we speak of that experience are lacking in harmony or are otherwise unsatisfactory. We are sometimes thrown into a mood of interrogation not because we are in quest of further facts, but because we are in quest of clearer, or less discordant, or merely different ways of verbally dealing with those facts. Such moods of questioning plainly have no answers, in any ordinary sense of 'answer'; we may nevertheless hope to relieve them by becoming clearly conscious of the underlying needs that prompt them, and by deliberately adopting ways of talking that provide appeasement for those needs.

There are other reasons why there is interest in our difficulties with regard to time. These difficulties form a relatively self-contained group of puzzles, which do not seem to share their entrails with too many other philosophical problems. We can find time difficult without finding anything else difficult, but we couldn't be puzzled by matter or mind or knowledge, without being puzzled by practically everything else. Hence we can deal more cleanly with these temporal puzzles than with other issues; they provide, accordingly, a simpler paradigm of method. These puzzles are also important in that philosophical difficulties seem to flourish more readily in the temporal field than in almost any other. It would be safe to say that rapid change and the 'nothingness of the past' are things which can always be relied on spontaneously to vex a large number of unsophisticated people, and so to constitute one of the standing mysteries of our universe. We have reason, of course, to suspect such generalizations; for we know nowadays that there is no way of ascertaining the philosophical reactions of unphilosophical common sense, except by testing and questioning large numbers of people.[1] But in the absence of such testing, vague experience certainly bears witness to the generality of such puzzlement.

We may now point to a circumstance which is certainly responsible for *some* of our difficulties with regard to time. This is the fact that it is possible to persuade a man, by an almost insensible process, to use certain familiar locutions in ways which become, on the one hand, steadily wider and more general, or, on the other hand, steadily narrower and stricter. This persuasive process is only one of the many processes by which an able dialectician can twist or stretch or shift or tear apart the web of words with which we overlay our world. In doing so, he relies on the fact that the boundaries of linguistic usage are seldom clear, that there are always ranges of cases in which it is simply doubtful whether a given locution is or is not applicable, and that there are, in addition, a number of deep-seated tendencies in language which facilitate linguistic shifts in certain directions. In the particular case we are now considering there are, it is plain, words and phrases whose use very readily widens: it is easy to persuade a man that they really *ought* to be used in cases in which it has never before occurred to anyone to use them. And it is also plain that there are words and phrases whose use very readily narrows, so that we are easily persuaded to say that it was 'wrong' or 'improper' to use them in cases where we previously used them without hesitation. And it is possible for the adroit dialectician, by making repeated use of a big stick called 'consistency', on the one hand, and another big stick called 'strictness', on the other hand, to persuade us to use such forms of speech so widely that they apply to everything, or so narrowly that they apply to nothing: the result in either case is to turn a serviceable mode of speaking into one that is totally unserviceable. Good examples of these dialectical processes would be arguments which led us to

[1] See, e.g., Arne Ness's *Truth as conceived by those who are not professional philosophers*, Oslo, 1938. [In *Skrifter utgitt av Det Norske Videnskaps—Akademi i Oslo*, II. *Hist.-Filos. Klasse*, Vol. IV.—Editor.]

use the term 'know' so widely, on the one hand, that we might be said, like the monads of Leibniz, always to know everything, or so narrowly, on the other hand, that we might never be said to know anything. There is, of course, nothing in such an exaggerated width or narrowness of reference which *necessarily* leads to paradoxes or problems. If we persuade a man to use words in new ways, we disorganize his linguistic habits for the time being, but there is no reason why he should not rapidly build up a new set of habits, which will enable him to talk of ordinary situations as plainly and as promptly as before. But the trouble is that such a sudden change of usage *may* produce a temporary disorientation, it is like a cerebral lesion from which an organism needs to recover, and in the interval before recovery sets in, and new connections take the place of the old, a man may readily become a prey to serious confusions. For even after a man has been persuaded to use certain phrases in totally new ways in certain contexts, he may still hark back to old uses in other contexts: he may even try to incorporate both uses in the same context, thus giving rise to statements and questions which cannot be interpreted in either way of speaking.

Now in regard to time it is plain that there is a strong tendency in language to use terms connected with the 'present' in an ever stricter manner, so that, if this tendency is carried to the limit, the terms in question cease to have *any* application, or, at best, a novel and artificial one. It is also plain that *some* of the problems of time are connected with this fact. We can readily be persuaded to use the present tense and the temporal adverb 'now' (as well as the imperfect past and imperfect future tenses and the words 'then', 'at that time', etc.) in stricter and stricter ways; and if we yield completely to such pressure, our normal habits of speech will be disorganized. Our use of the present tense and of the temporal adverb 'now' is not very strict in ordinary circumstances: we are prepared to say, even of happenings that last a considerable time, that they are happening *now*, e.g. we say 'The National Anthem is now being sung', 'The Derby is now being run', etc. Now the present tense and the temporal adverb 'now' *might* have been the sort of speech-form that we tended to use more and more widely, so that we might easily have been persuaded to say 'The history of England is now running its course', 'The heat death of the Universe is now taking place'. We might then have been persuaded to allow that, since a *whole* cannot be happening now, unless all its component *parts* are also happening now, John is now really signing Magna Carta, life on the earth is now really extinct, and so on. The problems that this way of speaking might occasion, would certainly be serious. The natural development of the speech-forms we are considering does not, however, lie in this direction. We tend rather, if pressed, to use the present tense and the temporal adverb 'now' more and more narrowly: thus if we had said that the National Anthem was being sung, and someone asked us 'But what are they singing *just now*?', we should not widen our reference to cover the whole evening's concert, but narrow it to apply to some line or phrase or word or note of the National Anthem. Now since our tendencies lie in *this* direction, we can readily be persuaded to give up saying that anything which takes an appreciable time is happening now. We can be bullied into admitting that this is a 'loose' and 'inaccurate' way of talking. And it is possible to force us to grant that the really strict speaker would not use these forms of speech in the case of anything but a happening which was so short that it took *no time at all*. Thus we might force a man first to admit that nothing which was *past*, nothing which was *no longer there*, could possibly be said to be happening now. We might then press him to admit the additional principle that nothing of which a *part* lay in the past could properly be said to be happening now. We might then persuade him to grant, with regard to any happening that 'takes time', that it doesn't happen 'all at once', but that it has parts which happen one after the other, and that, when any *one* of these parts *is* happening, all the *other* parts either *have* happened or *will* happen. It then becomes easy to prove that no happening which takes time can properly be said to *be* taking place, and that the only parts of it of which such a thing could ever be rightly said, would be parts that took *no time at all*.[1]

[1] The typical historical case of this argument is Augustine, *Confessions* (Book XI: 19, 20): 'Are an hundred years, when present, a long time? See first, whether an hundred years can be present. For if the first of these be now current, it is present, but the other ninety and nine are to come, and therefore are not yet, but if the second year be current, one is now past, another present, the rest to come. And so, if we assume any middle year of this hundred to be present, all before it are past; all after it to come; wherefore an

In all these arguments we are being persuaded to apply linguistic principles which are established in the case of happenings of *fairly long duration*, to happenings of very short duration; we are not obliged, but can be readily pressed, to be 'consistent' in this manner since there are no clear lines between the long and the short. But the result of yielding to this pressure is to turn a serviceable way of talking into one that has no use. For it is obvious that all the happenings that we can point to (in any ordinary sense of 'point to') take time, and that pointing itself takes time, so that if the only happenings of which we may say 'This is happening now' are happenings which take no time, there are no happenings which we can point to, of which we may say 'This is happening now'. Now this does not, of course, imply that a clear and useful meaning cannot be given to phrases and sentences which mention happenings that take no time: it is plain, in fact, that very clear and useful meanings *have* been given to them by a long succession of mathematicians and philosophers. But it is also plain that these new forms of diction may, at first, merely serve to disorganize existing speech-habits, and that, while this lasts, we may fail to give any clear or serviceable meaning to 'happenings which take no time'; we may tend to talk of them as if they were happenings we could point to, in the same sense in which we can point to happenings which *do* take time, and we may further credit them unthinkingly with many of the properties of happenings which *do* take time. Such ways of talking, it is plain, must lead to many quite unanswerable questions.

hundred years cannot be present. But see at least whether that one which is now current itself is present; for if the current month be its first, the rest are to come; if the second, the first is already past, and the rest are not yet. Therefore neither is the year now current present; and if not present as a whole, then is not the year present. For twelve months are a year; of which, whatever be the current month is present; the rest past, or to come. Although neither is that current month present; but one day only; the rest being to come, if it be the first; past, if the last; if any of the middle, then amid past and to come. See how the present time which alone we found could be called long, is abridged to the length scarce of one day. But let us examine that also; because neither is one day present as a whole. For it is made up of four and twenty hours of night and day: of which the first hath the rest to come; the last hath them past; and any of the middle hath those before it past, those behind it to come. Yea, that one hour passeth away in flying particles. Whatsoever of it hath flown away is past; whatever remaineth is to come. If an instant of time be conceived which cannot be divided into the smallest particles of moments, that alone is it, which may be called present, which yet flies with such speed from future to past, as not to be lengthened out with the least stay. For if it be, it is divided into past and future. The present hath no space. Where, then, is the time which we may call long?'

After this preliminary consideration of *one* source of our temporal difficulties, we may turn to Augustine's problem in the eleventh book of the *Confessions*. This we may phrase as follows: 'How can we say of anything that it lasts a long time or a short time? How can a time have length? And how can that length be measured?'[1] What was it, we may ask, that Augustine found so difficult in the length and measure of time? We may perhaps distinguish three aspects of his bewilderment, which might be grounds for anyone's bewilderment. He found it difficult, in the first place (we may suppose), to see how happenings which take *no* time could ever be 'added up' to make the happenings which *do* take time.[2] This difficulty is not peculiar to our thought of time, but applies to space as well. It seems absurd to say that an accumulation of events, the duration of each of which is zero, should have, together, a duration that is more than zero. The matter might be put more strongly. We are inclined to say that, if the duration of events were reduced to zero, 'there would be nothing left of them', they would 'just be nothing', and we obviously could not hope to make something out of an accumulation of nothings.[3] We may regard this as one side of the Augustinian problem. A second slightly different side consists in the fact that the stages of any happening that takes time are never there *together*. Now it seems absurd to say of a number of things which are never together, but always apart, that they can ever *amount* to anything, or form a *whole* of any kind: it would be as if one were to try to build a house with bricks that repelled each other, so that each one moved away when the next one was brought up to it. At such a rate, it would seem, one could build no house and no interval of time.[4] But Augustine's problem has a third side which seems to have worried him particularly: that if we measure an interval of time, we must be measuring something of which a vanishing section only has reality: all the other sections of it, which give it breadth and

[1] The interest in Augustine as a case of philosophical puzzlement is due to Wittgenstein.

[2] Augustine: 'The present hath no space. Where then is the time which we may call long?' See above.

[3] Augustine: 'If time present . . . only cometh into existence because it passeth into time past, how can we say that either this is, whose cause of being is that it shall not be' (XI, 17).

[4] Augustine: 'Therefore neither is the year now current present; and if not present *as a whole* (our italics) then is not the year present.' See above.

bulk, are either *not yet there* or *not there any longer*. Now it is hard to grasp how we can measure something which is no longer there, which is 'past and gone', of which we are tempted to say that it is 'simply nothing'. And it is also hard to grasp how we can measure something which is not yet there, which is merely expected, which we are likewise tempted to describe as 'nothing'. It would be like trying to measure a building of which all but the tiniest fragment had been blasted by a bomb, or existed merely in a builder's blue-print. In such a situation we should have no building to measure, and it seems we should be in the same position with regard to lengths of time.[1]

We shall now briefly point to some ways—there are an indefinite number of such ways—in which we might avoid these Augustinian perplexities. We might, first of all, evade the whole argument by which we have been bludgeoned into saying that there are some events that take no time, and that only these are ever truly present. We might refuse to say, of certain happenings which are very short, that any of their parts lie in the past or future; we do not normally, in fact, make use of the past and future tenses in speaking of the parts of very short events contemporary with our utterance. Alternatively we might say that some sufficiently short events can be 'present as wholes', though most of their parts are past or future; this too agrees with ordinary usage, for we say that many fairly long events *are* happening, though we should talk in the past or future tense of some of their remoter parts. Or again we might deny—as Whitehead in his doctrine of epochal durations has denied—that certain very brief events come into being *part by part*.[2] There is, in fact, no plain empirical meaning to be given to the supposition that all events come into being part by part, since there must necessarily be a limit to the division of events by human judgements or instruments. Or again we might choose to follow certain other trends of language, and to say, of certain very brief events, that they

[1] Augustine: 'In what space then do we measure time passing? In the future, whence it passeth through? But what is not yet we measure not. Or in the present by which it passes? But no space we do not measure. Or in the past to which it passes? But neither do we measure that, which now is not' (XI, 27).

[2] 'Accordingly we must not proceed to conceive time as another form of extensivenss. Time is sheer succession of epochal durations. . . . The epochal duration is not realized *via* its *successive* divisible parts, but is given *with* its parts' (*Science and the Modern World*, p. 158).

'took no time at all', thereby excluding from the start the whole issue of divisibility into successive parts.[1] It does not, in fact, matter, in all this choice of diction, *what* we say, provided only that we truly please ourselves: the facts are there, we can see and show them, and it is for us to talk of them in ways which will neither perplex nor embarrass us. It is desirable, in our choice of words, that we should be consistent, but it is not desirable that we should make a fetish of consistency. Consistency in language is most necessary if it means that we shall not, in a given context, fall victims to linguistic conflicts, that we shall not try to say something, while striving at the same time to unsay it.[2] Consistency is also very desirable if it means that we shall be guided by the analogies of things in what we say in *different* contexts; in the absence of *some* degree of such consistency, all language would be arbitrary and communication impossible. But consistency is wholly undesirable if it becomes a bogey, if it makes us say something in one context merely because we have said it in some other, more or less analogous context, and if it then leads us on to say further things which bewilder and confuse us. For the analogies of things are varied and conflicting, and it is impossible, without disrupting human language, to do justice to them all.

So far we have pursued a line which shakes the dialectic on which the Augustinian problem is founded. By so doing we avoid giving a sense to the phrase 'events which take no time', and are not obliged to say that these alone are truly present. Suppose however we are moved by this dialectic, or by some consideration of scientific convenience, to admit this talk of 'momentary presents', how then shall we proceed to deal with the various aspects of the Augustinian problem? As regards the first aspect, the building of a whole which has size out of parts which have *no* size, we may simply point out that it mixes up the familiar sense in which a pile of money is built up out of coins, with the new sense in which a happening which takes time may be built up out of happenings which take no time. Because one couldn't amass a fortune out of zero contributions, one tends to think one couldn't make a measurable duration out of parts

[1] *How* brief the happenings must be, of which we say any of these things, is of course a matter for arbitrary decision.

[2] Unless, indeed, a linguistic conflict is deliberately used to express some personal reaction to reality, as has been done by some philosophers.

with no duration. But the situations are quite different; no one has witnessed a lapse of time being built up out of instants, as he can witness a pile of money being built up out of coins, nor can the former be imagined as the latter is imagined.[1] Hence if we wish to speak of 'happenings which take no time', we are quite free to fix what may be said of them, and this means that we may simply rule that events which take time *are* made up of events which take no time. And once misleading pictures are avoided, we shall find no problem in this. We may in the same way dispose of the difficulties which spring from the tendency to say that an event which took no time would 'just be nothing'. Either we must restrain this inclination—to which we are not in duty bound to yield—or be prepared to say that certain parts of real temporal wholes are simply nothing, and that mere nothing can at times have definite properties. This way of talking would no doubt do violence to our habits, and abound in dangerous suggestions, but we should not, with a little practice, find it difficult.

The second aspect of the Augustinian problem involves a similar confusion. Because it would be absurd to say of certain wholes—houses, mountains or libraries, for instance—that they existed and were measurable, although their parts were never together, we think it would be absurd to say the same thing of happenings. But the fact that we shouldn't say that *some* of the things we call parts could constitute the things we call their wholes, unless they were present together, does not oblige us to say this in the case of *other* things we also call parts and wholes. For the sense in which the parts were parts, and the wholes wholes, and the former made up the latter, might be ruled to be different in the two sets of cases: we might say we were dealing with two totally different *sorts* of parts and wholes. And we do in fact rule so; for we regard it as nonsense to say of an event that takes time, that its parts are present together. And we recognize the difference between the two sets of cases by talking of *coexistent* parts in the one set of cases, and of successive parts in the other: the successive parts of a whole are, in fact, just those parts of it that *don't* need to be together. But if we feel ourselves unconquerably opposed to calling something a whole whose parts are

[1] Though a sense might be invented in which we could be said to witness or imagine the former.

not together, we may simply rule that some things may have magnitude although they are not wholes. And other similar expedients will meet other possible difficulties.

As regards the third difficulty of Augustine, how we manage to measure something which is in part past, we may again suggest a number of alternatives. We might, in the first place, reject the analogy between the measurement of a co-existent whole like a house, which isn't there to be measured if any parts of it lie in the past, and the measurement of a successive whole like a happening, which *must* have parts in the past. Or we might follow certain other trends of language, and say that we have succession *in the present*, and that certain happenings which are not too long are able to be present as wholes and so to be measured directly. Other longer happenings might then be measured by means of the briefer and directly measurable happenings which entered into their remembered history. Or if it is the 'nothingness of the past' that troubles us, we must remember that we are not compelled to say that the past is nothing: we may, if we like, credit it with existence or subsistence or any other suitable status. For we are only worried by the 'nothingness of the past' because we think it will stop us from finding out any facts about the past, just as the nothingness of a bachelor's children stops us from asking for their ages or appearance. But there are so many clear and agreed ways of establishing what has happened in the immediate or remoter past, that it would be nonsense to put past events in the position of a bachelor's children. So that if we wish to say that they exist or subsist, there is no good reason why we should not do so. But if the 'existence' of the past is going to suggest to us that we could by some device revive or revisit the past, as we could revive a drowned man or revisit Palermo, then it is perhaps better to go on saying that the past is nothing, allowing meanwhile that there may be measurable wholes which have certain parts that are nothing.

The puzzles of Augustine lead on very naturally to the problems of Zeno, or rather to a certain very general difficulty which seems to be involved in every one of Zeno's paradoxes. This is our difficulty in seeing how anything can happen, if *before* it happens something else must happen, and *before* that happens something else must happen, and so on indefinitely. If we make time continuous and infinitely divisible, we also feel obliged to say that before any happening is completed, an infinity of prior happenings must have been completed, and this seems to mean that *no* happening can ever be completed. We seem to be in the plight of a runner in a torch-race, who wants to hand on his torch to another runner A, but is told by A that he will only take it from B, who tells him he will only take it from C, who tells him he will only take it from D, and so on indefinitely. Or in the plight of a man who wants to interview a Cabinet Minister, and who is informed by the Minister that he must first discuss his business with the Under-Secretary, who informs him he must first discuss it with the Chief Clerk, etc., etc. Our runner obviously will never get rid of his torch, and our harassed petitioner will obviously never see his Minister, and it looks as if all happenings involve the same hopeless difficulty. The difficulty we are presenting is, of course, not identical with any one of Zeno's historical puzzles: in all of these the difficulties of duration are complicated by the introduction of change and motion. But it is plain that all these puzzles could be so restated as to deal with happenings without regard to whether those happenings were changes or persistent states, and without regard to whether they involved motion or not. A plum continuing to hang on a tree for a certain period affords, less dramatically, the same species of philosophical perplexity as an arrow in its flight. Moreover, when we strip Zeno's problem of its spatial and other wrappings, its significance becomes clearer. For it is not, essentially, a problem of space or quantity, but solely one of time: it is only because all motion is *successive*, because an infinity of positions must be passed *before* any subsequent position, that the possibility of such motion seems so utterly ruled out. If the infinite stages of a motion could be there all at once, as the parts of a piece of space are, we should feel no problem in their infinite number. It is therefore foolish to imagine that we can meet Zeno's puzzles by the modern theory of the continuum or by the facts of infinite convergent numerical series.[1] And the problem assumes its most vexing form if we allow that ordinary happenings have ultimate parts that take no time. For of such parts it seems most natural to say that none can be next to any

[1] This point is clearly brought out by Whitehead. See *Process and Reality*, p. 95.

other,[1] and once this is said it is hard to understand how any ultimate part can ever pass away or be replaced by any other. For before such a part can be replaced by any other similar part, it must first have been replaced by an infinity of other similar parts. Our admission seems to leave us with a world immobilized and paralyzed, in which every object and process, like the arrow of Zeno, stands still in the instant, for the simple reason that it has no way of passing on to other instants.

As before, we may deal with our difficulties in several different ways. We might, in the first place, deny that very short happenings are divisible as fairly long ones are divisible: the divisibility of *all* happenings is in any case without a definite meaning. This is the line followed by Professor Whitehead, who makes time flow in indivisible drops, and says that it is 'sheer succession of epochal durations'.[2] But, far less drastically, we might give to all this talk of instants and of infinite divisibility a sense consistent with the obvious facts of our experience, that things happen and that phases are outlived, that the world is not immobilized, and that we seldom have to cast about for ways of passing on to novel stages. For the infinite happenings that must first occur before a given thing can happen, are not like ordinary happenings we can see and show, of which it would be absurd to say that an infinite number ever were completed. They are happenings of a new sort to which a meaning must be arbitrarily given. And since *we* have to give a meaning to these happenings, it is for us to see that they mean nothing which conflicts with our established ways of saying things. And once we strip them of pictorial vividness, we also strip them of their puzzling character. Our problem also vanishes when we note that even to be 'desperately immobilized', to 'cast about in vain for means to pass to other stages', would both, if they were anything, be states that lasted and took time. Our problem therefore takes for granted the very thing it finds so difficult.

We turn, in conclusion, from these Augustinian and Zenonian difficulties, to a different set of temporal puzzles, quite unconnected with our tendency to use the present tense in more exact

[1] Unless we choose to say that there is a finite number of ultimate parts in any happening, or other queerer things.

[2] *Science and the Modern World*, quoted above.

and narrow ways. We shall consider briefly the very general wonderment which professes to find something 'unintelligible' or 'contradictory' in time and change. 'How is it possible', we sometimes like to ask, 'for all the solid objects and people around us to melt away into the past, and for a new order of objects and persons to emerge mysteriously from the future?' This kind of wonderment is most strongly stirred by processes of *rapid change*: we wonder at things which have no constant quality for any length of time however short, at things which only reach a state to leave it, and so forth. A similar perplexity besets us in regard to 'truths' or 'facts': we wonder how what *is* the case can ever cease to be the case, or how what was false *then* can come to be true *now*, and so on. This week the peaches in our garden are not ripe; next week we find them ripe; the following week they are no longer ripe, but rotten: in certain frames of mind we find this difficult. Our difficulty with regard to change may also be expressed in terms of 'happenings' and their 'properties' of 'pastness', 'presentness' and 'futurity', the form in which this problem was propounded by McTaggart. We wonder how it comes about that happenings which are at first remotely future, should steadily become more nearly future, how in the end they manage to be present, and how from being present they become past, and how they go on, ever afterwards, becoming more and more remotely past. McTaggart has shown plainly that we cannot solve this problem (if it is a problem) by bringing in the 'different times' at which events are present, past and future, since these themselves (whatever we may mean by them) have also to be present, past and future, and so involve the very difficulty they are called in to remove.

Now it is hard to see, if we remain in any ordinary, unreflective state of mind, what is the problem that is being raised by those who say they can't see how what *is* the case at one time, is not the case at other times, or that they can't see how a happening that is future can ever come to be a happening that is past. As we observed at the beginning of this paper, it should be possible to remove such difficulties by pointing to some ordinary happening around us, a man diving, for instance, and saying, as it happened, 'Now he's not yet diving', 'Now he's diving', 'Now he is no longer diving', or other similar phrases. And if a man were really puzzled by our usage in such situations, it would not take him very long to master it. We do not ordinarily have difficulty in knowing what to say of happenings as they pass, nor any tendency both to say and not to say the same thing in a given context, a kind of inconsistency that is seldom desirable. Occasionally, where change is rapid, we may find ourselves at a loss to say whether something is or is not yellow, or whether it is or was yellow: we may also have a tendency to say that it is both or neither. But all this only means we lack a settled and satisfactory way of talking about very swiftly changing things. But in the case of changes which are less rapid, we find ourselves quite free from conflict or confusion. *Before* an event occurs we say, if we have evidence that it is not yet happening, that it hasn't yet happened, but that it will happen, while if it *is* happening we say that it is now happening, that it hasn't ceased happening and that it isn't about to happen, and *after* it has happened we say that it has happened, that it is no longer happening and that it is not going to happen. Stated in words these semantic rules might seem circular, but taught in connection with a concrete situation they are wholly clear. And our conventions with regard to tenses are so well worked out that we have practically the materials in them for a formal calculus.[1] Where all is so desirably definite, what room is there for puzzles or perplexities?

To give an answer to this question, we must point to a certain aspiration which all our language to some extent fulfils, and which we are at times inclined to follow to unreasonable lengths. We desire to have in our language only those kinds of statement that are *not* dependent, as regards their truth or falsity, on any circumstance in which the statement happens to be made. We do not wish a statement which we call 'correct' and 'justified by fact' when made by one person, to be incorrect when made by another person, and to have to be superseded by some other statement. In the same way we do not wish a statement which we call 'correct' when made in one place, to be incorrect when made in

[1] The calculus of tenses should have been included in the modern development of modal logics. It includes such obvious propositions as that

x present = (x present) present;

x future = (x future) present = (x present) future;

also such comparatively recondite propositions as that

(x). (x past) future; i.e. all events, past, present and future, *will* be past.

another place, and to have to be superseded by some other statement. And there are occasions when we feel the same sort of thing about the *time* at which a statement is made: if we are right in saying something at a certain time, then, we sometimes feel, we must be right in saying the same thing at all other times. This means that we object, in certain frames of mind, even to the easy, systematic changes of tense which statements have to undergo when they are transmitted from period to period. We might express our general aspiration by saying that we wish our statements to be independent of 'extraneous circumstances' in regard to their truth or falsity: 'the facts' must settle whether what we say is true, and nothing else must come into consideration. But such a way of talking would be gravely question-begging, for it depends on the sort of language we are speaking whether a circumstance is or is not extraneous. If we spoke a language in which the statements permitted in one place differed systematically from the statements permitted in another place, then it wouldn't, in that language, be an extraneous circumstance, as regards the truth or falsity of a statement, whether that statement was made here or there. And those who used the language would protest quite legitimately that 'something was left out' by other languages which ignored all local circumstances of utterance. But the point is that we do *in part* say things which may be passed from man to man, or place to place, or time to time, without a change in their truth-value, and we look at things from *this* angle when we say that time, place and speaker are extraneous circumstances, and require our statements to ignore them.

Now the urge behind these austerities seems simply to be the urge towards more adequate communication, which is the fundamental impulse underlying language. We are prepared to sacrifice local and personal colour, or period flavour, in order that our statements may be handed on unaltered to other persons who are differently situated, or to ourselves in other situations. But it is not *this* sacrifice which gives rise to our perplexities: if we always spoke rigorously in the third person of everyone, ourselves included, if we avoided the adverbs 'here' and 'there', if we purged our language of tenses, and talked exclusively in terms of dates and tenseless participles, we should never be involved in difficulties. And for the purposes of science it is perhaps desirable that we should always talk in this manner. But our difficulty arises because we try to talk in this way but are also uneasy in doing so; we feel that something worth-while has been omitted, and try to combine our old way of talking with our new one. Thus McTaggart first offers us an order of events in which there are no differences of past, present and future, but only differences of earlier and later, in which every happening always stays the sort of happening it is, and always occupies the same position in the time-series: he then slides back into another way of talking in which events are present, past and future, and always *change* in these modalities. And his attempt to combine these ways of talking results in the unanswerable question: how can a single happening have the incompatible properties of being past and present and future? Whereas if we talk in the ordinary way we never have to say these things at once, and if we talk in an artificial, tenseless manner the question can't arise, since the modalities in question can't be mentioned. It is as if a man tried to retain the use of personal pronouns, such as 'I', 'you', 'he', etc., in a language in which everything that could truly be said by one man could be truly said by every other man, and were then led to ask: 'How can one and the same person be I and you and he?' And once we see the source of such perplexities, we should be easily rid of them.

CHAPTER IV

BERTRAND RUSSELL'S DOUBTS ABOUT INDUCTION

By Paul Edwards

I

A. In the celebrated chapter on induction in his *Problems of Philosophy*, Bertrand Russell asks the question: 'Have we any reason, assuming that they (laws like the law of gravitation) have always held in the past, to suppose that these laws will hold in the future?' (p. 100).[1] Earlier in the same chapter he raises the more specific question: 'Do *any* number of cases of a law being fulfilled in the past afford evidence that it will be fulfilled in the future?' (p. 96). We may reformulate these questions in a way which lends itself more easily to critical discussion as follows:

(1) Assuming that we possess n positive instances of a phenomenon, observed in extensively varied circumstances, and that we have not observed a single negative instance (where n is a large number), have we any reason to suppose that the $n+$ 1st instance will also be positive?

(2) Is there any number n of observed positive instances of a phenomenon which affords evidence that the $n+$ 1st instance will also be positive?

It is clear that Russell uses 'reason' synonymously with 'good reason' and 'evidence' with 'sufficient evidence'. I shall follow the same procedure throughout this article.

Russell asserts that unless we appeal to a non-empirical principle which he calls the 'principle of induction', both of his questions must be answered in the negative. 'Those who emphasized the scope of induction', he writes, 'wished to maintain that all logic is empirical, and therefore could not be expected to realize that induction itself, their own darling, required a logical

[1] The references are to the original edition of *The Problems of Philosophy*, the pagination of which differs from that of the reset edition first published in 1946.

principle which obviously could not be proved inductively, and must therefore be *a priori* if it could be known at all' (*Our Knowledge of the External World* (2nd edition), p. 226). 'We must either accept the inductive principle on the ground of its intrinsic evidence or forgo all justification of our expectations about the future' (*Problems of Philosophy*, p. 106; also *Outline of Philosophy*, p. 286).

In conjunction with the inductive principle, on the other hand, question (1) at least, he contends, can be answered in the affirmative. 'Whether inferences from past to future are valid depends wholly, if our discussion has been sound, upon the inductive principle: if it is true, such inferences are valid' (*External World*, p. 226). Unfortunately Russell does not make it clear whether in his opinion the same is true about question (2).

As against Russell, I shall try to show in this article that question (1) can be answered in the affirmative without in any way appealing to a non-empirical principle. I shall also attempt to show that, without in any way invoking a non-empirical principle, numbers of observed positive instances do frequently afford us evidence that unobserved instances of the same phenomenon are also positive. At the outset, I shall concentrate on question (1) since this is the more general question. Once we have answered question (1) it will require little further effort to answer question (2).

I want to emphasize here that, to keep this paper within manageable bounds, I shall refrain from discussing, at any rate explicitly, the questions 'Are any inductive conclusions probable?' and 'Are any inductive conclusions certain?' I hope to fill in this gap on another occasion.

It will be well to conduct our discussion in terms of a concrete example. Supposing a man jumps from a window on the fiftieth floor of the Empire State Building. Is there any reason to suppose that his body will move in the direction of the street rather than say in the direction of the sky or in a flat plane? There can be no doubt that any ordinary person and any philosophically unsophisticated scientist, would answer this question in the affirmative without in any way appealing to a non-empirical principle. He would say that there is an excellent reason to suppose that the man's body will move towards the street. This excellent reason, he would say, consists in the fact that whenever in the past a human being jumped out of a window of the Empire State Building his body moved in a downward direction; that whenever any human being anywhere jumped out of a house he moved in the direction of the ground; that, more generally, whenever a human body jumped or was thrown off an elevated locality in the neighbourhood of the earth, it moved downwards and not either upwards or at an angle of 180°; that the only objects which have been observed to be capable of moving upwards by themselves possess certain special characteristics which human beings lack; and finally in all the other observed confirmations of the theory of gravitation.

B. The philosophers who reject common-sense answers like the one just described, have relied mainly on three arguments. Russell himself explicitly employs two of them and some of his remarks make it clear that he also approves of the third. These three arguments are as follows: (*a*) Defenders of common sense point to the fact that many inferences to unobserved events were subsequently, by means of direct observation, found to have resulted in true conclusions. However, any such appeal to observed results of inductive inferences is irrelevant. For the question at stake is: Have we ever a reason, assuming that all the large number of observed instances of a phenomenon are positive, to suppose that an instance which is still unobserved is also positive? The question is not: Have we ever a reason for supposing that instances which have by now been observed but were at one time unobserved are positive? In Russell's own words: 'We have experience of past futures, but not of future futures, and the question is: Will future futures resemble past futures? This question is not to be answered by an argument which starts from past futures alone' (*Problems of Philosophy*, p. 100).

(*b*) Cases are known where at a certain time a large number of positive instances and not a single negative instance had been observed and where the next instance nevertheless turned out to be negative. 'We know that in spite of frequent repetitions there sometimes is a failure at the last' (*Problems of Philosophy*, p. 102). The man, for instance, 'who has fed the chicken every day throughout its life at last wrings its neck instead' (*Problems of Philosophy*, p. 98). Even in the case of the human being who is jumping out of the Empire State Building, 'we may be in no better position than the chicken which unexpectedly has its neck wrung' (*Problems of Philosophy*, p. 98).

(*c*) The number of positive and negative necessary conditions for the occurrence of any event is infinite or at any rate too large to be directly observed by a human being or indeed by all human beings put together. None of us, for example, has explored every corner of the universe to make sure that there nowhere exists a malicious but powerful individual who controls the movements of the sun by means of wires which are too fine to be detected by any of our microscopes. None of us can be sure that there is no such Controller who, in order to play a joke with the human race, will prevent the sun from rising to-morrow. Equally, none of us can be sure that there is nowhere a powerful individual who can, if he wishes, regulate the movement of human bodies by means of ropes which are too thin to be detected by any of our present instruments. None of us therefore can be sure that when a man jumps out of the Empire State Building he will not be drawn skyward by the Controller of Motion. Hence we have no reason to suppose that the man's body will move in the direction of the street and not in the direction of the sky.

In connection with the last of these three arguments attention ought to be drawn to a distinction which Russell makes between what he calls the 'interesting' and the 'uninteresting' doubt about induction (*Problems of Philosophy*, p. 95). The uninteresting doubt is doubt about the occurrence of a given event on the ground that not all the conditions which are known to be necessary are in fact known to be present. What Russell calls the interesting doubt is the doubt whether an event will take place although all the conditions known to be necessary are known to obtain. Russell's 'interesting doubt', if I am not mistaken, is identical with Donald Williams's 'tragic problem of induction' ('Induction and the Future', *Mind*, 1948, p. 227).

II

As I indicated above, it is my object in this article to defend the common-sense answers to both of Russell's questions. I propose to show, in other words, that, without in any way calling upon a non-empirical principle for assistance, we often have a reason for supposing that a generalization will be confirmed in the future as it has been confirmed in the past. I also propose to show that numbers 'of cases of a law being fulfilled in the past' do often afford evidence that it will be fulfilled in the future.

However, what I have to say in support of these answers is so exceedingly simple that I am afraid it will not impress the philosophers who are looking for elaborate and complicated theories to answer these questions. But I think I can make my case appear plausible even in the eyes of some of these philosophers if I describe at some length the general method of resolving philosophical puzzles which I shall apply to the problem of induction.

Let us consider a simple statement like 'there are several thousand physicians in New York'. We may call this a statement of common-sense, meaning thereby no more than that anybody above a certain very moderate level of instruction and intelligence would confidently give his assent to it.

The word 'physician', as ordinarily used, is not entirely free from ambiguity. At times it simply means 'person who possesses a medical degree from a recognized academic institution'. At other times, though less often, it means the same as 'person who possesses what is by ordinary standards a considerable skill in curing diseases'. On yet other occasions when people say about somebody that he is a physician they mean both that he has a medical degree and that he possesses a skill in curing diseases which considerably exceeds that of the average layman.

Let us suppose that in the common-sense statement 'there are several thousand physicians in New York' the word 'physician' is used exclusively in the last-mentioned sense. This assumption will simplify our discussion, but it is not at all essential to any of the points I am about to make. It is essential, however, to realize that when somebody asserts in ordinary life that there are several thousand physicians in New York, he is using the word 'physician' in one or other of the ordinary senses just listed. By 'physician' he does not mean for example 'person who can speedily repair bicycles' or 'person who can cure any conceivable illness in less than two minutes'.

Now, supposing somebody were to say 'Really, there are no physicians at all in New York', in the belief that he was contradicting and refuting common-sense. Supposing that on investigation it turns out that by 'physician' he does not mean 'person who has a medical degree and who has considerably more skill in curing disease than the average layman'. It turns out that by 'physician' he means 'person who has a medical degree and who can cure any conceivable illness in less than two minutes'.

What would be an adequate reply to such an 'enemy of common-sense'? Clearly it would be along the following lines: 'What you say is true. There are no physicians in New York—in *your* sense of the word. There are no persons in New York who can cure any conceivable disease in less than two minutes. But this in no way contradicts the common-sense view expressed by "there are several thousand physicians in New York". For the latter asserts no more than that there are several thousand people in New York who have a medical degree and who possess a skill in curing disease which considerably exceeds that of the average layman. You are guilty of *ignoratio elenchi* since the proposition you refute is different from the proposition you set out to refute.'

Our discussion from here on will be greatly simplified by introducing a few technical terms. Let us, firstly, call '*ignoratio elenchi* by *redefinition*' any instance of *ignoratio elenchi* in which (i) the same sentence expresses both the proposition which ought to be proved and the proposition which is confused with it and where (ii) in the latter employment of the sentence one or more of its parts are used in a sense which is different from their ordinary sense or senses. Secondly, let us refer to any redefinition of a word which includes all that the ordinary definition of the word includes but which includes something else as well as a '*high* redefinition'; and to the sense which is defined by a high redefinition we shall refer as a high sense of the word. Thus 'person who has a medical degree and who is capable of curing any conceivable disease in less than two minutes' is a high redefinition of 'physician' and anybody using the word in that fashion is using it in a high sense. Thirdly, we shall refer to a redefinition of a word which includes something but not all of what the ordinary definition includes and which includes nothing else as a '*low* redefinition'; and the sense which is defined by a low redefinition we shall call a low sense of the word. 'Person capable of giving first aid' or 'person who knows means of alleviating pain' would be low redefinitions of 'physician'. Finally, it will be convenient to call a statement in which a word is used in a high or in a low sense a *redefinitional statement*. If the word is used in a high sense we shall speak of a high-definitional statement; if it is used in a low sense we shall speak of a low-definitional statement.

A short while ago, I pointed out that the man who says 'there are no physicians in New York', meaning that there are no people in New York who have a medical degree and who can cure any conceivable illness in less than two minutes, is not really contradicting the common-sense view that there are physicians in New York. I pointed out that he would be guilty of what in our technical language is called an *ignoratio elenchi* by redefinition. Now, it seems to me that the relation between the assertion of various philosophers that past experience never constitutes a reason for prediction or generalization except perhaps in conjunction with a non-empirical principle and the common-sense view that past experience does often by itself constitute a reason for inferences to unobserved events has some striking resemblances to the relation between the redefinitional statement about physicians in New York and the common-sense view which this redefinitional statement fails to refute. And more generally, it strongly seems to me that almost all the bizarre pronouncements of philosophers—their 'paradoxes', their 'silly' theories—are in certain respects strikingly like the statement that there are no physicians in New York, made by one who means to assert that there are no people in New York who have medical degrees and who are capable of curing any conceivable disease in less than two minutes.

In making the last statement I do not mean to deny that there arc also important differences between philosophical paradoxes and the high-definitional statement about physicians. There are three differences in particular which have to be mentioned if my subsequent remarks are not to be seriously misleading. Firstly, many of the philosophical paradoxes are not without some point; they do often draw attention to likenesses and differences which ordinary usage obscures. Secondly, the redefinitions which are implicit in philosophical paradoxes do quite often, though by no means always, receive a certain backing from ordinary usage. Frequently, that is to say, there is a secondary sense or trend in ordinary usage which corresponds to the philosophical redefinition, the 'real' sense of the word.[1] Thirdly, philosophical paradoxes are invariably ambiguous in a sense in which the high-definitional statement about the physicians is not ambiguous.[2]

Now, while fully admitting all these (and other) differences, I wish to insist on the great likenesses between philosophical paradoxes and the redefinitional statement about the physicians. And in this article I am mainly concerned with the likenesses, not with the differences. My main object, of course, is to point out the likenesses between the high-definitional statement 'there are no physicians in New York' and the statement that past experience never by itself affords a reason for making inferences to unobserved events. However, my points there will be clearer if I first make them in connection with another celebrated paradox.

Following Plato, Berkeley[3] argued in favour of the view that heat and cold are not really 'in the object'. Ordinary people would unhesitatingly say that water of e.g. 50° C. is hot. Against this, Plato and Berkeley would point out that to a man who a moment before had held his hands in a jug of water with a temperature of 80° C., the water of 50° C. would appear cold. Similarly, to a race of individuals whose body-temperature was say 75° C., water of 50° would regularly appear cold. But the percepts of those to whom the water of 50° appears cold are just as genuine as the percepts of people to whom the water appears hot. Now, since it would be wrong to say that the water of 50° is really cold simply because of these genuine percepts of cold, it cannot any more rationally be said to be hot. The cold has 'just as good a right to be considered real' as the hot; and therefore, 'to avoid favouritism, we are compelled to deny that in itself'[4] the water is either hot or cold.

It is not difficult to show that this argument is a case of *ignoratio elenchi* by redefinition. When an ordinary person says that water

[1] Prominent instances of this phenomenon are 'real certainty', 'real knowledge', 'real sameness', 'real freedom', and 'really contemporaneous events'.

[2] The last of these points seems to me to be of enormous importance for understanding the phenomenon of philosophical paradoxes.

[3] *Three Dialogues between Hylas and Philonous*, p. 208 (Everyman edit.).

[4] The phrases are Russell's, used in a very similar context (*Problems*, p. 14).

of 50° C. is hot, all he means is that human beings, with their body-temperature being what it is, would in *all ordinary circumstances* have sense-impressions of heat on coming into contact with such water. In saying that water of 50° is hot, is *really* hot, an ordinary person in no way denies that under certain *special* conditions a human being would have genuine sense-impressions of cold. He also in no way denies that to a race of individuals whose body-temperature is 75° the water would genuinely appear cold. Pointing to these facts does not therefore refute the ordinary man. Berkeley is clearly guilty of a high redefinition of 'hot' or 'really hot'. To him something is hot only if, in addition to appearing hot to human beings in ordinary circumstances, it also appears hot to them under special circumstances and if it appears hot to beings with a body-temperature which is much greater than the actual body-temperature of human beings.

However, this is not quite accurate since, like most other philosophical paradoxes, the paradox about heat and cold has a double meaning. It would be inaccurate simply to say that Berkeley is guilty of *ignoratio elenchi* by redefinition. On the other hand, without in any way being inaccurate, it can be said that Berkeley and Plato have laid themselves open to the following dilemma: 'Either you mean by "hot" what is ordinarily meant by it—if you do, then what you say is plainly false; or else you are using "hot" in a high sense—if so what you say is true, but in that case you are guilty of *ignoratio elenchi* by redefinition. In either event you have failed to refute common-sense.' Very similar answers can also be made to Berkeley's and Russell's arguments concerning colours, shapes, and the other qualities which common-sense believes to exist independently of being perceived.

At the same time it must be admitted that Berkeley's arguments have a certain value. In ordinary speech we make a fairly rigid distinction between 'real' and 'unreal' data. Among the unreal data we lump together both the percepts which we have under special conditions (and percepts which do and would appear to beings differently constituted from ourselves) and what we experience e.g. in dreams and hallucinations. 'Real' we call only those percepts which a normal observer has under certain standard conditions.

A classification of this sort obscures the many likenesses between the 'real' percepts and percepts appearing under special conditions, while also hiding the many differences between the latter and data which are experienced in dreams and hallucinations.

The situation becomes quite clear if we divide data into three and not merely into two groups, as follows:

the R-data: percepts appearing to a normal observer under standard conditions,

the A-data: percepts appearing to a normal observer under special conditions or to an abnormal observer in cerain normal or special circumstances, and

the D-data: data appearing in dreams, hallucinations, etc.

It is unnecessary for our purposes to discuss exactly what are the likenesses between the R-data and the A-data. It is unnecessary, too, to discuss what exactly are the differences between the A-data and the D-data. It is sufficient to point out that while Berkeley is wrong in believing or suggesting that there are no differences between the R-data and the A-data, he is right in insisting that the differences between the R-data and the A-data are not nearly as great as ordinary speech suggests. In the case of colours, Berkeley's argument has the further merit of bringing out the fact that the expression 'X's real colour' has *two* perfectly proper senses. His argument helps one to realize that 'X's real colour' may mean 'the colour which X exhibits to a normal observer under certain standard conditions' *as well as* 'the colour which X exhibits to a normal observer under a finer instrument than the human eye, e.g. a microscope'.

III

A. Supposing a man, let us call him M, said to us 'I have not yet found any physicians in New York'. Suppose we take him to Park Avenue and introduce him to Brown, a man who has a medical degree and who has cured many people suffering from diseases of the ear. Brown admits, however, that he has not been able to cure *all* the patients who ever consulted him. He also admits that many of his cures took a long time, some as long as eight years. On hearing this, M says 'Brown certainly isn't a physician'.

Supposing we next take M to meet Black who has a medical degree and who can prove to M's and to our satisfaction that he has cured every patient who ever consulted him. Moreover, none of Black's cures took more than three years. However, on hearing that some of Black's cures took as long as two years and ten months, M says 'Black certainly isn't a physician either'.

Finally we introduce M to White who has a medical degree and who has cured every one of his patients in less than six months. When M hears that some of White's cures took as long as five and a half months, he is adamant and exclaims 'White—what a ridiculous error to call him a physician!'

At this stage, if not much sooner, all of us would impatiently ask M: What on earth do you mean by 'physician'? And we would plainly be justified in adding: Whatever you may mean by 'physician', in any sense in which we ever use the word, Black and Brown and White are physicians and very excellent ones at that.

Let us return now to Russell's doubt about the sun's rising to-morrow or about what would happen to a man who jumps out of the Empire State Building. Let us consider what Russell would say in reply to the following question: Supposing that the observed confirmatory instances for the theory of gravitation were a million or ten million times as extensive as they now are and that they were drawn from a very much wider field; would we then have a reason to suppose that the man will fall into the street and not move up into the sky? It is obvious that Russell and anybody taking his view would say 'No'. He would reply that though our *expectation* that the man's body will move in the direction of the street would be even stronger then than it is at present, we would still be without a *reason*.

Next, let us imagine ourselves to be putting the following question to Russell: Supposing the world were such that no accumulation of more than five hundred observed positive instances of a phenomenon has ever been found to be followed by a negative instance; supposing, for instance, that all the chickens who have ever been fed by the same man for 501 days in succession or more are still alive and that all the men too are still alive feeding the chickens every day—would the observed confirmations of the law of gravity in that case be a reason to suppose that the man jumping out of the Empire State Building will move in the direction of the street and not in the direction of the sky? I am not quite sure what Russell would say in reply to this question. Let us assume he would once again answer 'No—past experience would not even then ever be a *reason*'.

Thirdly and finally, we have to consider what Russell would say to the following question: Supposing we had explored every corner of the universe with instruments millions of times as fine and accurate as any we now possess and that we had yet failed to discover any Controller of the movements of human bodies—would we then in our predictions about the man jumping out of the Empire State Building be in a better position than the chicken is in predicting its meals? Would our past observations then be a reason for our prediction? Whatever Russell would in fact say to this, it is clear that his remarks concerning the 'interesting' doubt about induction require him to answer our question in the negative. He would have to say something like this: 'Our *expectation* that the man's body will move in a downward direction will be even stronger than it is now. However, without invoking a non-empirical principle, we shall not *really* be in a better position than the chicken. We should still fail to possess a *reason.*'

As in the case of the man who refused to say that Brown, Black, and White were doctors, our natural response to all this will be to turn to Russell and say: What do you mean by 'being in a better position'? What on earth do you mean by 'a reason'? And, furthermore, why should anybody be interested in a reason in your sense of the word?

Russell's remarks about the need for a general principle like his principle of induction to serve as major premiss in every inductive argument make it clear what he means by a reason: like the Rationalists and Hume (in most places), he means by 'reason' a *logically conclusive* reason and by 'evidence' *deductively conclusive* evidence. When 'reason' is used in this sense, it must be admitted that past observations can never by themselves be a reason for any prediction whatsoever. But 'reason' is not used in this sense when, in science or in ordinary life, people claim to have a reason for a prediction.

So far as I can see, there are three different trends in the ordinary usage of 'reason for an inductive conclusion' and according to none of them does the word mean 'logically conclusive reason'. Among the three trends one is much more prominent than the others. It may fitly be called the main sense of the word. According to this main sense, what we mean when we claim that we have a reason for a prediction is that the past observations of this phenomenon or of analogical phenomena are of a certain kind: they are exclusively or predominantly positive, the number of the positive observations is at least fairly large, and they come from extensively varied sets of circumstances. This is, of course, a very crude formulation. But for the purposes of this article it is, I think, sufficient.[1]

Next, there is a number of trends according to which we mean very much less than this. Occasionally, for instance, we simply mean that it is *reasonable* to infer the inductive conclusion. And clearly it may be reasonable to infer an inductive conclusion for which we have no reason in the main sense. Thus let us suppose I know that Parker will meet Schroeder in a game in the near future and that it is imperative for me not to suspend my judgement but to come to a conclusion as to who will win. Supposing I know nothing about their present form and nothing also about the type of court on which the match is to be played. All I know is that Parker and Schroeder have in the previous two seasons met six times, Parker scoring four victories to Schroeder's two. In these circumstances it would be reasonable for me to predict that Parker will win and unreasonable to predict that Schroeder will win. Clearly, however, in the main sense of the word I have no reason for either prediction.

Again there is a trend according to which any positive instance of a phenomenon is *a* reason for concluding that the next instance of the phenomenon will be positive. Thus in the circumstances described in the preceding paragraph, it would be quite proper to say we have *more reason* for supposing that Parker will win than

[1] I have so far left out one important element in the main sense of 'reason for an inductive conclusion'. I shall come to that in Section IV. In the meantime this omission will not affect any of my points.

for predicting Schroeder's victory. It would be quite proper also to say that we have *some reason* for supposing that Schroeder will win. It would be proper to say this even if Schroeder had won only one of the six matches. To all these and similar trends in the ordinary usage of 'reason for an inductive conclusion' I shall from now on refer as the second ordinary sense of the word.

There can be no doubt that in both these ordinary senses of the word, we frequently have a reason for an inductive conclusion. In these senses we have an excellent reason for supposing that the man jumping out of the Empire State Building will move in the direction of the street, that the sun will rise to-morrow and that Stalin will die before the year 2000. The answer to question (1) is therefore a firm and clear 'Yes': in many domains we have a multitude of exclusively positive instances coming from extensively different circumstances.

The same is true if 'reason' is used in the third ordinary sense. However, I propose to reserve our discussion of that sense for Section V below. For the time being it will be convenient and, I think, not at all misleading to speak as if what I have called the main sense is the *only* ordinary sense of 'reason for an inductive conclusion'.

It should now be clear that, when Russell says that observed instances are never by themselves a reason for an inductive conclusion, he is guilty of an *ignoratio elenchi* by redefinition. His assertion that the premisses of an inductive argument never by themselves constitute a *logically conclusive* reason for an inductive conclusion in no way contradicts the common-sense assertion that they frequently constitute a reason *in the ordinary sense of the word*. Russell's definition of 'reason' is indeed in one respect not a redefinition since in certain contexts we do use 'reason' to mean 'deductively conclusive reason'. However, it is a redefinition in that we never in ordinary life use 'reason' in Russell's sense when we are talking about inductive arguments.

Moreover, if 'reason' means 'deductively conclusive reason', Russell's questions are no more genuinely questions than e.g. the sentence 'Is a father a female parent?' For, since part of the definition of 'inductive inference' is inference from something observed to something unobserved, it is a *contradiction* to say that an inference is both inductive and at the same time in the same respect deductively conclusive. Russell's 'interesting' doubt, then, is no more sensible or interesting than the 'doubt' whether we shall ever see something invisible or find an object which is a father and also female or an object which is a man but not a human being.

In a similar fashion, Russell's remarks about the future future which we quoted in Section 1B constitute an *ignoratio elenchi* by redefinition.[1] If the word 'future' is used in its ordinary sense in the statement 'the future will resemble the past and the present in certain respects' then we have plenty of evidence to support it. For in the ordinary sense of the word, 'future' simply means 'period which has to the past and the present the relation of happening after it'. In its ordinary sense, 'future' does *not* mean 'period which has to the past and the present the relation of happening after it *and* which can never itself be experienced *as a present*'. The period which is referred to by 'future' in its ordinary sense may very well one day be experienced as a present.

In the ordinary sense of the word 'future' therefore, what Russell calls past futures *are* futures. They are futures in relation to certain other periods which preceded them. Now, the appeal to the fact that past futures resembled past pasts and past presents constitutes excellent inductive evidence for the conclusion that the future will resemble the past and the present. Stated fully, the argument is as follows: a period which has to the past and present the relation of happening after it will resemble the past and the present in certain respects because in the past periods which stood in the same temporal relation to other periods were found to resemble those periods in these respects.

It should be emphasized that in the conclusion of this argument 'future' means 'future future', as that phrase would normally be understood. It refers to a period which by the time at which the statement is made has not yet been experienced, i.e. has not yet become a present or a past.

The appeal to the resemblance between past futures and past pasts and presents is not to the point only if in the sentence 'the future will resemble the past and the present' the word 'future' means 'period which has to the present the relation of occurring

[1] The paragraphs which follow are a summary in my own words of the main point of F. L. Will's delightful article 'Will the Future be like the Past?' (*Mind*, 1947).

after it *and* which can never be experienced as a present'. In that case, of course, past futures are not really futures. For, when they were experienced they were experienced as presents. However, anybody who in ordinary life or in science says or implies that the future will resemble the past and the present does not use 'future' in this sense. He means to assert something about a future which may one day be experienced as a present.

B. If Russell had answered in the affirmative any of the three questions which we imagined ourselves to be addressing to him, his question (1) would be a genuine question in the sense that it could then not be disposed of by an examination of definitions alone. But even then Russell would have been guilty of *ignoratio elenchi* by high redefinition. For in order to have a reason, in the ordinary sense of the word, for inferring that the next instance of a certain phenomenon is positive it is not necessary to observe all the positive and negative necessary conditions for the occurrence of this instance. Nor is it necessary that the collection of positive observed instances should be larger or taken from more extensively different circumstances than many we actually have. Nor, finally, is it necessary that breakdowns should never have occurred in *any* domain. All that is necessary in this connection is that there should have been no breakdowns in the same domain. Or, if any did occur in the same domain they must have proved capable of correlation with certain special features which are known not to be present in the subject of the prediction.

Anybody who takes the trouble to observe the ordinary usage of the word 'reason' in connection with inductive arguments can easily check up on these claims.

It may be interesting to return for a moment to the case of the chicken which finally had its neck wrung. If we had explored every corner of the universe with wonderfully fine instruments and failed to discover a Controller of human movements, then in any ordinary sense of 'being in a better position' we should undoubtedly be in a better position in the case of the man jumping out of the Empire State Building than the chicken in regard to its meals. If Russell even then denied that we are in a better position he is surely using the phrase 'being in a better position' in a strange sense. Or else he is asserting a very plain falsehood. For to say that possession of one set of observed facts, say P, puts one in a better position with regard to a certain inductive conclusion, say *c*, than possession of another set of observed facts, say Q, simply means that P is a reason for *c* while Q is not, or that P is a better reason than Q.

Moreover, even without having explored every corner of the universe, we *are* in a very much better position in the case of predicting the sun's rising or the movement of a man jumping from the Empire State Building than the chicken is regarding its meals. The truth is that Russell's analogy, although it is not wholly pointless, is very weak indeed. Its only merit consists in bringing out the fact that neither we nor the chicken have explored every corner of the universe. On the other hand, there are two important differences which Russell obscures when he says that even in the case of our most trusted scientific theories we may be in no better a position than the chicken. Firstly, the number of observed instances supporting our prediction in a case like the man's jumping from the Empire State Building is obviously much greater than the number of positive instances observed by the chicken. And secondly, although we cannot definitely say that there is nowhere a Controller of human motions, we certainly have no reason whatsoever to suppose that one exists. We have no reason whatsoever to suppose that a living individual, in any ordinary sense of 'control', controls the movements of human beings who jump out of a house. The chicken, on the other hand, if it knows anything, knows that it depends for its meals on another living object.

C. Let us now turn to question (2): Is there any number, *n*, of observed positive instances of a phenomenon which affords evidence that the $n+1$st instance will also be positive? I have already mentioned the familiar fact that scientists as well as ordinary people of a certain level of intelligence do not rely for their inductive conclusions on the number of observed positive instances exclusively. However, it will be easier to discuss the question before us if we proceed on the assumption that according to common sense the strength of past experienee as evidence depends on the number of observed positive instances and on nothing else. All important points can be made more easily if we proceed on this assumption.

Now, in two senses the answer to question (2) must be admitted to be a clear 'No'. Firstly, even if there were in every domain or in some domains a number of observed positive instances which constitutes the dividing line between evidence and non-evidence or, as it is more commonly expressed, between sufficient and insufficient evidence, there is no reason whatsoever to suppose that the number would be the same for different domains. There is no reason to suppose that in the domain of animal learning, for example, the number is the same as in the domain of the movements of the heavenly bodies. But, secondly, there is no such number in *any* domain. For we are here clearly faced with a case of what is sometimes called 'continuous variation'. There is no more *a* number dividing sufficient from insufficient evidence than there is a number dividing bald people from those who are not bald or poor people from people who are not poor.

These facts, however, imply nothing against common-sense. For, from the fact that there is no rigid division between sufficient and insufficient evidence it does not follow that there are no cases of sufficient evidence. From the fact that there is no number which constitutes the borderline between adequate collections of positive instances and those which are not adequate it does not follow that no number of positive instances is adequate. Although we cannot point to a number which divides bald people from people who are not bald, we can without any hesitation say that a man without a single hair on his head is bald while one with a million hairs on his head is not bald.

Furthermore, just as we can say about many people that they are bald and about many others that they are not bald although we have not counted the number of hairs on their heads and just as we can say that Rockefeller is rich although we cannot even approximately say what is the dollar-equivalent of his total possessions, so we can very often say *that* a number of observed instances constitutes sufficient evidence although we cannot say *what* this number is. The number of instances supporting the theory of gravitation which human beings have observed is for example more than sufficient evidence—in any ordinary sense of the word—for supposing that the man jumping out of the Empire State Building will move in a downward direction. But nobody knows what this number is. Human beings simply do not bother to keep records of all instances which confirm the law of gravity.

IV

A few words must now be said about the claim, made by Russell, Ewing and others, that empiricism cannot provide a justification of induction since any inductive or empirical justification of induction would necessarily beg the question. If the principle of induction 'is not true', to use Russell's words, 'every attempt to arrive at general scientific laws from particular observations is fallacious, and Hume's scepticism is inescapable for an empiricist'. But 'the principle itself cannot, without circularity, be inferred from observed uniformities, since it is required to justify any such inference' (*History of Western Philosophy*, p. 699).

In the light of our remarks about redefinitions it is easy to see that all claims of this nature are either mistaken or else cases of *ignoratio elenchi* by redefinition. Before showing this, it will be well to restate the principle of induction in a form which is less confusing than that which Russell uses. Let us try the following formulation:

'The greater the number of positive instances of a phenomenon which have been observed, assuming that no or none except easily explicable negative instances have been found, *and* the greater the number of kinds from which the positive instances are drawn, the less often does it happen that a new instance of the phenomenon turns out to be negative.'[1]

I admit that this statement is rather vague and I also admit that, unless one qualifies it so as to deprive it of all factual significance, one can find exceptions to it.

At the same time, it seems plain that the principle as here stated is very much closer to the truth than its contrary. Furthermore, whether or not it would be correct to regard the inductive principle as a *premiss* of all inductive arguments, it does seem to me part of the *reason* for every inductive conclusion. I mean by this that we would not apply 'reason' to a large number of positive and widely varied instances if the contrary of the inductive principle were true or nearer the truth than the inductive principle. Supposing, for example, it had been found in all domains that after 10,000 instances had been observed, all of them

[1] Cf. Ernest Nagel, *Principles of the Theory of Probability*, p. 72.

positive and gathered from very varied circumstances, chaos was found among the rest. After the 10,000th instance, in other words, predictions always became thoroughly unreliable. Supposing that in these circumstances we discover a new species of animal—let us call them grats. We want to find how long it takes the grats to solve a certain puzzle and find that all our first 10,000 subjects can solve it in less than an hour. Would we say, knowing what happened in all the many observed domains after the 10,000th instance, we had a reason for supposing that the 10,001st grat would also solve the puzzle in less than an hour? It seems clear that most of us would refuse to say this.

It is now apparent that my analysis in Section III of the main sense and also of the second ordinary sense of 'reason for an inductive conclusion' was incomplete. It will be sufficient here to indicate how my analysis requires to be supplemented in the case of the main sense. To say that *p* is a reason for an inductive conclusion, in the main sense of 'reason', is to say firstly that part of *p* asserts what I earlier claimed the whole of *p* to assert *and* secondly that the rest of *p* asserts the inductive principle. Part of *p* asserts the inductive principle at least in the sense of asserting that it is much closer the truth than its contrary.

Miss Ambrose, in her splendid article on induction, has tried to meet the charge of *petitio principii* by contending that the principle of induction is not a premiss of inductive arguments, but a principle of inference or substitution *according* to which 'inductive inferences are made'.[1] But this seems to me an inadequate reply to the charge. For the enemies of common-sense might admit that what Miss Ambrose says is true of the principle as Russell is in the habit of formulating it. But they might then proceed to restate it in some such way as I have done, maintaining that in this sense it does form part of the reason for every inductive conclusion. At this stage they would undoubtedly renew their charge that the inductive argument cannot be supported by an inductive argument without begging the question.

And I want to show now that my admission that the inductive principle is part of the reason for every inductive conclusion

[1] 'The Problem of Justifying Inductive Inference', *Journal of Philosophy*, 1947, pp. 260 ff. Miss Ambrose's point is not actually made in order to answer the charge of *petitio principii*. However, if what she says were true of all possible forms of the inductive principle, the charge would have been implicitly disposed of.

implies nothing against common-sense or against empiricism. For this purpose it is necessary to distinguish two possible senses of any statement of the form 'All S are P'. Such a statement may either mean 'All *observed* S are P'; or it may mean 'All S *whatsoever* are P'. I propose to refer to statements of the first class as 'universal premisses' and to statements of the second class as 'universal conclusions'. Now, the charge of *petitio principii* could be sustained only if the inductive principle were meant as a universal *conclusion* when forming part of the evidence of inductive conclusions. But it is clear that when it forms part of the evidence of inductive conclusions, the inductive principle is or requires to be meant only as a universal *premiss*. We would refuse to regard a large collection of exclusively positive and widely varied instances of a phenomenon as a good reason for predicting that the next instance will also be positive if in all or most previous cases large collections of exclusively positive and widely varied instances turned out to be a thoroughly unreliable basis for prediction. However, given a large collection of exclusively positive and widely varied instances of a phenomenon, it would be sufficient for a correct application of 'reason' that in all or most *observed* cases large collections of exclusively positive and widely varied instances turned out to be a reliable basis for prediction. Any opinion to the contrary rests on the belief, exploded in the previous section, that according to ordinary usage 'reason for an inductive conclusion' means 'deductively conclusive reason for the inductive conclusion'.

V

I can well imagine that some people will not be moved by what I have said. Even if Russell himself were convinced, there are undoubtedly other philosophers who would take me to task for evading what they would declare to be the real issue. 'You may have shown,' it would be said, 'that in the ordinary sense of "reason" and "evidence" past observations do often constitute a good reason and sufficient evidence. But how do you know that what is a reason in the ordinary sense is *really a reason*? The fact that the sun has risen every day so far is admittedly a reason, in the ordinary sense, for supposing that it will again rise to-morrow. For to say this is simply to say that it has always risen in the past.

But *can you predict* that the sun will again rise to-morrow simply because it has always risen in the past? The question, the interesting doubt about induction in this instance is not: Have we any reason in the ordinary sense for supposing that the sun will rise to-morrow? To this, we agree, the answer is 'Yes'. The real question is: Having a reason, in the ordinary sense, for believing that the sun will rise to-morrow, can we infer from this with any reliability that the sun will again rise to-morrow?

Before I take up this objection I should like to fill in a gap in my analysis of the ordinary usage of the phrase 'reason for an inductive conclusion'. It will be remembered that in Section III I distinguished between three trends in the ordinary usage of this phrase. Firstly there is what I called the main sense of the word; secondly there is a set of trends which I grouped together as the second sense of the word; and finally there is a trend or sense to which I alluded but which I have so far not attempted to analyse. According to both senses I analysed, '*p* constitutes a reason for *c*' (where *c* stands for some inductive conclusion) asserts the existence of *observed* events exclusively. Its truth need not at all be affected by the discovery that *c* is false.

Now, the third sense which I have not yet analysed is much less prominent than the main sense but, so far as I can see, much more prominent than the trends which I have grouped together as the second sense. When 'reason' is used in this third sense the observed facts referred to by 'reason' in the main sense are part of its referent, but they are not the whole of it. It is not indeed a necessary condition for the application of 'reason' (in this sense) to a set of propositions, say *p*, that the prediction based on *p* be *true*. But, where the prediction refers to a multitude of events, it is a necessary condition that it be considerably nearer the truth than its contrary. Where the prediction explicitly refers to a single event only, it is a necessary condition that a considerable majority of instantial predictions having the same relation to *p* be true. Thus, according to the third sense, we would have had a reason for believing that the man jumping out of the Empire State Building will move in a downward direction although subsequent observation shows him to move into the sky—provided that in most other cases, as yet unobserved at the time of making our prediction, human bodies did in similar circumstances move downwards. With our large collection of exclusively positive and widely varied past instances, we would have had a reason for believing that all men who will jump out of houses are going to move in a downward direction even if a few of them disappeared in the sky so long as *most* of them moved as we predicted. We would have had no reason in this third sense if in the case of a large proportion of subsequent jumps—approaching half the total number of new jumps—bodies failed to move in a downward direction.

It will be helpful to use different signs to distinguish between a reason in the main and a reason in the third sense. Let us use the sign 'reason *m*' to stand for reasons in the main sense and the sign 'reason *f*' to signify reasons in the third sense. Using this terminology, we may restate the objection outlined at the beginning of the present section as follows: 'You have shown that frequently people have reasons *m* for believing in inductive conclusions. However, the real question is whether, without appealing to a non-empirical principle, they ever have reasons *f*; and this you have not shown'. I could have stated this charge more easily by using the words 'probable' and 'certain'. But, as I explained earlier, an explicit discussion of the questions 'Are any inductive conclusions probable?' and 'Are any inductive conclusions certain?' is beyond my scope.

In reply to this charge, I wish to make two comments. The first of these is as follows: it simply is a fact that, given certain sets of observations, human beings can make true predictions. It simply is a fact that given reasons in the sense of reason *m* we very often also have reasons in the sense of reason *f*. This is a fact just as it is a fact that human beings can make genuine observations and just as it is a fact that certain objects have certain spatial relations to one another and that some events happen after other events. It is logically and also I think factually possible to have feelings of doubt and anxiety concerning the outcome of any prediction whatsoever. But it is also possible to have such doubts about the genuineness of observations at the present moment and about the reality of spatial and temporal relations. The possibility or the actual existence of such feelings no more implies that human beings cannot in certain circumstances make true predictions than it implies that they never make genuine observations or that there are no real relations in space and time.

Secondly, it seems to me that a person who has all the information which ordinary mortals have but who nevertheless asks, with an air of infinite puzzlement 'How can we now predict something which is not yet?' is tacitly confusing the statement '*c* is true' with the statement '*c* has been or is being directly verified'.[1] '*c* can now be correctly predicted' does indeed imply '*c* is true', but it does not imply '*c* has been directly verified'. To say that we have a reason *f* for *c* does imply that *c* is at least probable. It does not imply that *c* has already been directly tested. Now, if 'correctly predict' is used in any ordinary sense, then the question 'How can we now predict an event which is not yet?' produces no cramps and can easily be answered by referring to the truth of past predictions in certain circumstances. Questions like 'How can we now predict something which is not yet?' give rise to headaches only if '*c* can now be correctly predicted' is used in such a way as to imply '*c* has been directly verified'. Sentences like this then produce cramps and headaches because they are not really questions at all. They are like rhetorical questions. The sentence 'How can we now predict something which is not yet?' is then another way of *asserting the necessary* proposition that in the high sense of 'predict' in which '*c* can now be correctly predicted' implies '*c* has been directly verified', it is impossible ever to predict a future event. But this, of course, does not at all contradict the common-sense view that in the ordinary sense of 'predict' we can frequently predict future events. This objection, too, is therefore an *ignoratio elenchi* by redefinition.

To be more precise: the sentence 'How can we now predict something which is not yet?' produces a cramp if one believes oneself to be asking the (easy) question which the sentence expresses with every word in it used in its ordinary sense when one is in fact *asserting* the necessary proposition that in a certain high sense of 'predict' we can never predict anything at all.

Following Moore, Mr. J. N. Findlay has forcibly drawn attention to the queerness of the philosopher's doubt when he utters sentences like 'But how can any one set of facts furnish a

[1] This distinction is brought out very lucidly by Sydney Hook in his *John Dewey*, p. 79

valid basis for an inference concerning another set of facts?'[1], 'How do you know that one thing ever happens after another?' or 'How do you know that one thing is ever to the left of another?' Findlay suggests that we take a specific instance—e.g. what we would normally describe as a pencil lying to the left of a pen—, point it out to the doubting philosopher, and say 'This is how'.[2] In the case of predictions we could take a piece of chalk and call out 'I now predict that when I release this piece of chalk it will move in a downward direction'. We would then release it, and, as it falls in a downward direction, we would point to it and say 'This is how we can know in advance'. Since the philosopher is just as familiar with these facts as we are and since he does not, in one important sense at least, query any of them, it is apparent that, without realizing it, he is using one or more of his words in a strange sense.

[1] Williams, 'Induction and the Future', *Mind*, 1948, p. 227.

[2] 'Time: A Treatment of Some Puzzles', *Australasian Journal of Psychology and Philosophy*, 1941, p. 217 (reprinted as Chapter III in this volume); cf. also Friedrich Waismann's introduction to Schlick's *Gesammelte Aufsätze*, pp. xxi ff.

CHAPTER V

THE PHILOSOPHER'S USE OF ANALOGY

By Margaret Macdonald

VIEWS about the nature of philosophy and philosophical method do not appear to permit of demonstration. As Mill said of a similar topic, 'it is possible only to give considerations capable of determining the intellect either to give or withhold its consent to the doctrine'. The method of science is justified in practice. The scientist shows that he has the correct method for discovering new facts by indisputably presenting more and more of them. No one would dispute that we know more about physics, chemistry, and psychology than we did a hundred years ago. The philosopher has no such means of conviction. For one of the points at issue is whether he discovers any facts at all. He may recommend a philosophical method, but whether he convinces will depend as much on his audience and the general climate of opinion as on his own reasoning. For there seems to be no accepted criterion of when a philosophical question has been answered and what satisfies one generation, it seems, does not satisfy another. But everyone who was not satisfied that the problem of combustion had, in essentials, been settled by Lavoisier would rightly be considered incompetent or irrational. We are not even sure whether this is because philosophical questions are more difficult than scientific questions or because they are not questions at all. Certainly, we have not decided what sort of questions they are. I wish to invite, or strengthen, your consent to the view that philosophical propositions are not factual but verbal. That is itself a bald and misleading statement. I shall try to recommend it with the help of an example. Philosophical questions, it is suggested, arise from certain apparent peculiarities of ordinary statements. E.g., 'This is red' and 'That is red', yet they are not two colours but 'the same colour' (problem of universals); 'We have both got toothache but I can only feel my own' (problem of solipsism); 'That is a mirage though it looks exactly like an oasis' (problem of the existence of physical objects),[1] etc. We certainly understand these propositions and use them in ordinary conversation without any difficulty. Yet to the philosopher they appear queer and inconsistent. But, obviously, not in the sense in which 'He has gone out but is still at home' is inconsistent, for everyone would immediately agree that this was so. It is when, as we say, we reflect on statements of the first kind that they seem peculiar and puzzling. When we consider some of their implications and compare them with those of other statements. We consider, e.g., that two red flags may be in different places at the same time but that it would be nonsense to say of either of them that it could be in the same place and equal nonsense to say of their colour that it could not characterize at the same time many different objects in different places. 'What a peculiar thing a colour is', says the philosopher. 'How does it manage to multiply itself in a way impossible to coloured objects?' 'Perhaps it is like the day which is everywhere at once, or a very ethereal vapour which pervades visual space and becomes perceptible in different parts of it', etc. The same sort of remarks are made about the other statements. 'How queer that what we perceive now is exactly like what we have perceived when dreaming or deluded. Perhaps we are always deluded though some dreams and hallucinations last longer and are more coherent than others', etc. In making such remarks, what has the philosopher said? Does he make them as the result of a more profound study of the nature of colours and physical objects or has he analysed facts about them more carefully than the ordinary man? Has he discovered, e.g. a number of objects called *universals* with peculiar characteristics, signified by our use of general terms, of whose existence we were previously ignorant? Or has he (as the Nominalists supposed) discovered that since there *cannot* be general objects our use of general terms *must* refer only to groups of objects resembling each other? Is it his superior knowledge of human perceptions which makes him insist that since we *may* always be dreaming, drunk, or deluded whenever we perceive—however much we may protest on many particular occasions that we are not—we are for ever prevented from knowing whether

[1] I wish only to suggest that these are of the type of statement which (among others) have caused these problems.

physical objects exist? In other words, does he give us reason to believe that we always use ordinary language *wrongly*, or that all ordinary propositions are false, and, if so, what does he mean? Many philosophers have, I think, supposed that ordinary language is very inexact and misleading; that it needs to be refined, or a new, improved symbolism substituted for the purposes of philosophy. A symbolism which would express more accurately certain facts about the situations in which ordinary language is used and which that language either fails to express or expresses very loosely and vaguely. But this new and perfect language has never been achieved although the sciences bristle with technical terms for the expression of their discoveries. For a non-verbalist this ought to be somewhat surprising. But it would be a necessary consequence if the philosopher's puzzles which were generated by the known uses of words are capable only of a verbal solution. If philosophical questions, i.e. are never answered by producing more empirical facts but either by misusing words or by examining their already known, correct usage. The informative air, the plausibility and the paradoxes of most philosophical theories may not be due to any astonishing information acquired by the philosopher but to a curious practice of using words by analogy without giving the analogy any intelligible application. Philosophical theories which claim to state facts in much the same sense as physical theories will be found, I suggest, to appeal for evidence not to experience but to 'what we say' in certain relevant circumstances. They depend for their understanding, as scientific theories do not, *entirely* upon the known uses of ordinary words. They do not extend the use of these words but generally only misuse them. It is for this reason that such philosophical propositions have been called senseless. They try to operate with ordinary words when they have deprived them of their ordinary functions. They recombine known words in an unfamiliar way while trading on their familiar meanings. But these analogies lead to hopeless difficulties and so it seems that philosophical problems are never solved at all. Nor could they be solved, or even tackled satisfactorily, while the verbal character of both questions and answers was realized only half, or not at all. But if it is realized and is correct, then the only help we can get in tackling philosophical problems is from understanding the uses of words and their use and misuse by philosophers. But this conclusion certainly disgusts many philosophers. To be concerned 'merely with words' seems trivial and unimportant. Surely philosophy is not a branch of philology or grammar! Certainly it is not. Philology is an empirical science. Philologists formulate laws, e.g. Grimm's Law, from which they predict future forms of speech, etc. This is not philosophy. Nor does the philologist consider sentences of the form 'S is P' to elucidate the problem of substance. For the philologist or grammarian 'Substance is causa sui' is as good a grammatical sentence as 'St. Paul's is large', but for the philosopher they are very different. Yet it does not follow that philosophy is concerned with 'something more' than the uses of words. It is concerned with them differently and for a different purpose. Or rather, when it is said that philosophers study not words but *facts* it must be asked in what sense the word 'fact' is being used. In one of the commonest uses of 'fact' the empirical sciences state matters of fact. Consider therefore the difference between the introduction of a word like 'chromosome' and that of a phrase like 'sense-datum'. The first could not be completely defined, its use could not be wholly given, by other terms already in use. It could not be, we should say, because the biologists first gave a use to 'chromosome' by discovering chromosomes. But the philosophers did not similarly define 'sense-datum' as the result of discovering sense-data. They did not because 'sense datum' can be understood only in terms of words already used in describing what we perceive, viz., words and phrases like 'seeing', 'looking', 'looking as if', etc. As Mr. Paul and Professor Murphy have pointed out,[1] 'I am seeing an elliptical sense-datum of a penny' or 'I am seeing a tree-like sense-datum although there is no tree there' are, or can be considered as, only more misleading ways of saying 'That penny looks elliptical' or 'It looks as if there is a tree there but there isn't' and do not represent the discovery by the philosopher of an element in the perceptual situation as the use of the word 'chromosome' represents the discovery of a genetical element by the biologist. Again, consider the difference between what

[1] Cf. 'Is there a Problem about Sense-Data?' by G. A. Paul (*Proceedings of the Aristotelean Society*, Supp. Vol. XV, p. 61 *et seq.*), reprinted as Chapter VI in this volume.
'Two Versions of Critical Philosophy', by A. E. Murphy (*Proceedings of the Aristotelean Society*, 1937–38, p. 143 *et seq.*).

Lavoisier was doing when he discovered oxygen and the nature of combustion and when he reformulated the chemical vocabulary. The second involved defining new chemical terms and redefining old ones. It was wholly concerned with the uses of words and so far resembled philosophical activity. But it resulted from the first activity of empirical discovery which was not verbal. There is, I suggest, no such distinction in the activities of philosophers. Scientists use words to state facts. They do not consider, except in special circumstances, their uses. Philosophers use words entirely in order to make propositions about their uses however much their propositions seem to resemble scientific statements of fact. This is shown by the kind of assertions made and the reasons with which they are supported. The philosophers who dispute about universals, e.g., have not discovered that *red* or *redness* is or is not 'something more' than its instances. They have not discovered this in the sense in which Stalin is 'something more' than the whole collection of his photographs or 'Mrs. Harris' was 'nothing more' than the frequent references and descriptions of Mrs. Gamp. For if they had there would no longer be a dispute. But the Nominalist says: 'A universal cannot be something over and above its instances for (1) we use general terms when we have been acquainted with instances of their application and (2) we commonly use the word "object" for something having unique spatio-temporal position and this is just how we do not use general terms. General terms, therefore, refer to classes of resembling instances.' The Realist asserts: 'A universal cannot be identical with the class of its instances for a universal term may be significant when it has no instances. If everything green disappeared "Leaves are green" would still be significant though false and though we might still "think of" green we should not be having green thoughts. Moreover, some universals, e.g. *perfection*, may never have had instances and yet we can sometimes use the word "perfect" significantly. We must be referring to something. A universal must therefore be more than its instances and some universals are not even instantiated.' The dispute turns clearly on the uses of words and what must exist or not exist is deduced from these uses. And both disputants seem to be right, which would be impossible if they were in fact disputing the existence of something. For it is clearly true that we do not use general terms as we ordinarily use words for objects. They are indeed precisely those to which we oppose them. A tree is an object, a person is an object, a red patch is an object, but what is meant by saying that 'red' must name an object if it is used with none of the criteria with which the word 'object' is ordinarily used? But neither is a general term used for the class of its instances since it may have significance but no present application. The nominalist seems superficial since he stresses only part of the usage of general terms. The realist seems mystical because although he correctly emphasizes what the nominalist overlooks he combines this with a misuse of the word 'object' which causes more puzzles. Neither is content merely to describe for us the use of general terms, contrasting it with the use of words for objects, in the ordinary sense, but without offering pseudo-scientific explanations of these differences. Yet this may be the only business of the philosopher faced with the peculiar problems called philosophical.

Matter and Form

A similar account could be given of the problems of solipsism and perceptual illusion, but I wish to take as my chief example of philosophical analogy and linguistic misusage the ancient antithesis of matter and form and especially its application by philosophers to the physical world. Materialists have asserted and idealists denied the existence of matter or material substance. Both have assumed that the world must be made of *something*. For Thales the world was made of water; for Russell[1] events are the 'real stuff' of the world. To what questions are such peculiar statements the answer?

There seem to be three kinds of proposition which have puzzled philosophers into making such remarks. (1) Propositions of the forms 'There is an *x*' or '*x* exists', and (2) '*x* has the property ϕ'. Or, in traditional language, propositions ascribing the essence of a thing, connoted by its class name, and those ascribing its accidental qualities. (3) Propositions asserting change.

The third problem is logically subsidiary to the first two, if

[1] Cf. *An Outline of Philosophy*, p. 291.

not part of them, but since it has troubles of its own it is usually treated separately.

We say, then, 'That man is a millionaire' and 'That is a man'. A millionaire is a man having the quality of owning at least a million pounds. But whatever is a man must have certain qualities, e.g. human shape, reason, speech, etc. Even if we could not give a complete list of them which would cover all borderline cases we could say within very wide limits what they are. We can all recognize men and know how to use the word 'man'. Now 'being rich', says the philosopher, is predicated of a man. And 'man' also connotes a set of qualities. But of what are these predicated in the sense in which 'being rich' is, e.g., predicated of this man, viz., Lord Nuffield? We can think of the quality of 'being rich' and imagine Lord Nuffield to be poor. We can 'abstract' the quality. We can also think of all the qualities which we generally mean by 'man'. But when we have abstracted them all, of what do we think as having these qualities in the sense in which we think of Lord Nuffield as wealthy? This sounds extremely crude but I think it fairly represents what many philosophers have thought as the following highly respectable quotations may show. They could easily be multiplied.

'When all else is stripped off evidently nothing but matter remains . . . by matter I mean that which in itself is neither a particular thing nor of a certain quantity nor assigned to any of the other categories by which being is determined . . . for the predicates other than substance are predicated of substance while substance is predicated of matter.'[1]

'When I distinguish the wax from its exterior forms and when, as if I had stripped it of its vestments, I consider it quite naked . . . it is certain that nothing remains except something extended, flexible and movable . . . of which the perception is neither an act of sight, of touch, nor of imagination . . . but is simply an intuition of the mind.'[2]

This is surely a very curious proceeding. When its sensible qualities have been 'stripped' from a perceptual object nothing remains which could conceivably be perceived at all. When a man's hair is shorn he is left bald. How is he left when shorn of

[1] Aristotle, *Metaphysics*, trans. Ross, 1029a, 10–20.
[2] Descartes, *Meditation* 2, trans. Veitch.

all qualities, we may ask. It may be objected that this is just stupid literalism. Of course, no one supposes that qualities are taken from objects as skins from an onion. They are simply abstracted, thought of apart from the objects, and that is perfectly possible. But I wish to concentrate on the metaphors for I believe they are important and have been very misleading. For the metaphor suggests and was undoubtedly intended to suggest that by abstraction an intellectual analysis of objects was performed which showed their composition in a way analogous to that in which a chemical analysis reveals their chemical composition. Thus it seemed plausible that an object should consist of perceived qualities attached to or 'informing' something logically imperceptible. For, by definition, for Aristotle, Descartes, Locke, and many other philosophers we cannot perceive the subject of all sensible qualities. We can know only that it *must* exist as their substratum. But this analogy is an attempt to apply an ordinary use of the word 'analysis', viz., that in which a complex object, e.g. a machine, is decomposed or separated into its parts or a compound resolved into its elements. But for these operations we have sensible criteria for recognizing the whole, the process of separation and the parts when separated. It is logically impossible to apply any such criteria to the separation of matter from its qualities. The analogy, therefore, does not apply; it is not properly to be called an analogy at all and it gives a wholly wrong and misleading picture of the philosopher's problem and its solution. For when we 'abstract' red from this object we do not leave it colourless, nor when we think of all its properties do we leave it formless materia prima, intelligible extension or 'something we know not what'. To abstract qualities is to recognize that quality-words may be used in many different contexts. It is wrongly pictured as separating an element from a compound and then naming it, as if it resembled separating a gas from water and calling it oxygen. Such a picture gives the problem a pseudo-scientific air. But that it is not and does not resemble a scientific problem is shown by the admission that it would be logically impossible to verify the existence of material substance or of the abstracted qualities in the sense required and thus to apply the analogy of stripping, analysing, finding the 'base' of sensible qualities, which this language suggests. For the problem is not one of analysing objects or facts about them but of understanding the use of the subject term in certain propositions. This involves also examining the use of predicates or words for qualities. Moreover, since such propositions are used for what exists it is easy to confuse a scientific statement about what exists with a linguistic statement about the use of words for what exists, or to suppose that a proposition about what exists can be deduced from such a linguistic statement. That this is not so, again, can be seen by examining the use of the words in which such an alleged deduction is expressed. The linguistic nature of the problem was partly realized by Aristotle for he expressed it in terms of the categories. And the categories are forms of speech. True, they are, also, the clue to the nature of being, but since they appear to be the only clue, i.e. nothing could be expressed about being except by a proposition in one of the categories, it is not clear in what sense problems about being are more than problems about the uses of the categories.

The solution is that existence propositions like 'That is a man', 'There are men', 'Men exist' are different from subject-predicate positions like 'That man is a millionaire', 'All men are gullible', and cannot be simply reduced to the subject-predicate form. It is quite clear that the category of substance does not ascribe a set of predicates to a subject other than a substance as Aristotle supposed. If we ask, 'What is called Bois Roussel and won the Derby in 1938?' the correct reply is 'a horse'. If we ask, 'What has the defining properties of a horse?' again the only sensible reply is 'a horse', not 'a piece of matter' or 'material substance'. But if we had asked, 'What horse won the Derby in 1938', the reply 'a horse' would have been absurd. Again, 'This piece of matter has the defining properties of a horse but is not itself a horse' is nonsense while 'This horse has a mane but is not itself a mane' is, I think, sensible and true. For propositions like 'This horse won the Derby', 'This man is wealthy' we have separate criteria for the use of the subject and predicate. We know how to distinguish a horse from its achievement of winning a race and a man from his possession of great wealth. But in one sense at least no such distinction is possible for existence propositions. To ascribe the defining properties of an object is to state what is correctly called by the name of that object. And whatever is correctly called, e.g. a man or a horse is just a man or a horse, not something else to which these properties are ascribed. For they are ascribed to men and horses and 'That is a man' or 'There are men' translated into the subject-predicate form would give the tautologies 'That man is a man' and 'Men are men'. Since existence propositions are never tautological it seems important to emphasize their difference from those which ascribe a predicate to a subject as well as for the reason that the denial of this difference has led philosophers to pseudo-theories of material substance. For matter is, on these views, the ultimate subject of all propositions about the physical world. But this is unintelligible. We must then recognize a difference between propositions which assert that an object of a certain sort exists and those which assert that such an object has various 'accidental' properties. Nothing is gained by denying their differences but something may be by understanding how they are significantly asserted.

This may sound platitudinous. Have we not been told by Kant and certainly by Russell of the difference in logical type between existence and subject-predicate propositions? We have certainly been told that existence is not a predicate, which is true. But I do not think we have been so clearly told how existence propositions ascribe predicates at all in the sense in which subject-predicate propositions, in the ordinary sense, do so. According to Russell,[1] 'There are men' or 'A man exists' means 'The property of being human belongs to something'[2] or '*x* is human' is sometimes true, and that 'All horses neigh' means 'Whatever is equine neighs' or '*x* is equine and *x* neighs' is always true. According to this they are similar in type though one is more complex than the other since it is a compound of two or more propositional functions. But we might be inclined to ask (assuming that 'man' here means 'man or woman, i.e. human being') what is the something that has the property of being human except a man? What is it that is equine except a horse which also neighs? That this view did lead to a more sophisticated attempt to find ultimate subjects for predicates seems to be shown by Russell's doctrine that the ultimate elements of facts are logical atoms named by logically proper names unadulterated

[1] *Introduction to Mathematical Philosophy*, pp. 171–2.
[2] I think this is Prof. Moore's formulation.

by any description. The purified symbolism in which these objects were to be expressed does not, however, seem to have been formulated.

But although there seem to be important differences between existence propositions and those which ascribe predicates to subjects, in the ordinary sense, I do not myself profess to be able to state them adequately. I can indicate only what seem to be one or two marks of such differences. It might be said, e.g., that in order to know whether there are men we must make certain observations, viz., of human shape and behaviour. To know whether men are tall and die we must make these plus other observations which verify 'being tall' and 'being mortal'. How then can it be said that although we observe that Mr. Chamberlain is tall and thin, we do not similarly observe that he has the property of being human, i.e. that he exists? For these seem to be similar activities. How then can they result in the assertion of two different types of proposition? The answer can be found only by considering further how we use these propositions, i.e. what else we say about them. We should say that to make humanish observations is just the same thing as to observe that there are human beings; it is not to observe that there are objects which have the property of being human for that suggests that there are separate criteria for the use of the word 'object' in this connection. But observations of tallness and mortality would not be described as observation of the objects 'a tall man' and 'a mortal man'. For a tall man just is a man who is tall and a mortal man is one who will die. They are not different objects from men. But that men are tall and mortal does justify the assertion that certain properties belong to something, viz., mortality and exceptional height to men. Again, it would be true to say, pointing to Mr. Chamberlain, 'He (or "that man") might not have been so tall' and also 'He might not have existed' but it would, I think, be nonsense to say, 'He might not have been human'. So that in one sense 'A man exists' and 'x is human' do not mean the same since a true value for the propositional function would give a tautology while an existence proposition is never tautologous. This last statement may seem false. For we may, e.g., ask from a distance 'Is that a man or a tree?' and, on coming closer, remark, 'Yes, that is a man'. Of a monstrous birth we may decide that it is not human, etc. But we are not here doubtfully ascribing predicates to objects, as we might wonder whether a person's eyes are blue or brown; we are wondering whether they are certain objects, which is different. So that either, e.g. 'That has the property of being human' or '*x* has the property of being human' simply means 'That man exists' or 'A man exists', for which it is a misleading reformulation, or it is a tautology which fails to give the meaning of an existence proposition. For it is not about the existence of anything but about the meaning of a word, e.g. 'man'. Existence propositions do not ascribe their defining properties to subjects and the search for such subjects by philosophers is due to this typical confusion of propositions. Nor does it follow that they have no subjects. Their subjects are things which are asserted to exist.

The third class of proposition which has provoked philosophical theories of material substance is that of those asserting change. That change presupposes an unchangeable substance as its subject is asserted by many philosophers. It is vehemently denied by others from Heraclitus to the Dialectical Materialists. Indeed, the word 'change' rouses the passions of philosophers to a curious degree. For some change is a shifty business to be shunned by searchers for eternal truth, equated with logical certainty. For others it is the mysterious source of novelty, incapable of prediction and therefore free from the shackles of logic and reason. Both attitudes seem absurd though it is not difficult to see the sort of propositions which have tempted philosophers to make such remarks. But, of course, propositions about change are not logically certain, irrational nor non-rational. They are used with the criteria of reasonable assertion appropriate to their type as a class of contingent propositions, and that is all. Bergsonian eulogy and platonic denunciation are both irrelevant.

It is clear that we frequently use in describing processes of change the same subject in the same sense throughout. We say, e.g., that this apple was green but has ripened and is now red; that it has grown larger in the last six weeks; that it was picked from that tree and placed in this bowl, etc. We should say that it was 'the same apple' to which all these changes occurred and we could give sensible criteria for determining the respects in which it was the same and those in which it had altered. In Aristotle's language, change can occur to a substance in any of the categories except substance without causing much philosophical trouble. The criteria may vary in difficulty. An object which has changed its place only is more easily recognized than one which has also changed its size, shape, and colour, but as long as the same class name is applicable both before and after change the difficulties do not seem insuperable or even very puzzling. I may not be sure whether this is Smith whom I have not seen for twenty years when he was young and is now old, but he is at least a man of about the right age and I can find out whether he is Smith. But we should scarcely ask of a heap of earth in the churchyard whether it is Smith who has been dead for twenty years. Yet Smith (or his body) dies and becomes ashes just as he grows and becomes old. What is the surviving subject of this change in the sense in which Smith recognizably survives all other changes which occur to him? How do we describe change of substance or the transformation of one object into another? A favourite answer of philosophers has been: ' "X changes into Y" means "There is something called 'matter' or 'material substance' which at time t has or is informed by x qualities and at t^1 (later than t) has or is informed by y qualities. Matter itself does not change, neither do the qualities, but change consists in the qualitative re-shaping or re-forming of matter into different objects at different times. Just as "this apple" is the subject when we say "This apple was green and is now red and it is 'the same apple' though it now has a different colour", so "matter" is the subject when we say "The water that was in this bowl has been changed into two gases" because this means "A certain portion of matter had the qualities of water and now has those of oxygen and hydrogen and it is the same piece of matter although all its qualities are different".' But is this suggested translation a proposition which we should ever ordinarily assert and, if not, what does it mean? The following quotations illustrate this view, which is common to many philosophers:

' "Matter", in the most proper sense of the term, is to be identified with the *substratum* which is receptive of coming-to-be and passing-away: but the *substratum* of the remaining kinds of change is also, in a certain sense, "matter".'[1]

[1] Aristotle, *De Generatione et Corruptione*, trans. Joachim, Oxford Press, §320a.

'Does the same wax remain after this change? It must be admitted that it does remain; no one doubts it or judges otherwise. What, then, was it I knew with so much distinctness in the piece of wax? . . . It was perhaps . . . only a body that a little before appeared to me conspicuous under these forms, and which now is perceived under others.'[1]

What is the significance of the words 'matter', 'material', stuff', etc., which are frequently used by philosophers of very different schools?

There are a number of propositions which we ordinarily make in which we distinguish a material or stuff, what is made of it, and the design or pattern according to which it is made. An architect examines the plans or specifications of a building and decides whether to build in brick or concrete. A dress pattern is made up in silk or cotton material. We choose 'exactly the same' ornament in platinum instead of gold, etc. Moreover, the material can be made into something else of a different form. The guinea is melted down and the gold re-made into a ring; souvenirs are made of wood from a famous ship, etc. In all these homely examples the distinction between what is matter and what is form is quite clear. We make it constantly and know how it is verified. When Aristotle wants an example of the distinction this is the kind of example he constantly gives. If we wished to teach a child the distinction we should do so by such examples. We know, too, from such examples, what it means to say that the material of a thing may remain unchanged though taking a different form and so becoming a different object. If the same gold is first a coin and then a ring we could say quite sensibly that one object has become another though its material has remained the same throughout these changes. We might describe this by saying 'This gold was a coin and is now a ring'. The use of the words 'matter' and 'material substance' is intended to suggest by analogy that an 'ultimate' *something* is related to different sets of 'essential' predicates at different times as a piece of gold is related to different shapes at different times. 'Being X' and 'being Y' are successively ascribed to a piece of matter as 'being coin-shaped' and 'being ring-shaped' are successively ascribed to a piece of gold. Further, matter is 'made into' different objects by its

[1] Descartes, *loc. cit.*, p. 91.

different predicates as gold is made into different objects by giving it different shapes. This is the analogy employed by all those philosophers who search for the 'ultimate stuff' of the physical world or the nature of the 'ultimate' constituents of physical objects or of facts about them. This is true whether they call what they have claimed to discover, materia prima, extension, events, sense data or even mental states. The picture is that of a material made into different objects as a roll of cloth is made into different garments. It is important to state it thus as crudely as possible. Philosophers who extol change like to emphasize their denial that any permanent material substance exists. But what are they denying and what are those who assert it, asserting? They are not surely denying that we can sometimes say truly, e.g. 'This is the same house although it has been re-painted'? If so, they are denying that the word 'same' is significant in ordinary usage, which is absurd. For if 'same' has no significance neither has 'change'. To say that something has changed is to say that it is not the same as it was and this would be nonsensical if 'being the same' had *no* meaning. If, however, they are denying the contention of those philosophers who assert that an unchangeable matter or substance is the ultimate material of the world, what is the meaning of the assertion which is being denied? Where are the verifiable distinctions which gave 'material' and 'design' their significance in ordinary usage? Since matter or material substance is that which receives all forms or predicates and nothing which is known can be described except by ascribing predicates, no description or knowledge of matter is possible. It is 'pure potentiality', 'something we know not what'. We know only that it *must* exist as the subject of all predicates and the material of all forms. Obviously, therefore, it is logically impossible to apply any sensible criteria whatever for the distinction of material and design. But such criteria are part of what we *mean* by such words; they give the words their use and philosophers who attempt to apply them by analogy without indicating similar criteria or, indeed, any sensible criteria whatever are not using an analogy but simply misusing these ordinary words while trading on the association of their ordinary meanings in appearing to give some subtle information about the world where the conditions of such information are absent.

But neither is the philosopher *merely* gibbering. To say that such metaphysical assertions are nonsense is true but inadequate. They are not meaningless as a string of nonsense words is meaningless simply because they are or can be translated into syntactically correct arrangements of ordinary words of which we already know the meanings. Moreover, the propositions which tempt philosophers to make these assertions are themselves, as we have seen, perfectly ordinary propositions about the characters of things and their changes. What the philosopher does is to notice certain differences in our use of ordinary words which seem to require explanation by a theory about that to which the words are said to refer. But it may be that what is required is just a description of these different uses and their criteria. If this is to be called a 'theory', very well, but it must be noticed that this is a very different use of 'theory' from that employed by science and the C.I.D. or even in ordinary life when we contrast 'theory' and 'practice'. But it is in this second sense of 'theory' that philosophical doctrines of matter claim to be theories. For their authors and many other philosophers have thought that they gave at least a plausible account of what the facts *must* be even though we could never know them more directly and even when the account implied that all ordinary propositions must be false or, at least, very inexact and misleading. But if, as suggested, these doctrines are non-significant they cannot, in this sense, be plausible or unplausible theories for they cannot be theories at all.

I hope this illustration may have helped to make clear why and in what sense philosophical propositions are linguistic and not informative in the ordinary sense. It might, perhaps, be argued that the puzzle about change is not a genuine philosophical problem. It is a scientific problem which some philosophers have tried to solve without the necessary technique or for which others, e.g. Kant, have just adopted a solution from scientific practice. To ask for the substratum of substantial change is a queer way of asking for a connection between, e.g., the liquid state of water and the gaseous states of oxygen and hydrogen into which it is decomposed. Moreover, scientists do connect these by means of other bodies, molecules, atoms, etc., which function as the substratum of change and do assert that the quantity of matter remains constant throughout all changes. The difference is, of course, that propositions about the connection and prediction of changes, the existence of molecules, atoms, etc., are verifiable empirical statements, though the criteria for 'There are molecules' may be very different from those for 'There are apples' or even for 'There are chromosomes'. Similarly, to the truth of the law of the conservation of matter a large number of propositions asserting the equality of weight between substances before and after experiment is relevant. It certainly does not assert that a fixed amount of something which could never be weighed at all is preserved as the substratum of all equality of weight. And equality of weight itself cannot sensibly be called a *substance*. The law is, in fact, a compressed hypothetical proposition about physical operations and their results. But sensible observations and physical operations, as already shown, could never provide criteria for the meaning or use of the philosophical proposition that material substance exists.

The philosopher is not asking a scientific question, for of any scientific proposition it would be possible to ask similar questions about the use of the subject term and no propositions expressing sensible evidence would obviate this difficulty. Nor does the philosopher ever seek such evidence. The question, as we have seen, is asked in terms of categories which are forms of speech or forms of judgement. Aristotle knew as well as we do that much was yet to be sensibly discovered about the laws of physical changes but no such discovery, he thought, would settle the question of the subject of the category of substance. Descartes appeals only to the fact that 'we should all judge', or say, that it was 'the same wax' which remained after melting. The investigation of physical changes is a different undertaking from the investigation of philosophical puzzles which arise from the language used to describe such changes. These puzzles may differ with different terminologies used. They may sometimes be resolved by inventing a new terminology into which the propositions which suggested them can be translated, or by describing how these propositions are actually used. What is important is to notice the difference between this activity and that of the scientific investigation of changing objects. For this difference is all that is meant by saying that philosophy is verbal and not factual.

That different predicates at different times can be ascribed to the same subject, i.e. that things remain recognizable after many changes, is true, and examples of this have been given from ordinary usage. Nor, in spite of Plato and Bergson and their followers, does it appear to be either more difficult or less rational to know that people grow old, apples turn red, and societies change their forms of government than to know that $2 + 2 = 4$. But that all change *must* be ascribed to a permanent substance as subject in this sense is false if intended to describe our ordinary usage and, if not, is a linguistic recommendation by some philosophers which may or may not be accepted. It is certainly not a contingent proposition about what *exists* as the substratum of all change. Scientists may resolve gross bodies into microscopic ones in the course of investigating change and transformation, but no proposition about such scientific objects is, I think, part of what we mean by any ordinary propositions about change such as those responsible for the philosophical puzzles we are considering. Similarly, 'water' does not *mean* 'compound of oxygen and hydrogen', for if it did no one who did not know chemistry would know what water is, but we all do know what water is. And if we did not we could not come to know its composition.

No ordinary person has any difficulty with Aristotle's substantial change for the propositions describing it are used differently from those describing other kinds of change. They are used in different circumstances and with different verification. But grammatical similarities in expression may promote philosophical questions about the use of such expressions though this use itself is habitual and easy. What, then, is the difference in use between, e.g., 'The tree planted by the Mayor is taller than it was last year' and 'The tree planted by the Mayor was struck by lightning and it is now a heap of ashes'? One difference which may be indicated is that the descriptive phrase in the first example could be replaced by 'This' together with a pointing to a particular tree, viz., 'This tree was planted by the Mayor and is taller than it was last year'. A similar translation is not possible for the second example, although we might, e.g., point to a photograph and say 'This is the tree which the Mayor planted and it was burned last night'. The use of 'this' is clearly different from its use in the first example.

More usually one would say 'The tree which stood here was planted by the Mayor and, etc.', or, pointing to the ashes, 'This is all that remains of the tree which was planted by the Mayor, etc.' The verification of the second example is different from and more complicated than that of the first. It is achieved not by searching for a permanent, imperceptible substance which survives change but by recognizing location, environment, etc. These may remain 'the same' but they are not the subject of change in the sense in which the tree is. There is not, in the ordinary usage, *something else* which survives transformation as the tree survives growth. There are only different ways of verifying propositions which assert that objects have changed. It has been supposed that the second example must have a different subject which is first a tree and then ashes as the tree is first 2 ft. and then 6 ft. tall. But this is not so. The tree is as much the subject of 'The tree has been burned' as it is of 'The tree has grown', but to verify whether it has grown we look for *it* and measure *it*. To verify whether it has been destroyed we do not look for it nor for something else which had its characters and now has others, but we look for a number of different circumstances which are evidence that the tree has been destroyed. That is to say, the propositions, including their subject terms, are used differently and may be said to be of different logical forms. For its destruction is ascribed to a tree in a very different sense from that in which its size is. It seems much too simple to suppose that propositions asserting change ascribe different predicates to subjects at different times as different coats of paint are applied to a wall at different times.

There seem to be other propositions about change which do not ascribe predicates to any substance. If you watch a green after-image, shut your eyes, and open them to find it has disappeared or to find a blue flash succeeding a red, you will certainly observe changes but not changes which would properly be described as occurring to any substance which remains in other respects unchanged. There just was a change in your experience but not a change *of* anything. That all change *must* be ascribed to a substance, therefore, seems to be false, for very often it is, but sometimes it is not.

The obvious reply to this account of philosophical propositions may be a *tu quoque*. Philosophers are condemned for using analogies and yet this method constantly employs them. If an inquirer asks 'Do philosophical propositions give information?' he is not answered with a plain 'Yes' or 'No' but referred to other examples for comparison. 'Do they give information in the sense in which this proposition (e.g. a scientific proposition) does? If not, then if you wish to say that they give information you must be careful to specify the sense in which they do and you must compare your use of "giving information" with other uses, etc.' Does not this also apply to the statement 'Philosophical propositions are verbal or about the uses of words'? I think it does and that one must be careful to show by examples how philosophical propositions differ, e.g., from grammatical propositions and the statements of philologists, and, one might add, from the utterances of poets. I indicated one such difference at the beginning of this paper. Nor is the statement that philosophical propositions are verbal to be taken as a piece of brand new information about them as the composition of water was a piece of new information for eighteenth-century chemists. But it draws attention to the fact that the criteria for the truth or falsity of philosophical propositions are the uses of language. 'What we say' in certain circumstances is explicitly appealed to in the arguments of most philosophers although they often go on to try to deduce what must be the case from what we say. Since, however, these deductions are never empirically verifiable, we can test them only by considering how the words in which they are expressed are otherwise used and what uses of the propositions from which they are said to be derived have tempted philosophers to these alleged deductions.

I do not at all wish to disparage the making of comparisons and analogies which are often very useful. But as misused by philosophers in giving pseudo-scientific explanations of ordinary propositions they are non-significant. A comparison of propositions with a view to understanding the misuse of analogy and to resolving the puzzles which have caused it seems to me harmless for it does not attempt to re-define ordinary words. Most philosophers, on the contrary, seem to have supposed that they could correct and enlarge our ordinary and technical vocabularies. If, as suggested, they make no factual discoveries, it is not clear how this improvement is to be made. Indeed, the suggestion that anyone can prove that all ordinary language is incorrect and all ordinary propositions are false seems to be nonsense unless we are told how the improved language is to be understood. Philosophers who held this view seem only to have succeeded in misusing ordinary words. Against this, it is suggested that philosophical problems can be solved by understanding how language is ordinarily used, how certain uses of it have provoked these problems and how it has been misused in many alleged solutions.

CHAPTER VI

IS THERE A PROBLEM ABOUT SENSE-DATA?

By G. A. Paul

(That there must be sense-data had been suggested in, for example: 'The Ultimate Constituents of Matter', 'The Relation of Sense-data to Physics' and 'Knowledge by Acquaintance and Knowledge by Description' (in Bertrand Russell, *Mysticism and Logic*), 'On our Knowledge of the External World' and 'The World of Physics and the World of Sense' (in his *Our Knowledge of the External World*), 'The Refutation of Idealism', 'The Nature and Reality of Objects of Perception', 'The Status of Sense-Data', and 'Some Judgements of Perception' (in G. E. Moore, *Philosophical Studies*), 'A Defence of Common Sense' (by Moore in *Contemporary British Philosophy*, second series, ed. Muirhead, pp. 217 ff.), 'Sense-Perception and Matter' (in C. D. Broad, *The Mind and its Place in Nature*), 'The Given' (in H. H. Price, *Perception*), and A. J. Ayer, *Language, Truth and Logic*, passim.)

THE problem with which we shall be principally concerned is 'Are there such things as sense-data?' We shall go on to consider also the questions, supposing there are such things, whether they are private, whether they can exist unsensed, and whether they can continue to exist throughout a period of time or are merely momentary.

About these last problems I shall perhaps be able to say something definite, but about the first I am unable to come to any decision. The difficulty about it is not that there is a problem which we can understand and to which we are unable to find the answer; the difficulty is on the contrary to find out clearly what the problem is itself. It is the difficulty of understanding what anyone is saying who says that there *are* such things as sense-data, and is due partly to the fact that not all the words used occur in everyday speech, a new technical term 'sense-datum' having been brought into use. It is not, however, due solely to the fact that a word is being introduced which has not been used before, for there are many cases in which this is done where there is no such difficulty. For example the physiologists who wished to introduce the word 'fovea' to describe a certain peculiarity of the structure of the eye can have encountered no such difficulty. They could say that they were using 'fovea' as a name for the slight depression in the retina diametrically opposite to the pupil, and by dissecting eyes could point to instances of this depression. When they had done this no one would have any difficulty in answering the question 'Are there such things as foveas?' This is the sort of question with which, because of its linguistic similarity, we are apt to compare our question 'Are there such things as sense-data?' and in case we should be misled by this similarity we require to point out the differences which also exist between them. Once we know that 'fovea' is being used to mean 'the slight depression in the retina diametrically opposite to the pupil' we can find the answer to Qf * by dissecting some eyes and finding in each case whether there is an object which answers to this description. Before we even start the experiment of dissecting we have some idea of what it will be like to find such a depression and of what it will be like to be unable to find such a depression or to find that there is no such depression.

On the other hand if we are to find whether there are such things as sense-data we need make no experiment, and no experiment of any kind will help us. Sense-data, if there are such things, are objects which, so far from needing to seek by making an experiment, we cannot help seeing every time we see anything at all. It is sometimes said that we have only to inspect what happens whenever we have any visual experience of any kind to become aware that on such occasions we always do see an object of the sort which is being called the 'sense-datum' sort. For example, it is said, you know what it is to look from an angle at the top surface of a penny lying flat on a table; in such a case the surface which you can see of the penny is round but you see it by means of an object which is not round but elliptical. A great difference becomes quickly obvious between this and the answer to Qf, where the point of asking whether there were such things as foveas was that you would know what it was like to discover a retina which lacked a depression opposite to the lens, whereas in this case you do not know what it would be like to be seeing anything whatever and not be perceiving an object of the sort in question. It then seems that either there was no point in asking Qs† (since you can have no idea what it would be like for

* 'Qf' = 'the question "Are there such things as foveas?"'
† 'Qs' = 'the question "Are there such things as sense-data?"'

the answer to be 'No') or that the point of asking such a question is very different from the point of asking such a question as Qf. If this is not obvious, we can try to make it so by further consideration of the situation where you look at a penny from an angle. Sometimes in such a case it is true to say 'I see the round top surface of this penny, and I see that it is round, but it looks elliptical', and what some philosophers say is that you can become aware on inspection that it is true not only that you are seeing a round object but also that you are seeing an object which is elliptical (the elliptical object being related to the round object in a certain intimate way which we have expressed by saying that the round object is seen 'by means of it').

Some people have claimed that they are unable to find such an object, and others have claimed that they do not understand how the existence of such an object can be doubted, which drives one to ask what it would be like to be unable to find such an object and what it is like to find one. A clue is given by the fact that the claim generally made is not what would sometimes be called the 'more moderate' one that whenever we see a physical object we do in fact see a sense-datum but the 'less moderate' claim that it is logically impossible that we should see a physical object and not see a sense-datum. To call one the 'more' and the other the 'less' moderate claim is misleading, for it obscures the fact that while the 'more' moderate would be a simple empirical statement the 'less' moderate is a statement that so and so is logically impossible, i.e., in this case, a statement about the way a certain expression is to be used, viz., that 'I saw a circular penny, and I saw an elliptical object (by means of which I saw it)' is to be another way of saying 'I saw a round penny, and it looked elliptical to me'.

Is there any test which would be relevant to whether it is true that in such a case there is an object which is round and also that there is an object which is elliptical?

This brings us to the question what it means to say of a sense-datum that it is an object. To say that there are such objects as foveas is to say that in eyes there is a shallow depression opposite to the lens; to say that a fovea is an object is to say that it is a physical object or at least a depression in a physical object, that it is the sort of thing that several people can see at once, and can be pointed to by, for example, placing a probe in it. It is not in the same way clear what is meant by saying of a *sense-datum* that it is an object, for people ask about it 'is it a physical part of a physical object?', 'is it private to one percipient?', 'is it the sort of thing one can point to?' Such questions have the usual empirical look, but if we consider what facts we should consider relevant to their truth or falsity we see that they are not asking for information about 'objects' but about the uses of words, viz., 'is "observed surface" of a physical object replaceable in all sentences in which it occurs by "corresponding sense-datum"?', 'does it mean anything to say "More than one person is seeing the same sense-datum at the same time"?', 'is there anything which is (to be) called "pointing to a sense-datum"?' In saying that the word 'fovea' is to stand for a *thing* of a certain sort, meaning a *physical* thing, and at the same time *pointing* to an instance of a fovea, we say a great deal about the way the word is to be used—in fact we say all that any physiologist requires in order to be able to use the word successfully, i.e., from our pointing only to one instance of a fovea and calling it 'fovea' he knows at once what is meant by saying ever so many things about foveas, e.g., that there are and have been foveas which no one ever has or will see, that a given fovea is the same one as we examined yesterday, that it continued to exist overnight when no one was looking at it, that the person standing beside me is looking at the same fovea as I am, that it is turning a deeper yellow, and so on. This is a simple thing to point out, but it is of importance here. All that seems to happen is that someone points to an object, and says the name of the object, whereupon by watching the behaviour of the object we are enabled to make all sorts of true statements about it. Similarly it seems in telling us what sense-data are, someone refers to a situation with which we are all familiar, viz., seeing a penny obliquely, and says 'the elliptical object which is related in such and such a way to the observed surface of the penny is a sense-datum.' One is thereupon inclined to behave in the way one is justified in doing when such a thing as a fovea is pointed out to one, viz., to suppose that one knows what is to be meant by saying of such an object that, for example, objects of the same sort have existed which no one ever has or will see, that this object is the same one as I saw a short time ago, that it does or does not continue to exist when no one is looking at the penny from this angle, that it is turning a darker brown, and so on. That is, one is inclined to go on and talk as if one had just learned the name of some new kind of physical object which has just been brought to light. We know in the case of physical objects what it means to say '*this object* has such and such properties', and when someone tries to point out to us an object of the sort that is to be called a 'sense-datum' we go on as if we knew in the same way what it means to say '*this object* has such and such properties', 'this sense-datum has such and such properties'. But in fact the case is very different: the word 'fovea' was introduced as a name for a physical object, and we know how to use it in new cases because we know in general how words for physical objects are used in English. This statement is the crux of the present paper. There are certain general criteria which ordinarily enable us to decide whether a given physical object is the same object as we saw at a given previous time, whether it is the same object even though many of its properties are different, whether it is a different object from one we saw previously although it has very much the same properties, whether it is now changing its colour and shape, and so on. This being so, we are apt to think that all we have to do is to give a name to an object and then examine this object and watch its behaviour in order to be able to make up true statements about it in which this name occurs: we forget that the name-word is being brought into use as a member of a class of words whose use in certain contexts is already given. E.g., everyone can imagine circumstances in which it would be true to say 'He opened his eyes, saw a certain fovea, closed his eyes and did not see it for five seconds, opened them again and saw *the same fovea* again', and circumstances in which it would be false to say this (e.g. if during the five seconds someone cunningly replaced the eye-dissection he had been examining by another exactly similar). On the other hand, can anyone describe or imagine circumstances in which it would be true to say 'He saw a certain sense-datum, ceased to see it for five seconds, and then saw *the same sense-datum* again'? Would it be true to say this, for example, if it were true to say 'He saw a certain penny from a certain angle, and it looked elliptical to him, he closed his eyes and did not see it for five seconds, opened them again and saw the same penny looking exactly the same to him'? The answer is that no examination of such a situation will provide us with an answer: in the one case it seems that examination of the situation in question *will* provide an answer; in the other that it will not. It seems that in one case examination of the object in question will tell us whether it continued to exist throughout a period; but that in the other it will not. In a sense it does not do so in either case; but in the case where we introduce the word 'fovea' by pointing to one or more foveas everyone does as a matter of fact know under what conditions it is to be true to say that this is the same fovea as I saw five seconds ago, this fovea has been on this table for the last half-hour although no one has been in the room, and so on. They know this because they know under what circumstances it is true to say such things of other physical objects; but it is not *necessary* that the word 'fovea' should behave like other words for physical objects. We might, for example, say 'No fovea lasts longer than a single specious present' meaning this not as an empirical statement but as a statement of how the word fovea is to be used. We might have some good reason for adopting such a way of speaking; e.g., suppose certain minute structures in the fovea were, we discovered, annihilated and replaced every five minutes, then we might very well say 'During the last half-hour I have observed five foveas succeed one another here, each differing from the last one in respect of the minute structures (M)' or 'During the last half-hour I have observed the same fovea, the minute structures (M) in it being replaced every five minutes' and mean the same by these two statements.

The word 'sense-datum' as people have employed it does not fall into a fully-prepared scheme for its usage as a word for a physical object does, but its usage is not purely arbitrary. By this I mean that its use is connected with the use of certain words which *are* in ordinary language, e.g. 'looks', 'appears', 'appearance', and with certain uses of 'this', 'after-image', and 'image'. We shall now consider some uses of such words with which it is connected, and how it is connected with them.

We so use language that whenever it is true that I am seeing the round top surface of a penny, and know that it is round, it is true to say that the penny *looks* (e.g.) elliptical to me, in a sense in which this does not entail that I am in any way deceived about the real shape of the penny. (I shall indicate this sense by means of a suffix: 'looks^1'.) The rule which has generally been adopted is that the sense-datum is correctly said to have whatever shape and colour-property the corresponding surface of the physical object looks^1 to me to have. E.g., suppose a red light is cast upon the penny as I view it obliquely, then if it is true that the surface which I see is round and brown, and looks^1 to be elliptical and red, then according to our rule it is true to say that the corresponding sense-datum *is* elliptical and red.

Those who have in practice used the word 'sense-datum' have not spoken as if what they were doing was introducing *merely* an alternative way of saying this same thing over again, but as if this new sentence which they substitute were in some way nearer to the facts. They have the idea that in some sense when a physical object looks^1 red to someone then something really is red, i.e., that there really are in such cases two *objects*, one which looks^1 red and one which *is* red, and that somehow the one which *is* red has generally been overlooked, and its existence has now for the first time been recognized. It is said that its existence cannot be doubted, for if we carefully inspect what happens when a physical object appears red to us we shall come to realize that we can see this object, and further that, while in every such case it is academically possible to doubt whether there really is a physical object which is appearing red, it is academically impossible to doubt that there is an object which *is* red. The point is that although I may have been mistaken in supposing that there was a round surface of a penny looking^1 elliptical to me, yet it is quite certain that there was an elliptical appearance (and that it is logically impossible that this appearance should merely have *looked* elliptical to me). I shall only point out that another way of describing the same situation is 'I thought I was seeing a round surface of a penny, which was looking elliptical to me, but in fact there was no penny there at all.' It is then asked: 'If there was no penny there at all, what was really happening? what were the elements of the situation?' and it is answered that what I was really seeing was a sense-datum which was elliptical, but was not a sense-datum 'of' a physical object (or at least not 'of' a penny). It is an equally good answer to say 'It only seemed to me as if there was a round penny which looked[1] elliptical. I was really not seeing anything at all.' This says just the same as the statement which contained the word 'sense-datum', and there is no question of the one saying it less or more adequately than the other.

Sometimes people explain how they are going to use 'sense-datum' by taking the case when I have an after-image with my eyes closed, in which case it is quite certain that there is no external object which is appearing, say, red. They then say that a sense-datum is any object which is seen in the sense in which the after-image is seen, and ask us to notice that whenever we see a physical object we see[1] an object (in this sense, which I am going to call 'see[1]'). It is, however, not at all clear what this means. For it is not certain that whenever I see a physical object I see any *other* object in any sense of see. What is certain is that, suppose the physical object looks[1] red, there is nothing to prevent me from expressing that by saying that an object which is red corresponds to the physical object, and nothing to prevent me from saying that I see[1] that object. Such a notation might be convenient for certain purposes, and is unlikely to mislead, because (1) it makes no sense to say of an after-image that it looks different from what it really is, and we are not tempted to say such a thing of a sense-datum, and certainly have not given any meaning to saying it of a sense-datum, and (2) it is possible, and may sometimes happen, that what we took to be an after-image turns out to be an appearance of a physical object, and vice versa. This way of talking at once suggests that there really is in such a case an object (viz., a sense-datum) about which it is doubtful whether it is an after-image, or an appearance (sense-datum) of a physical object.

My intention has not been to deny that there are sense-data, if by that is meant that (1) we can understand, to some extent at least, how people wish to use the word 'sense-datum' who have introduced it in philosophy, and that (2) sometimes statements of a certain form containing the word 'sense-datum' are true, e.g., 'I am seeing[1] an elliptical sense-datum "of" a round penny.' Nor do I wish to deny that the introduction of this terminology may be useful in helping to solve some philosophical problems about perception; but I do wish to deny that there is any sense in which this terminology is nearer to reality than any other which may be used to express the same facts; in particular I wish to deny that in order to give a complete and accurate account of any perceptual situation it is necessary to use a noun in the way in which 'sense-datum' is used,* for this leads to the notion that there are entities of a curious sort over and above physical objects which can 'have' sensible properties but cannot 'appear to have' sensible properties which they have not got.

We shall consider now certain puzzles to which the use of 'sense-datum' has given rise.

There is first the idea of the sense-datum as a sort of barrier, an entity which gets between us and the physical object. In trying to overcome the idea of its being a barrier people ask 'Is the corresponding sense-datum identical with the observed surface of the physical object?' An answer to this question is relevant to many questions commonly asked, viz., are sense-data mental or physical, are they private or public, do they exist only when someone is seeing[1] them or can they exist while no one is seeing[1] them, are they merely momentary or can they continue to exist throughout a time? In order to be able to answer 'Yes' to it philosophers have even been prepared to alter their use of 'sense-datum' so that it makes sense to say that such and such a sense-datum appears to have sensible qualities it does not in fact have'†; for if the answer were 'Yes', not only would the idea of a barrier be overcome, but also the second of each of these alternatives would be true, for we should say that what is a part of the surface of a physical object in this sense is physical, and we know what it is for more than one person to see the same part of the surface of a physical object, and for such a part to exist while no one is perceiving it, and for it to continue to exist throughout a period of time. The question whether a given sense-datum is identical with the corresponding surface has the air of being a question about two objects (or about one object) which is to be settled by inspecting the object or objects. Actually it is to be settled by examining not an object but our use of the two words 'sense-datum' and 'surface'; if we find some sentence which says some-

* I.e., there are no facts of visual experience in order to express which it is necessary to use a noun functioning in the way 'sense-datum' does.

† E.g. John Wisdom, *Problems of Mind and Matter*, pp. 156–7, and Cp. IX passim.

thing true about the sense-datum such that if the sentence which results from replacing the word 'sense-datum' in that sentence by the word 'surface' is either false or meaningless, that is what we shall call the sense-datum and the surface being not identical. Thus if *ex hypothesi* the corresponding surface is really round, and the sense-datum I see of it is elliptical, to say 'the sense-datum is round' is either false or nonsense; and so is 'the corresponding surface is elliptical'. This is what we call the sense-datum and the surface being not identical. Thus it is not true to say that in this case the sense-datum is physical if we mean by that that it is a part of the surface of a physical object in the sense in which the corresponding part of the surface is a part of the surface of a physical object.

It is suggested that in certain favoured cases it may yet be true that the sense-datum is identical with the corresponding surface. E.g., suppose I am looking at the penny in such a way that it looks[1] to me the same shape as it really is, i.e., the corresponding surface is round and the sense-datum of it is round. We have now to try and show a further difference between the way the two words behave, and at this point the most useful thing to consider is that future experience might lead us to believe that the surface in question had not been really round, whereas this same evidence would not lead us to doubt that it had looked[1] round to me, i.e., that the sense-datum I saw of it had been round. That is, what is evidence in such a case against the truth of 'the surface is round' is not evidence against the truth of 'the sense-datum is round'.

It is, however, not impossible to hold that in such a case it is the same object which is being called 'round', but that it is being called 'round' in two different senses, and that all that has been shown is that it is not round in one sense but may yet be round in the other.

This urges us to try to point out further differences in usage between the two words, and so we come to a problem which is thorny indeed. It is suggested that, say, a minute ago the surface, in question, of the penny was in existence but the sense-datum was not, that it only came into existence when I looked at the penny. If one takes one's cue for the use of 'sense-datum' from the use of 'looks[1]' this is the natural thing to say. Suppose that a minute ago the penny was in my pocket out of sight, then it is not true that 'the penny really was round and looked[1] ϕ to so and so', and we incline to say that if it was not looking[1] ϕ to anybody then there was no sense-datum of it. We ask 'How *can* there be a sense-datum which no one is seeing?' and get the answer 'A sense-datum is an object which you see. You know that other objects which you see exist while no one is seeing them. So why should not sense-data do so likewise?' We may then say: 'Sense-data are only products, which are made by certain physical processes involved in seeing. They can have no existence apart from such processes.' To this it will perhaps be answered 'There is no reason to suppose that sense-data are manufactured by these processes. We may suppose that our sense-data exist unsensed and that all that the processes involved in seeing do is to select from among those already there.' This sort of argument arises from considering sense-data as if they were a sort of physical objects. We know what it is for physical objects, which we see, to exist during times when we are not seeing them. We often do things which we call observing that a given physical object has continued to exist unperceived throughout a given period of time; but there is nothing which we similarly call observing that a given sense-datum has continued to exist unperceived throughout a given period of time. There are certain criteria which are ordinarily used as criteria for whether a physical object has gone on existing unperceived throughout a time; but there is nothing which is a criterion of this in the case of sense-data. We may if we care introduce such criteria, i.e., we may describe what we are going to call 'observing that a sense-datum has gone on existing unperceived throughout such and such a time'; but probably we are strongly disinclined to do so, because we incline to take our use of the word 'sense-datum' from that of 'looks[1]', 'appears', and 'appearance'.

It does not make sense to say that a sense-datum has existed unperceived; in giving the usage of the word we have not given a use to this, but it is open to us to do so if we care.

Perhaps it will be useful here to give an example of something which similarly does not make sense, but which we require to contemplate a little before we become quite clear that it doesn't. Whether rightly or wrongly, there is attributed to the President of this session the remark: 'It is not true that I sleep *more* than other people, I only sleep *more slowly*.' It takes just a moment or two to see that sleeping is not the sort of thing that one *can* do more slowly than other people, and perhaps another moment or two to see that this means that to say that one person sleeps more slowly than another is to say something which has no meaning. The world being as it is we are not inclined to give a use to this phrase; on the other hand it is easy to describe circumstances in which we would be so inclined. Suppose, for example, that human beings were clearly divided into two kinds, those who walked and ate slowly and required a long sleep to recover from a given amount of exercise, and those who walked and ate quickly and required only a short sleep to recover from a given amount of exercise, then we should be very inclined to say that people of the first kind slept more slowly than people of the second kind.

Similarly, to say that a sense-datum has existed unperceived is to say something to which no meaning is given, but to which in certain circumstances we might be strongly inclined to give meaning. It is worth pointing out, for example, that sometimes we speak of an 'appearance' of a thing which is not an appearance to anyone. E.g., 'What a fine sunset. It must present a wonderful appearance from the top of Mochrum hill' does not imply that there is anyone there to whom it would be presented. On the other hand, we frequently use 'appearance' in a different way. E.g., suppose I look at the round surface of the penny from a certain angle, then shut my eyes or go away for five minutes, then look at it again under similar conditions from the same place, we might describe this correctly by saying that 'I saw two different appearances of it which were exactly the same in shape and colour'. We do not describe it by saying that 'I saw twice the same appearance which continued to exist during the period when I was not seeing it'. Whether we are to say that in this case I saw numerically the same sense-datum twice or that I saw two sense-data which had the same qualities is a matter of indifference, and perhaps we will never require to use 'sense-datum' in such a case and so need never make any decision on the matter. The important point is that whatever we do is not demanded by the nature of objects which we are calling 'sense-data', but that we have a choice of different notations for describing the same observations, the choice being determined only by the greater convenience of one notation, or our personal inclination, or by tossing a coin.

Whether the sense-datum in question is to be said to have existed between the times when it was observed is also, as I have tried to show, a matter for the people who wish to use the terminology to decide, should occasion arise. What is important is that whatever criteria are laid down for the existence of a sense-datum during a time when it is unobserved, to say that since these criteria are fulfilled *therefore* it is the case that there is an object exactly like a sense-datum, only that it is unobserved, is misleading. That there is such an object is not a further fact inferred from them. It is better to say that these criteria being fulfilled is what we *call* a sense-datum's existing unobserved. This is particularly important in considering theories which say that an unsensed sense-datum exists at a certain place if an observer at that place would see a sense-datum answering to the given description. We may use the fact that if an observer were to be at a given place he would see a sense-datum of a given sort as a criterion for there existing an unsensed sense-datum of that sort; but if that is all we use, the fact that an observer at that place would see such and such a sense-datum is what we *call* a sense-datum of that sort's existing at that time. This is extremely important in considering the kind of view which tries to 'mitigate the severities of phenomenalism' by saying that physical objects are groups of actual and possible (or unsensed) sense-data. The attractiveness of such a view fades when one considers what is the criterion which is being used for the existence of unsensed sense-data, and what is the relation between the criterion and the object of whose existence it is a criterion.

It is also important in considering another thing which is said, viz., that sense-data are a sort of things which only one person can ever see, i.e. that it is impossible that you should ever see my sense-data, i.e. that you should ever see a sense-datum which I see, and vice versa. People have the idea of sense-data as sort of private physical objects which each person keeps behind a high wall, and that although two people never see the same sense-datum the order in which I see my sense-data is connected in a fortunate fashion with the order in which you see yours and other people see theirs; but it is with a feeling of regret that people say 'content can't be communicated, only structure can', and it is with a feeling of discomfort that they contemplate the possibility that although when an object looks to me green, I have a green sense-datum, yet it may always be the case that when an object looks to *you* green you may have a red sense-datum, and so long as the error is systematic it is undiscoverable.

In the first place we have to consider what is meant by saying that 'content can't be communicated'. This suggests that there is some process which we can describe but can't do, viz., communicate content. It suggests that the walls between our private collections of sense-data are so high that we can't see over, but that it is not inconceivable that we should. That, however, is misleading. It makes us feel 'If only I could show you my sense-datum, we could decide whether we see the same or not'. But in fact there is nothing I can't do. I could show you all my sense-data if the words 'showing you a sense-datum of mine' had any meaning. To say that content can't be communicated is to say that 'one person has communicated the content of his sense-experiences to another' means nothing at all. To suppose otherwise is to treat sense-data as if they were a sort of physical objects, and so to assume that it makes sense to say that two people see the same sense-datum.

Ingenious circumstances have been described in which we *should* feel urged to say that one person was having another's sense-datum; but I do not propose to give such an example here. I wish to consider only two things: (1) suppose I look over your shoulder at a gas fire some feet in front of us both, and suppose that when I move my head into the position where yours is there is no difference in the way the fire looks[1] to me, and suppose when you move your head into the place where mine was you say that there is no difference in the way the fire looks[1] to you. Now suppose that we both have good eyes and have shown no signs of abnormal colour-vision. Then it is true that the gas fire looks[1] the same to both of us, and there is a sense in which it is true that it presents the same appearance to both of us; but do we see the same sense-datum of the fire? I.e., numerically the same sense-datum of it? Most people who have used the term 'sense-datum' would with little hesitation say that the sense-datum you see is not identical with the sense-datum I see. Why? Not because they see something about the nature of such objects which shows that they are not numerically the same, but simply because no meaning is given to 'two people are seeing the same sense-datum'.

(2) This raises the problem, what is meant by saying of *someone else* that he is seeing a sense-datum of a certain sort? When we think of such a thing we all think of a sort of inner vision inside the man's head directed on an object which we picture as a sort of screen, the whole thing being cut off from the outside world by a high barrier. We think that a man's behaving or not behaving in such and such ways is a symptom of some inner condition, viz., whether he has in fact such an object before his inner eye behind the barrier, and we regard this thing of which his behaviour is a symptom as something which we can never directly observe, but as something which might conceivably not exist even if his behaviour were exactly what it is. Such imagery is pointless. If this entity which he alone sees did not exist and his behaviour were no different from what it is, the world would appear to us to go on just the same, except that he would never really see things as they are, but only appear to. This shows that we have made a mistake about the use of such a phrase as 'other people see sense-data similar to mine'. The mistake is, as before, the one about the relation between the criterion for a thing's existence and the thing's existence. What we call someone else's seeing a sense-datum is his behaving in certain ways in certain situations, his reacting in certain ways to certain stimuli. A man's being colour-blind is not his having pictures of *only* certain sorts in his private collection, at whose absence we can guess more or less reliably by certain tests. His being colour-blind is his behaving in certain ways. Similarly your seeing the same colour as I do on looking at a certain object, or seeing a different colour when we should expect to see the same, is not my having in my collection a differently coloured picture from what you have in yours, but my behaving in a certain way. We could easily mention tests which would ordinarily be taken as tests for deciding whether people have the same (i.e., exactly similar) sense-data under such and such conditions. (E.g., colour-choosing tests for colour-blindness.)

I do not deal with *the* problem about sense-data, which gives point to the introduction of the word at all. I mean 'How are sense-data related to physical objects?' I.e., how does our use of the word 'sense-datum' compare with our use of our words for physical objects? and does the use of the word 'sense-datum' help to free us from any of the difficulties we get into about our use of words for physical objects?

And I have not touched upon how our use of the word 'sense-datum' is related to our use of the word 'sensation'.

All I have done is to consider a number of questions about the way 'sense-datum' is brought into use, which it seems to me must be considered before anything is said about the larger problems it was introduced to deal with.

CHAPTER VII

VERIFIABILITY

By Dr. Friedrich Waismann

(This paper was originally the second part of a Symposium in which the first symposiast was Mr. (now Professor) D. M. MacKinnon. It therefore naturally contained several polemical references to Professor MacKinnon's contribution. In tearing the present paper from that context in order to reprint it in this collection, we tried to remove as many of these references as possible; but unfortunately it was not practicable to remove them all without re-writing the entire paper. So we must apologize to Professor MacKinnon; and remind readers that in the interests of the unity of this book he has been denied the right to speak in his own cause.)

I

WHEN we reflect on such a sentence as 'The meaning of a statement is the method of its verification', we should, first of all, be quite clear as to what we mean by the term 'method of verification'. From a logical point of view we are not interested in the various activities that are involved in verifying a statement. What, then, is it we have in mind when we talk of such things? Take an example. Suppose there is a metal ball in front of me, and I have the task of finding out whether the ball is charged with electricity. To do that I connect the ball with an electroscope and watch whether the gold leaves diverge. The statement 'The gold leaves of the instrument diverge' (*s*) describes the verification of the statement 'The ball is charged' (*p*). Now what exactly am I doing when I describe the verification of the statement *p*? I establish a connection between two statements by declaring that the one (*s*) is to follow from the other (*p*). In other words, I lay down a *rule of inference* which allows me to pass from the statement 'The ball is charged with electricity' to another that describes an observable situation. By doing this I connect the statement with another one, I make it part of a system of operations, I incorporate it into language, in short, *I determine the way it is to be used.* In this sense giving the verification of a statement is an important part of giving its use, or, to put it differently, explaining its verification is a contribution to its grammar.

In everyday life we understand sentences without bothering

much as to the way they are verified. We understand them because we understand the single words which occur in them and grasp the grammatical structure of the sentence as a whole. The question of the verification arises only when we come across a new sort of combination of words. If, for instance, someone were to tell us that he owned a dog that was able to think, we should at first not quite understand what he was talking about and would ask him some further questions. Suppose he described to us in detail the dog's behaviour in certain circumstances, then we should say 'Ah, now we understand you, that's what you call thinking'. There is no need to inquire into the verification of such sentences as 'The dog barks', 'He runs', 'He is playful', and so on, as the words are then used as we may say in their *normal* way. But when we say 'The dog thinks', we create a new context, we step outside the boundaries of common speech, and then the question arises as to what is meant by such a word series. In such cases explaining the verification is explaining the meaning, and changing the verification is changing the meaning. Obviously meaning and verification *are* connected—so why say they are not?

But when I say that the statement p is connected with the statements $s_1, s_2 \ldots s_n$ which describe evidences for it, I do *not* say that p is *identical* with $s_1, s_2 \ldots s_n$ or their conjunction.[1] To say this would only be true if $s_1, s_2 \ldots s_n$ or their conjunction entailed p. Now is that so? There *may* be statements which are nothing more than abbreviations for all that which is unfolded in their verification. There are, however, other sorts of statements of which this is certainly not true. Recent discussions on phenomenalism, for example, tend to show that no conjunction or disjunction of sense-datum statements, however complex, entails the existence or the non-existence of a certain material object. If that is so, a material object statement, though it *is* connected with sense-datum statements, is not just an abbreviation for them, rather has it a logical status of its own, and is not equivalent to any truth-function of the latter ones. I think that the result of these discussions is essentially right, and I ask for permission, to make my point quite clear, to add one word more.

The failure of the phenomenalist to translate a material object

[1] This symbolism, and the other symbolism used in this article, is explained as it is introduced, and no knowledge of technical logic is required to understand it.—EDITOR.

statement into terms of sense-data is not, as has been suggested, due to the poverty of our language which lacks the vocabulary for describing all the minute details of sense experience, nor is it due to the difficulties inherent in producing an *infinite* combination of sense-datum statements though all these things may contribute to it. In the main it is due to a factor which, though it is very important and really quite obvious, has to my knowledge never been noticed—to the 'open texture'[1] of most of our empirical concepts. What I mean is this: Suppose I have to verify a statement such as 'There is a cat next door'; suppose I go over to the next room, open the door, look into it and actually see a cat. Is this enough to prove my statement? Or must I, in addition to it, touch the cat, pat him and induce him to purr? And supposing that I had done all these things, can I then be absolutely certain that my statement was true? Instantly we come up against the well-known battery of sceptical arguments mustered since ancient times. What, for instance, should I say when that creature later on grew to a gigantic size? Or if it showed some queer behaviour usually not to be found with cats, say, if, under certain conditions, it could be revived from death whereas normal cats could not? Shall I, in such a case, say that a new species has come into being? Or that it was a cat with extraordinary properties? Again, suppose I say 'There is my friend over there'. What if on drawing closer in order to shake hands with him he suddenly disappeared? 'Therefore it was not my friend but some delusion or other.' But suppose a few seconds later I saw him again, could grasp his hand, etc. What then? 'Therefore my friend was nevertheless there and his disappearance was some delusion or other.' But imagine after a while he disappeared again, or seemed to disappear—what shall I say now? Have we rules ready for all imaginable possibilities?

An example of the first sort tends to show that we can think of situations in which we couldn't be certain whether something was a cat or some other animal (or a *jinni*). An example of the second sort tends to show that we can consider circumstances in which we couldn't be certain whether something was real or a delusion. The fact that in many cases there is no such thing as a

[1] I owe this term to Mr. Kneale who suggested it to me as a translation of *Porosität der Begriffe*, a term coined by me in German.

conclusive verification is connected with the fact that most of our empirical concepts are not delimited in all possible directions. Suppose I come across a being that looks like a man, speaks like a man, behaves like a man, and is only one span tall—shall I say it *is* a man? Or what about the case of a person who is so old as to remember King Darius? Would you say he is an immortal? Is there anything like an exhaustive definition that finally and once for all sets our mind at rest? 'But are there not exact definitions at least in science?' Let's see. The notion of gold seems to be defined with absolute precision, say by the spectrum of gold with its characteristic lines. Now what would you say if a substance was discovered that looked like gold, satisfied all the chemical tests for gold, whilst it emitted a new sort of radiation? 'But such things do not happen.' Quite so; but they *might* happen, and that is enough to show that we can never exclude altogether the possibility of some unforeseen situation arising in which we shall have to modify our definition. Try as we may, no concept is limited in such a way that there is no room for any doubt. We introduce a concept and limit it in *some* directions; for instance, we define gold in contrast to some other metals such as alloys. This suffices for our present needs, and we do not probe any farther. We tend to *overlook* the fact that there are always other directions in which the concept has not been defined. And if we did, we could easily imagine conditions which would necessitate new limitations. In short, it is not possible to define a concept like gold with absolute precision, i.e. in such a way that every nook and cranny is blocked against entry of doubt. That is what is meant by the open texture of a concept.

Vagueness should be distinguished from *open texture*. A word which is actually used in a fluctuating way (such as 'heap' or 'pink') is said to be vague; a term like 'gold', though its actual use may not be vague, is non-exhaustive or of an open texture in that we can never fill up all the possible gaps through which a doubt may seep in. Open texture, then, is something like *possibility of vagueness*. Vagueness can be remedied by giving more accurate rules, open texture cannot. An alternative way of stating this would be to say that definitions of open terms are *always* corrigible or emendable.

Open texture is a very fundamental characteristic of most,

though not of all, empirical concepts, and it is this texture which prevents us from verifying conclusively most of our empirical statements. Take any material object statement. The terms which occur in it are non-exhaustive; that means that we cannot foresee completely all possible conditions in which they are to be used; there will always remain a possibility, however faint, that we have not taken into account something or other that may be relevant to their usage; and that means that we cannot foresee completely all the possible circumstances in which the statement is true or in which it is false. There will always remain a margin of uncertainty. Thus the absence of a conclusive verification is directly due to the open texture of the terms concerned.

This has an important consequence. Phenomenalists have tried to translate what we mean by a material object statement into terms of sense experience. Now such a translation would be possible only if the terms of a material object statement were completely definable. For only then could we describe completely all the possible evidences which would make the statement true or false. As this condition is not fulfilled, the programme of phenomenalism falls flat, and in consequence the attempts at analysing chairs and tables into patterns of sense-data—which has become something of a national sport in this country—are doomed to fail. Similar remarks apply to certain psychological statements such as 'He is an intelligent person'; here again it is due to the open texture of a term like 'intelligent' that the statement cannot be reduced to a conjunction or disjunction of statements which specify the way a man would behave in such-and-such circumstances.

It may have been a dim awareness of this fact that induced Locke to insist on corporeal, and Berkeley on mental substance. Doing away with their metaphysical fog, we may restate what seems to be the grain of truth in their views by saying that a material object statement, or a psychological statement has a logic of its own, and for this reason cannot be reduced to the level of other statements.

But there is a deeper reason for all that, and this consists in what I venture to call the *essential incompleteness* of an empirical description. To explain more fully: If I had to describe the right hand of mine which I am now holding up, I may say different things of it: I may state its size, its shape, its colour, its tissue, the chemical compound of its bones, its cells, and perhaps add some more particulars; but however far I go, I shall never reach a point where my description will be completed: logically speaking, it is always possible to extend the description by adding some detail or other. Every description stretches, as it were, into a horizon of open possibilities: however far I go, I shall always carry this horizon with me. Contrast this case with others in which completeness is attainable. If, in geometry, I describe a triangle, e.g. by giving its three sides, the description is *complete*: nothing can be added to it that is not included in, or at variance with, the data. Again, there is a sense in which it may be said that a melody is described completely in the musical notation (disregarding, for the moment, the question of its interpretation); a figure on a carpet, viewed as an ornament, may be described in some geometrical notation; and in this case, too, there is a sense in which the description may be called complete. (I do not mean the *physical* carpet, but its pattern.) The same applies to a game of chess: it can be described, move by move, from the beginning to the end. Such cases serve merely to set off the nature of an empirical description by the contrast: there is no such thing as completeness in the case in which I describe my right hand, or the character of a person; I can never exhaust all the details nor foresee all possible circumstances which would make me modify or retract my statement. (This was already seen by Leibniz when he said that anything actual is always inexhaustible in its properties and a true image of the Infinite Mind.)

The situation described has a direct bearing on the open texture of concepts. A term is defined when the sort of situation is described in which it is to be used. Suppose for a moment that we were able to describe situatios completely without omitting anything (as in chess), then we could produce an exhaustive list of all the circumstances in which the term is to be used so that nothing is left to doubt; in other words, we could construct a *complete definition*, i.e. a thought model which anticipates and settles once for all every possible question of usage. As, in fact, we can never eliminate the possibility of some unforeseen factor emerging, we can never be quite sure that we have included in our definition everything that should be included, and thus the process of defining and refining an idea will go on without ever reaching a final stage. In other words, every definition stretches into an open horizon. Try as we may, the situation will always remain the same: no definition of an empirical term will cover all possibilities. Thus the result is that the incompleteness of our verification is rooted in the incompleteness of the definition of the terms involved, and the incompleteness of the definition is rooted in the incompleteness of empirical description; that is one of the grounds why a material object statement p can *not* be verified conclusively, nor be resolved into statements $s_1, s_2 \ldots s_n$ which describe evidences for it. (In mathematics such a reduction is often possible: thus a statement about rational numbers *can*, without loss of meaning, be translated into statements about integers; but here you have complete description, complete definition and conclusive proof and refutation.)

One word more. Why is it that, as a rule, an experiential statement is not verifiable in a conclusive way? Is it because I can never exhaust the description of a material object or of a situation, since I may always add something to it—something that, in principle, can be foreseen? Or is it because something quite new and unforeseen may occur? In the first case, though I know all the tests, I may still be unable to perform them, say, for lack of time. In the second case I cannot even be sure that I know all the tests that may be required; in other words, the difficulty is to state completely what a verification would be in this case. (Can you foresee all circumstances which would turn a putative fact into a delusion?) Now the answer to the question is that *both factors combine* to prevent a verification from being conclusive. *But they play a very different part*. It is due to the first factor that, in verifying a statement, we can never finish the job. But it is the second that is responsible for the open texture of our terms which is so characteristic of all factual knowledge. To see this more clearly, compare the situation in mathematics: here a theorem, say Goldbach's hypothesis, which says that every even number can be represented as the sum of two primes, may be undecidable as we cannot go through all the integers in order to try it out. But this in no way detracts from the *closed* texture of the mathematical concepts. If there was no such thing as the (always present) possibility of the emergence of something new, there could be nothing like the open texture of concepts; and if there was no such thing as the open texture of concepts, verification would be incomplete only in the sense that it could never be finished (just as in the case of Goldbach).

To sum up: An experiential statement is, as a rule, not conclusively verifiable for two different reasons:

(1) because of the existence of an unlimited number of tests;
(2) because of the open texture of the terms involved.

These two reasons correspond to two different senses of 'incompleteness'. The first is related to the fact that I can never conclude the description of a material object, or of a situation. I may, for instance, look at my table from ever new points in space without ever exhausting all the possibilities. The second (and more exciting one) is due to the fact that our factual knowledge is incomplete in another dimension: there is always a chance that something unforeseen may occur. That again may mean two different things:

(*a*) that I should get acquainted with some totally new experience such as at present I cannot even imagine;

(*b*) that some new discovery was made which would affect our whole interpretation of certain facts.

An illustration of the first sort would be supplied by a man born blind who later obtained the experience of seeing. An illustration of the second sort would be the change brought about by the discovery of a new agent of nature, such as electricity. In this case we perceive that the data of observation are connected in a new and unforeseen way, that, as it were, new lines can now be traced through the field of experience. So we can say more exactly that the open texture of concepts is rooted in that particular incompleteness of our factual knowledge which I have just adumbrated.

What I have said modifies to a more or less extent the account I have given of verification. I said that in giving the method of verification we lay down a rule (or rules) of inference. We should, however, feel grave doubts whether that is so. If a material object statement were to entail a sense datum statement, to entail it in a strictly *logical* sense, then the premiss would be cancelled together with the conclusion: or, to put it differently, a single negative instance would suffice to refute the premiss. Suppose someone told me, 'Look, there is your friend, he is just crossing the street'. Now if I looked in the direction indicated, but failed to perceive the person who is my friend, would I say that the statement was refuted beyond the shadow of a doubt? There may be cases in which I may say that. But there are others in which I would certainly not think that the statement was refuted on the strength of such a single glance (for instance, when I was led to expect my friend at this hour, or received a letter from him saying that he will arrive at that time, and the like). A discrepancy between a material object statement and a single sense experience may always be explained away by some accessory assumption: I haven't looked thoroughly, my friend happened in this very second to be behind someone else, he just stepped into a doorway, and so on, not to mention more fanciful theories. I can never exclude the possibility that, though the evidence was against it, the statement may be true.

Whoever considers these facts with unbiassed eyes will, I trust, assent to the conclusion that a single sense experience, strictly speaking, never excludes a material object statement in the sense in which the negation of p excludes p. That means that no sense-datum statement s can ever come into *sharp logical conflict* with a material object statement p; in other words: $p . \sim s$ never represents a *contradiction* in the sense that $p . \sim p$ does. In the light of this we can no longer adhere to the view that p entails s. How, then, should we formulate the 'method of verification'—that is, the connection between a proposition p and the statements $s_1, s_2 \ldots s_n$ which are evidences for it? I propose to say that the evidences $s_1, s_2 \ldots s_n$, *speak for* or *against* the proposition p, that they *strengthen* or *weaken* it, which does not mean that they prove or disprove it strictly.

There is a striking analogy to that in the relation that holds between a law of nature L and certain observational statements $s_1, s_2 \ldots s_n$, an analogy which may help to clarify the situation. It is often said that the statements of observation *follow* from the law (the latter being regarded as a sort of universal premiss). Since an unlimited number of consequences can be derived from a law, the ideal of complete verification is, of course, unattainable; whereas, on the other hand, a single counter observation seems to suffice to overthrow the law. From this it would follow that, while a law cannot be strictly verified, it can be strictly confuted; or that it can be decided only one way.[1] That is unrealistic. What astronomer would abandon Kepler's laws on the strength of a single observation? If, in fact, some anomaly in a planet's behaviour were detected, the most varied attempts at explaining the phenomenon would first be made (such as the presence of unknown heavy masses, friction with rarefied gases, etc.). Only if the edifice of hypotheses thus erected has too little support in experience, if it becomes too complex and artificial, if it no longer satisfies our demand for simplicity, or again if a better hypothesis presents itself to us, such as Einstein's theory, would we resolve to drop those laws. And even then the refutation would not be valid finally and once for all: it may still turn out that some circumstance had escaped our notice which, when taken into consideration, would cast a different light upon the whole. Indeed, the history of science exhibits cases (Olaf Römer, Leverrier) in which the apparent defeat of a theory later turned into complete victory. Who can say that such a situation will not repeat itself?

Here again the view suggests itself strongly that the relationship between a statement and what serves to verify it was too crudely represented in the past; that it was a mistake to describe it in logical terms such as 'entailment'; that a law is not a sort of universal statement from which particular statements follow; that its logic is still unexplored, and that it may possibly take the form of rules according to which the law's truth-weight—if I am allowed to use such a term—is increased or lessened by the data of observation. Be that as it may, the mere fact that a single counter observation $\sim s$ can always be reconciled with a general law L by some accessory assumption shows that the true relation between a law and the experiential evidence for it is much more complicated and only superficially in accord with the customary account.

It will be said that this is due to our representing the case in too simple a manner. In reality the observational statement s does not follow from L alone, but from L plus a number of further premisses which are often not expressly stated. So that,

[1] See Karl Popper, *Logik der Forschung*.

if the observation *s* which we expected fails to materialize, we may say that any of the other premisses is false.

Now this would be perfectly correct if the system of premisses could be stated accurately and completely in every single case. But can it? Can we ever be certain of knowing all, really all the conditions on which the result of even the simplest experiment depends? Plainly not; what is stated is only a *part* of the conditions, viz., those which, e.g., can be isolated in experimental technique and subjected to our will, or which can readily be surveyed, etc. The others merge into one indistinct mass: the vague supposition that 'a normal situation subsists', that 'no disturbing factors are present' or in whatever way we may hint at the possibility of intervention of some unforeseen conditions. The relation between L and s, then, when exactly stated, is this: Given such-and-such laws $L_1, L_2 \ldots L_m$, given such-and-such initial and boundary conditions $c_1, c_2 \ldots c_n$ and *no other disturbing factors being present*, so-and-so will happen. And here it must be stressed that behind the words italicized a presupposition is concealed which cannot be split up into clear, separate statements. When actually deducing a consequence from a physical law we never make use of this premiss: it never forms part of the body of premisses: it does not enter the process of deduction. But then it should not be termed a premiss at all; what a queer sort of premiss this is, which is never made use of! What is, in fact, conveyed by these words is only that, in case of a conflict between theory and observation, we shall *search* for disturbing factors whilst considering ourselves free to adhere to the theory. The question at issue is *not* whether a certain system of assumption is sufficiently comprehensive—that is a question of fact which may be left to the expert; the question is rather whether there is a *criterion* which assures us that a system of premisses is complete. To this there is no answer; nay, more, we cannot even form any conception of such a criterion; we cannot think of a situation in which a physicist would tell us, 'Well, I have finished the job; now I have discovered the last law of nature, and no more is to be found'. But if this is devoid of meaning, there is no point in insisting, '*If* all the conditions in the universe, and *if* all the laws governing them were known to us, then—'. As the boundary regions of our knowledge are always enveloped in a dust cloud—

out of which something new may emerge—we are left with the fact that *s* is not a strict logical consequence of *L* together with the initial conditions. Saying that the class of premisses is not 'closed' and that *therefore* the conclusion is lacking in stringency comes, in my view, to the same thing as saying that *s* is *not* a logical consequence of the premisses as far as they are stated. And that is all I wanted to say.

All this tends to suggest that the relation between a law of nature and the evidences for it, or between a material object statement and a sense-datum statement, or again between a psychological statement and the evidence concerning a person's behaviour is a looser one than had been hitherto imagined. If that is correct, the application of logic seems to be limited in an important sense. We may say that the known relations of logic can only hold between statements which belong to a *homogeneous* domain; or that the deductive nexus never extends beyond the limits of such a domain.

Accordingly we may set ourselves the task of arranging the statements of our language in distinct strata, grouping in the same stratum all those statements linked by clearly apprehended logical relations. It is in this way, for instance, that the theorems of mechanics are organized in a system the elements of which stand in known logical relations with one another and where it is always possible to decide of two theorems in what logical relation they stand—whether one is a consequence of the other, whether they are equivalent, or independent of, or in contradiction with each other. In like manner the statements of a physicist in describing certain data of observation (such as the position of a pointer on his gauges) stand in exactly defined relations to one another. Thus a pointer on a scale cannot possibly be opposite 3 and 5 at the same time: here you have a relation of strict exclusion. On the other hand, no statement of mechanics can ever come into sharp logical conflict with a statement of observation, and this implies that between these two kinds of statements there exist no relations of the sort supplied to us by classical logic. So long as we move only among the statements of a single stratum, all the relations provided by logic remain valid. The real problem arises where two such strata make contact, so to speak; it is the problem of these planes of contact which to-day should claim the attention of the logician. We may, in this context, speak of the looseness of the chains of inference which lead from statements of one stratum to those of another; the connection is no longer coercive—owing to the incompleteness of all our data.

You will find that it is this fact to which the rise of philosophical troubles often can be traced. (Think of how confusing it is to assert or to dispute the statement, 'The floor is not solid', as it belongs to two quite distinct strata.) The fracture lines of the strata of language are marked by philosophical problems: the problem of perception, of verification, of induction, the problem of the relation between mind and body, and so on.

You will have noticed that I have used the term 'incompleteness' in very different senses. In one sense we may say of a description of a material object that it is incomplete; in another sense we may say that of our knowledge of the boundary conditions in a field of force. There is a sense in which we say that a list of laws of nature is always incomplete, and another sense in which even our knowledge of the agents of nature is so; and you may easily find more senses. They all combine, to a varying degree, to create what I have called the open texture of concepts and the looseness of inferences.

Incompleteness, in the senses referred to, is the mark of empirical knowledge as opposed to *a priori* knowledge such as mathematics. In fact, it is the criterion by which we can distinguish perfectly *formalized* languages constructed by logicians from *natural* languages as used in describing reality. In a formalized system the use of each symbol is governed by a definite number of rules, and further, all the rules of inference and procedure can be stated completely. In view of the incompleteness which permeates empirical knowledge such a demand cannot be fulfilled by any language we may use to express it.

That there is a very close relation between content and verification is an important insight which has been brought to light by empiricists. Only one has to be very careful how to formulate it. Far from identifying the meaning of a statement with the evidences we have for it, the view I tried to sketch leads to a sort of many-level-theory of language in which 'every sort of statement has its own sort of logic'.

II

In the second part of his paper Mr. MacKinnon is anxious to relate the notions of reality and causality by admitting as real only those objects (or events, or processes) which satisfy the conditions of causality. What he says is 'that the manner of discursive thought . . . reveals itself as an obstinate resolve . . . to admit nothing as real that does not manifest some ground of its occurrence'. That is part of Kant's doctrine according to which nothing can ever become object of our knowledge which did not conform to certain *a priori* forms of our intuition and our understanding. Such an attempt, if it succeeded, would be of tremendous importance. Think how miraculous it would be, using this method, to deduce from it causality, premisses of induction as well as other enjoyable things—I had almost said to *pro*duce them out of the conjuror's hat called the Transcendental Argument. How comforting would be the belief that we know the nature of space and time through and through so that we are able to enunciate the principles of geometry without fear of ever being defeated by experience. How reassuring it would be to say that nature *must* obey causal laws—and so on, you know the tune. The question is only whether Nature will conform to Kant. You will realize that such over-confidence is no longer permissible to-day, in the age of quantum mechanics. We arc told by Mr. MacKinnon that 'we display an unwillingness to admit the completely random' (by the bye, what does he mean by that?) 'and discontinuous as objectively real'. But our protest, however strongly worded, would be of no avail if Nature was willing to baffle us. The words Mr. MacKinnon has been using state precisely the sort of situation with which we have come face to face in modern physics: things do happen without ground of their occurrence. May I be allowed to say a few words on this subject?

There are people who think that physicists have just not succeeded in discovering laws which tell us why things happen in the atomic world, in the cheerful hope that someone some day will have a brain-wave which will enable him to fill the gaps in wave mechanics; on this day the latter will turn into a completely deterministic theory. Let these people realize how wide the cleavage is that separates us from the good old days. The hope they cherish is based on an illusion: it has been proved[1] that the structure of quantum mechanics is such that no further laws can be added to it which would make the whole theory deterministic; for if we could, we should, owing to the uncertainty principle, get entangled in contradictions. (The situation is, in fact, more intricate, but this is not the place to go into it.) So we are faced with the dilemma that quantum mechanics is *either* self-consistent *or* deterministic: you can't have it both ways. The crack in the wall of Determinism is definitive, and there is no way out of the situation.

According to Kant causality is an inescapable form which the nature of our understanding imposes on any given material. If this were so, it would be inconceivable—against the conditions of possible experience—ever to come across any events which did not conform to the principle of causality. Quantum phenomena, however, have forced physicists to depart from this principle, or better, to *restrict* it, whilst a torso of it is retained. Though the fate of a single electron is not governed by causal laws, the particle being free to move about, for instance, to 'jump' in a collision with light waves however it pleases, the behaviour of millions of electrons is statistically predictable. Not exactly that quantum mechanics confronts us with a mathematician's dream of chaos come true. For, as I said, there is a causal aspect in the new theory, namely this: there are certain waves connected with the motion of particles, the de Broglie waves, which obey rigorous 'causal' laws. That is, the propagation of these waves is governed by a differential equation of the respectable old type such as you find in the classical physics of fields. Hence we can, given the initial conditions and the values over the boundary of a region during a certain interval of time, predict with absolute precision the propagation of the waves. That is exactly what any causal theory achieves. What is new, however, is the interpretation we must give to these waves: they are a sort of 'probability clouds' the density of which at each point signifies the probability of the occurrence of a particle. So what we can deduce from the theory are only *probability statements* regarding the presence of a particle in a given place at a given time. Such a statement can be tested, not by making a single experiment such as observing a single

[1] See, for instance, J. v. Neumann, *Mathematische Grundlagen der Quantenmechanik.*

electron through a microscope, but by repeating the experiment a large number of times, or observing a large number of electrons and forming the mean value of all the data thus obtained. Therefore we cannot say where exactly a certain electron will be, but only with what probability, i.e. in what percentage of cases we may expect to find it at a certain place. In other words, the theory can be used only to predict the *average behaviour* of particles. That is the statistical aspect of the theory.

To sum up: quantum mechanics is neither a theory of the causal, deterministic type nor an indeterministic theory, whatever this may be taken to mean. The new physics combines deterministic and indeterministic features. What is deterministic is the law for the propagation of the de Broglie waves. That is, the propagation of these waves is *causally determined* in much the same way as, e.g., the propagation of electromagnetic waves is in the classical theories. What is indeterministic is the *interpretation* of these waves, that is, their connection with the facts of observation. Such an interpretation can only be given in statistical terms, and any attempt at interpreting it differently so as to reinstate causality would only lead to conflict with other well-established parts of the theory. Thus we have the curious result that causality holds for the de Broglie waves, which are no more than a purely symbolic and formal representation of certain probabilities, whereas the particles themselves obey no causal laws.

To bring home the last point let me add this: If it were possible to repeat exactly the same experiment and to bring about exactly the same conditions, the result would each time be a different one. Therefore the principle 'Like causes—like effects' no longer holds. *Lasciate ogni speranza . . .*

But may not quantum mechanics one day be superseded by a better theory that meets our demand for causal explanation? Certainly; no theory is sacrosanct and infallible. This, however, is not the point. What matters is, not whether quantum mechanics draws a true picture of reality, but only whether it draws a *permissible* one. About that there can be little doubt. Kant was of the opinion that if there was no such thing as causality science would simply break down. Now the important thing that has emerged is the *possibility* of constructing a theory along different lines, the *legitimacy* of departing from causality, while science has not died or committed suicide on that account. This suffices to disown any claim on the part of Kant to regard causality as an *indispensable* form of our knowledge of the world. Had he been right, we could not even *entertain* such views as physicists do to-day; to give up causality, even if in part, would mean robbing ourselves of the very condition for gaining knowledge; which could end in one result only, in complete confusion. But that is not so. Though causality has been severely limited, quantum mechanics is a useful tool. Kant did not foresee the possible forms of physical laws; by laying too much stress on the scheme of causality, by claiming for it an *a priori* status, he unduly narrowed the field of research.

The conclusion to be drawn for the preceding seems to me this: Even if quantum mechanics should one day be found wanting and be superseded by another theory, it still offers a *possible picture* of the material world. This picture is neither self-contradictory nor unintelligible, though it may not be the sort of picture to which we are accustomed; anyhow, it is a working hypothesis which serves its purpose in that it is fruitful, i.e. that it leads to new discoveries. Whether it contains the ultimate truth we cannot tell (nor can we in the case of the deterministic theories). It's only experience that can bring forward evidence against it. But the very fact that we *can* turn to experience is significant: in doing so we grant that quantum mechanics, and consequently the limits of causality, *can* be tested in experiment. Hence every attempt at raising the principle of causality to the status of a neccssary truth is irreconcilable with the situation as it has emerged in science. No matter whether quantum mechanics will stand its ground or will have to undergo some modification or other, the mere fact that the construction of such a theory is legitimate should settle the dispute: it proves that Kant's argument is based on a fallacy.

It was indeed an important step when man learnt to ask, Why? But it was also a great step when he learnt to drop this question. But leaving quantum mechanics and turning to the common world of sense, I still fail to see any ground for accepting Kant's position. True, in order to get our bearings in the world we must presuppose that there is some sort of order in it so that we may anticipate the course of events and act accordingly. What I fail to see, however, is why this order should be a strictly *causal* one. Suppose, for the sake of argument, that the objects around us were, *on the average*, to display an orderly behaviour, then the world may still be a liveable place. Suppose, for instance, the behaviour of chairs and the support they give us could be foreseen with much the same accuracy as can the behaviour of Tory and Labour candidates in election times, may we then not make use of them just the same? Or suppose they were to conduct themselves as our best friends do—they won't let us down, no; still, you never know—then, as far as I can see, this would be quite enough for all our practical ends. And as to the theoretical ones—well, go to the scientist and you will hear a sorry tale of nature's trickery. I cannot see why such a world should not be possible.

This brings me to the topic in which Mr. MacKinnon is so much interested—are there any *necessary* conditions which must be fulfilled if we are to attain knowledge of the external world? I propose to drop for the moment the subject of causality and to tackle the problem from a broader angle. Let me begin with some observations on the terms 'reality' and 'knowledge'.

Mr. MacKinnon, in his paper, repeatedly speaks of 'the real', 'the reality', he asks, for instance, whether 'the completely random' can be admitted as 'objectively real'. He blames Berkeley for having omitted 'to face the question of the rules whereby the inclusion in or exclusion from reality was determined; in consequence of which', we are told, 'his theory of knowledge flags'. In another passage he speaks of 'the task of compelling the actual to disclose itself'. My impression is that he talks as if there was a clearly bounded domain called 'the real' or 'the actual' with the implication that it is one of the tasks of the philosopher to define it sharply. Unfortunately the belief that there is such a domain is very slender. Not that I deny for a minute that a word like 'reality' is a blessing; it definitely is. Look at such phrases as 'A tautology doesn't say anything about reality', 'Pure mathematics is not concerned with reality', 'In reality it was not Smith I saw but his brother'. It would be silly to put such a word on an *Index Prohibitorum Verborum* as though it were a sin to use it. It is very handy—if it were not in use, we should have to invent it. On the other hand, when a philosopher looks closely at it, tears it from the context and asks himself, 'Now what *is* reality?' he has successfully manœuvred himself into a fairly awkward position. For it is surprisingly easy to ask a number of questions which are more or less embarrassing; for instance, 'Is the elastic force present in a spring something real?' I suppose some people would answer Yes, some No. The fact is that there simply are no fixed rules that govern the use of the word. To go on—'Is a magnetic field something real?' 'Is energy? and entropy?' Again, I may ask, 'Is the power of my memory real?', 'Is the genius of a people, is the spirit of an age, is the beauty of a spring day real?' Now we begin to see how the idea is lost in indeterminacy. What we must understand is that such a word is used on many different levels and with many different shades of meaning. It has a *systematic ambiguity*. At the same time there is a sort of family likeness between all these uses, and it is that which makes us denote them by one word.

The same applies to a verb like 'to exist'. We use the word in many different senses: we may, for instance, say of a memory picture, an after-image, a mirror image, or again of a material object that it 'exists'; again, we may say of a wave-motion in a space of many dimensions, or of a law of nature, or of a number satisfying certain conditions that it 'exists'; and it is quite obvious that we do use the word in each case according to totally different criteria. So again we have a case of systematic ambiguity.

Next take the term 'knowledge'. Everyone is familiar with the distinction between knowledge by acquaintance and knowledge by description. This division is not fine enough. When I know something by acquaintance, I may know it in very different senses, as when I say 'I know sweetness' (meaning 'I am acquainted with the taste of sweetness'), 'I know misery', 'I know him', 'I know his writings'. In this series we go progressively farther away from simple acquaintance. In a case like 'I know his motives', it is doubtful whether I should say this unless I had experienced some such motive myself. Moreover, there are cases which fall under none of the two groups; so, for instance, when I say 'I know French', 'I know how to deal with that man'. Again, we may speak in different senses of knowledge by description. Compare the case of a reporter who gained knowledge of some hush-hush affair with that of a scientist who claims to possess knowledge of nature. Now is this knowledge in the same sense? And mark, in the latter case there are again subtle differences. Compare knowledge of the history of certain birds as based on observation with knowledge of the history of our solar system as based on some hypothesis; again knowledge of a natural law of the causal type with knowledge of a statistical law. Quantum mechanics, though it is based on the assumption of a randomness in the behaviour of electrons (and other particles), leads to a lot of predictions. On this ground physicists do not hesitate to honour the newly discovered laws by awarding them the degree of knowledge; whereas Mr. MacKinnon thinks 'that we do concede the title unintelligible to any field . . . where such (causal) lines have not been traced'. Well, I shall not argue about that; my sole object is to call attention to the fact that the actual usage is unsettled, that there are many different types of knowledge, and that, by talking of knowledge *in general*, we are liable to overlook the very important differences between them. Suppose that someone has a vague awareness of the direction in which history moves—shall, or shall I not call this knowledge? Can you draw a clear line to mark where such vague awareness ends and where true knowledge begins? Knowledge as supplied by quantum mechanics was unknown two or three decades ago. Who can tell what forms of knowledge may emerge in the future? Can you anticipate all possible cases in which you may wish to use that term? To say that knowledge is embodied in true propositions does not get you any farther; for there are many different structures that are called 'propositions'—different, because they are verified in different senses of the word and governed by different sets of logical rules. (Incidentally speaking, the failure to draw a clear line between the meaningful and the meaningless is due to the fact that these terms have themselves a systematic ambiguity, and so has the term 'verifiable'.)

There is a group of words such as 'fact', 'event', 'situation', 'case', 'circumstance', which display a queer sort of behaviour. One might say of such words that they serve as pegs: it's marvellous what a lot of things you can put on them ('the fact that—'). So far they are very handy; but as soon as one focusses on them and asks, e.g., 'What *is* a fact?' they betray a tendency of melting away. The peg-aspect is by far the most important of all. It's just as in the case of the word 'reality': in reality, e.g., 'in reality' is an adverb.

Again, there are many different types of fact; there are many different types of statement which are called 'empirical'; there are many different things which are called 'experience'; and there are many different senses of communication and clarity.

Now if I am to contribute to the main subject of this symposium, that is, to the question whether there are any *necessary conditions* for *gaining knowledge of reality*—what am I to reply? Knowledge of reality! Of *what* sort of reality, and *what* sort of knowledge? As a logician I am bound to say that the notions of reality and knowledge have a systematic ambiguity and, moreover, that they are on each level extremely vague and hazy. I am even not quite clear as to what a condition is, let alone a 'necessary condition'. How questionable all these ideas are! How can I be expected to answer a question which consists only of a series of question marks?

III

So far my criticism was mainly negative. In conclusion I should like to offer some constructive suggestions. Before doing so, I must warn you that I can't see any ground whatever for renouncing one of the most fundamental rights of man, the right of talking nonsense. And now I suppose I may go on.

People are inclined to think that there is a world of facts as opposed to a world of words which describe these facts. I am not too happy about that. Consider an example. We are accustomed to see colour as a 'quality' of objects. That is, colour cannot subsist by itself, but must inhere in a thing. This conception springs from the way we express ourselves. When colour is rendered by an adjective, colour is conceived as an attribute of things, i.e. as something that can have no independent existence. That, however, is not the only way of conceiving colour. There are languages such as Russian, German, Italian, which render colour by means of verbs. If we were to imitate this usage in English by allowing some such form as 'The sky blues', we should come face to face with the question, Do I mean the same fact when I say 'The sky blues' as when I say 'The sky is blue'? I don't think so. We say 'The sun shines', 'Jewels glitter', 'The river shimmers', 'Windows gleam', 'Stars twinkle', etc.; that is, in the case of phenomena of lustre we make use of a verbal mode of expression. Now in rendering colour phenomena by verbs we assimilate them more closely to the phenomena of lustre; and in doing so we alter not only our manner of speaking but our entire way of apprehending colour. We *see* the blue differently now—a hint that language affects our whole mode of apprehension. In the word 'blueing' we are clearly aware of an active, verbal element. On that account 'being blue' is not quite equivalent to 'blueing', since it lacks what is peculiar to the verbal mode of expression. The sky which 'blues' is seen as something that continually brings forth blueness—it radiates blueness, so to speak; blue does not inhere in it as a mere quality, rather is it felt as the vital pulse of the sky; there is a faint suggestion of the operating of some force behind the phenomenon. It's hard to get the feel of it in English; perhaps it may help you to liken this mode of expression to the impressionist way of painting which is at bottom a new way of seeing: the impressionist sees in colour an immediate manifestation of reality, a free agent no longer bound up with things.

There are, then, different linguistic means of rendering colour. When this is done by means of adjectives, colour is conceived as an attribute of things. The learning of such a language involves for everyone who speaks it his being habituated to see colour as a 'quality' of objects. This conception becomes thus incorporated into his picture of the world. The verbal mode of expression detaches colour from things: it enables us to see colour as a phenomenon with a life of its own. Adjective and verb thus represent two different worlds of thought.

There is also an adverbial way of talking about colour. Imagine a language with a wealth of expressions for all shades of lustre, but without adjectives for colours; colours, as a rule, are ignored; *when* they are expressed, this is done by adding an adverb to the word that specifies the sort of lustre. Thus the people who use this sort of language would say, 'The sea is glittering golden in the sunshine', 'The evening clouds glow redly', 'There in the depth a shadow greenly gleams'. In such phrases colour would lose the last trace of independence and be reduced to a mere modification of lustre. Just as we in our language cannot say

'That's very', but only some such thing as 'That's very brilliant', so in the language considered we could not say 'That's bluish', but only, e.g., 'That's shining bluishly'. There can be little doubt that, owing to this circumstance, the users of such language would find it very hard to see colour as a quality of things. For them it would not be the *things* that are coloured, rather colour would reside in the lustre as it glows and darkens and changes—evidence that they would see the world with different eyes.

'But isn't it still true to say that I have the same experience whenever I look up at the sky?' You would be less happy if you were asked, 'Do you have the same experience when you look at a picture puzzle and see a figure in it as before, when you didn't see it?' You may, perhaps, say you see the same lines, though each time in a different arrangement. Now what exactly corresponds to this different arrangement in the case when I look up at the sky? One might say: we are aware of the blue, but this awareness is itself tinged and coloured by the whole linguistic background which brings into prominence, or weakens and hides certain analogies. In this sense language does affect the whole manner in which we become aware of a fact: the fact articulates itself differently, so to speak. In urging that you *must* have the same experience whenever you look at the sky you forget that the term 'experience' is itself ambiguous: whether it is taken, e.g., to include or to exclude all the various analogies which a certain mode of expression calls up.

Again, consider this case: Suppose there is a number of languages *A*, *B*, *C* . . . in each of which a proposition is used according to a slightly different logic. Consequently a proposition in the language *A* is not a proposition in exactly the same sense as a proposition in the language *B*, etc. And not only this: what is described by a statement in the language *A*, i.e., if you like, the 'fact', is not a fact in the same sense as a fact described in the language *B*, etc.; which tends to show that what is called a fact depends on the linguistic medium through which we see it.

I have observed that when the clock strikes in the night and I, already half asleep, am too tired to count the strokes, I am seized by an impression that the sequence will never end—as though it would go on, stroke after stroke, in an unending measureless procession. The whole thing vanishes as soon as I *count*. Counting frees me, as it were, from the dark formlessness impending over me. (Is this not a parable of the rational?) It seems to me that one could say here that counting *alters* the quality of the experience. Now is it the same fact which I perceive when counting and when not counting?

Again, suppose there is a tribe whose members count 'one, two, three, a few, many'. Suppose a man of this tribe looking at a flock of birds said 'A few birds' whereas I should say 'Five birds'—is it the same fact for him as it is for me? If in such a case I pass to a language of a different structure, I can no longer describe 'the same' fact, but only another one more or less resembling the first. What, then, is the objective reality supposed to be described by language?

What rebels in us against such a suggestion is the feeling that the fact is there objectively no matter in which way we render it. I perceive something that exists and put it into words. From this it seems to follow that fact is something that exists independent of, and prior to language; language merely serves the end of communication. What we are liable to overlook here is that the way we see a fact—i.e. what we emphasize and what we disregard—is *our* work. 'The sun-beams trembling on the floating tides' (Pope). Here a fact is something that emerges out from, and takes shape against a background. The background may be, e.g., my visual field; something that rouses my attention detaches itself from this field, is brought into focus and apprehended linguistically; that is what we call a fact. A fact is noticed; and by being noticed it becomes a fact. 'Was it then no fact before you noticed it?' It was, if I *could* have noticed it. In a language in which there is only the number series 'one, two, three, a few, many', a fact such as 'There are five birds' is imperceptible.

To make my meaning still clearer consider a language in which description does not take the form of sentences. Examples of such a description would be supplied by a map, a picture language, a film, the musical notation. A map, for instance, should not be taken as a conjunction of single statements each of which describes a separate fact. For what, would you say, is the boundary of a fact? Where does the one end and the other begin? If we think of such types of description, we are no longer tempted to say that a country, or a story told in a film, or a melody must consist of 'facts'. Here we begin to see how confusing the idea is according to which the world is a cluster of facts—just as if it were a sort of mosaic made up of little coloured stones. Reality is undivided. What we may have in mind is perhaps that *language* contains units, viz. *sentences*. In describing reality, by using sentences, we draw, as it were, lines through it, limit a part and call what corresponds with such a sentence a fact. In other words, language is the knife with which we cut out facts. (This account is over-simplified as it doesn't take notice of *false* statements.)

Reality, then, is not made up of facts in the sense in which a plant is made up of cells, a house of bricks, a stone of molecules; rather, if you want a simile, a fact is present, in much the same sense in which a character manifests itself in a face. Not that I invent the character and read it into the face; no, the character is somehow written on the face but no one would on that account say that a face is 'made up' of features symbolic of such-and-such traits. Just as we have to interpret a face, so we have to interpret reality. The elements of such an interpretation, without our being aware of it, are already present in language—for instance, in such moulds as the notion of thinghood, of causality, of number, or again in the way we render colour, etc.

Noticing a fact may be likened to seeing a face in a cloud, or a figure in an arrangement of dots, or suddenly becoming aware of the solution of a picture puzzle: one views a complex of elements as one, reads a sort of unity into it, etc. Language supplies us with a means of comprehending and categorizing; and different languages categorize differently.

'But surely noticing a face in a cloud is not inventing it?' Certainly not; only you might not have noticed it unless you had already had the experience of human faces somewhere else. Does this not throw a light on what constitutes the noticing of facts? I would not dream for a moment of saying that I *invent* them; I might, however, be unable to perceive them if I had not certain moulds of comprehension ready at hand. These forms I borrow from language. Language, then, *contributes to the formation and participates in the constitution* of a fact; which, of course, does not mean that it *produces* the fact.

So far I have dealt with perceptual situations only. This, I am afraid, will not satisfy Mr. MacKinnon. What he wants to know is whether there are any *general* conditions of the possibility of factual knowledge. We have seen some of the fallacies involved in putting this question. Still we may ask ourselves whether there are any methodological rules which guide us in gaining knowledge. All I can hope to do here is to throw out some hints.

The empiricist has a let-the-facts-speak-for-themselves attitude. Well, this is his faith; what about his works? Remember, a scientific theory is never a slavish imitation of certain features of reality, a dead, passive replica. It is essentially a *construction* which to a more or less degree reflects our own activity. When, for instance, we represent a number of observations made in the laboratory by a corresponding number of dots and connect them by a graph, we assume, as a rule, that the curve is continuous and analytic. Such an assumption goes far beyond any possible experience. There will always be infinitely many other possible curves which accord with the facts equally well; the totality of these curves is included within a certain narrow strip. The ordinary mathematical treatment substitutes an exact law for the blurred data of observation and deduces from such laws strict mathematical conclusions. This shows that there is an element of convention inherent in the formulation of a law. The way we single out one particular law from infinitely many possible ones shows that in our theoretical construction of reality we are guided by certain principles—*regulative principles* as we may call them. If I were asked what these principles are, I should tentatively list the following:

(1) Simplicity or economy—the demand that the laws should be as simple as possible.

(2) Demands suggested by the requirements of the symbolism we use—for instance, that the graph should represent an analytic function so as to lend itself readily to the carrying out of certain mathematical operations such as differentiation.

(3) Aesthetic principles ('mathematical harmony' as envisaged by Pythagoras, Kepler, Einstein) though it is difficult to say what they are.

(4) A principle which so regulates the formation of our concepts that as many alternatives as possible become decidable. This tendency is embodied in the whole structure of Aristotelian logic, especially in the law of excluded middle.[1]

(5) There is a further factor elusive and most difficult to pin down: a mere tone of thought which, though not explicitly stated, permeates the air of a historical period and inspires its leading figures. It is a sort of field organizing and directing the ideas of an age. (The time from Descartes to Newton, for instance, was animated by an instinctive belief in an Order of Things accessible to the human mind. Though the thinkers of that time have tried to render this tone of thought into a rationalistic system, they failed: for that which is the living spark of rationalism is irrational.)

Such, I think, are some of the regulative principles. The formulation of some of them is very vague, and advisedly so: it wouldn't be good policy to reduce mathematical harmony, consonance with the whole background of an age, etc., to fixed rules. It's better to have them elastic. Principle (5) should perhaps better be described as a condition for making—and missing—discoveries.

Now none of these principles is *indispensable*, imposed on us by the nature of our understanding. Kant has tried to condense the tone of thought of the Newtonian age into strict rules—into *necessary conditions* of factual knowledge; with what success can be seen from the subsequent development: the belief in synthetic *a priori* judgements soon became something of a brake to research, discouraging such lines of approach as non-Euclidean geometry, and later non-causal laws in physics. Let this be a warning.

Writers on the history of philosophy are inclined to attend too exclusively to one aspect only—to the ideas explicitly stated, canvassing their fabric, but disregarding the tone of thought which gives them their impetus. The deeper significance of rationalism, for instance, lies in the fact that it corresponds to what the scientist *does*, strengthening his belief that, if he only

[1] A more detailed account of this is given in my article on 'Alternative Logics' in *Proceedings of the Aristotelian Society*, 1945–6.

tries hard, he *can* get to the bottom of things. But slowly and gradually the mental climate changes, and then a philosophy may find itself out of tune with its time.

I do not think for a minute that what I have said is a conclusive refutation of Kant. On the other hand—you may confute and kill a scientific theory; a philosophy dies only of old age.

CHAPTER VIII

THE ASCRIPTION OF RESPONSIBILITY AND RIGHTS

By H. L. A. Hart

THERE are in our ordinary language sentences whose primary function is not to describe things, events, or persons or anything else, nor to express or kindle feelings or emotions, but to do such things as claim rights ('This is mine'), recognize rights when claimed by others ('Very well, this is yours'), ascribe rights whether claimed or not ('This is his'), transfer rights ('This is now yours'), and also to admit or ascribe or make accusations of responsibility ('I did it', 'He did it', 'You did it'). My main purpose in this article is to suggest that the philosophical analysis of the concept of a human action has been inadequate and confusing, at least in part because sentences of the form 'He did it' have been traditionally regarded as primarily descriptive whereas their principal function is what I venture to call *ascriptive*, being quite literally to ascribe responsibility for actions much as the principal function of sentences of the form 'This is his' is to ascribe rights in property. Now ascriptive sentences and the other kinds of sentence quoted above, though they may form only a small part of our ordinary language, resemble in some important respects the formal statements of claim, the indictments, the admissions, the judgements, and the verdicts which constitute so large and so important a part of the language of lawyers; and the logical peculiarities which distinguish these kinds of sentences from descriptive sentences, or rather from the theoretical model of descriptive sentences with which philosophers often work, can best be grasped by considering certain characteristics of legal concepts, as these appear in the practice and procedure of the law rather than in the theoretical discussions of legal concepts by jurists who are apt to be influenced by philosophical theories. Accordingly, in the first part of this paper I attempt to bring out some of these characteristics of legal concepts; in the second, I attempt to show how sentences ascribing rights function in our ordinary language and also why their distinctive function is overlooked; and in the third part I attempt to make good my claim that sentences of the form 'He did it' are fundamentally ascriptive and that some at any rate of the philosophical puzzles concerning 'action' have resulted from inattention to this fact.

I

As everyone knows, the decisive stage in the proceedings of an English law court is normally a *judgement* given by the court to the effect that certain facts (Smith put arsenic in his wife's coffee and as a result she died) are true and that certain legal consequences (Smith is guilty of murder) are attached to those facts. Such a judgement is therefore a compound or blend of facts and law; and, of course, the claims and the indictments upon which law courts adjudicate are also blends of facts and law, though claims, indictments, and judgements are different from each other. Now there are several characteristics of the legal element in these compounds or blends which conspire to make the way in which facts support or fail to support legal conclusions, or refute or fail to refute them, unlike certain standard models of how one kind of statement supports or refutes another upon which philosophers are apt to concentrate attention. This is not apparent at once: for when the judge decides that on the facts which he has found there is a contract for sale between A and B, or that B, a publican, is guilty of the offence[1] of supplying liquor to a constable on duty, or that B is liable for trespass because of what his horse has done on his neighbour's land, *it looks* from the terminology as if the law must consist of a set, if not a system, of legal concepts such as 'contract', 'the offence of supplying liquor to a constable on duty', 'trespass', invented and defined by the legislature or some other 'source', and as if the function of the judge was simply to say 'Yes' or 'No' to the question: 'Do the facts come within the scope of the formula defining the necessary and sufficient conditions of "contract", "trespass", or "the offence of supplying liquor to a constable on duty"?'

But this is for many reasons a disastrous over-simplification

[1] S. 16 of the Licensing Act, 1872.

and indeed distortion, because there are characteristics of legal concepts which make it often absurd to use in connection with them the language of necessary and sufficient conditions. One important characteristic which I do not discuss in detail is no doubt vaguely familiar to most people. In England, the judge is not supplied with explicitly formulated general criteria defining 'contract', or 'trespass'; instead he has to decide by reference to past cases or precedents whether on the facts before him a contract has been made or a trespass committed; and in doing this he has a wide freedom, in judging whether the present case is sufficiently near to a past precedent, and also in determining what the past precedent in fact amounts to, or, as lawyers say, in identifying the *ratio decidendi* of past cases. This imports to legal concepts a vagueness of character very loosely controlled by judicial traditions of interpretation, and it has the consequence that usually the request for a definition of a legal concept—'What is a trespass?' 'What is a contract?'—cannot be answered by the provision of a verbal rule for the translation of a legal expression into other terms or one specifying a set of necessary and sufficient conditions. *Something* can be done in the way of providing an outline, in the form of a general statement of the effect of past cases, and that is how the student starts to learn the law. But beyond a point, answers to the questions 'What is trespass?', 'What is contract?', if they are not to mislead, must take the form of references to the leading cases on the subject, coupled with the use of the word 'etcetera'.

But there is another characteristic of legal concepts, of more importance for my present purpose, which makes the word 'unless' as indispensable as the word 'etcetera' in any explanation or definition of them; and the necessity for this can be seen by examining the distinctive ways in which legal utterances can be challenged. For the accusations or claims upon which law courts adjudicate can usually be challenged or opposed in two ways. First, by a denial of the facts upon which they are based (technically called a traverse or joinder of issue) and secondly by something quite different, namely, a plea that although all the circumstances on which a claim could succeed are present, yet in the particular case, the claim or accusation should not succeed because other circumstances are present which brings the case under some recognized head of exception, the effect of which is either to defeat the claim or accusation altogether, or to 'reduce' it so that only a weaker claim can be sustained. Thus a plea of 'provocation' in murder cases, if successful, 'reduces' what would otherwise be murder to manslaughter; and so in a case of contract a defence that the defendant has been deceived by a material fraudulent misrepresentation made by the plaintiff entitles the defendant in certain cases to say that the contract is not valid as claimed, nor 'void', but 'voidable' at his option. In consequence, it is usually not possible to define a legal concept such as 'trespass' or 'contract' by specifying the necessary and sufficient conditions for its application. For any set of conditions may be adequate in some cases but not in others, and such concepts can only be explained with the aid of a list of exceptions or negative examples showing where the concept may not be applied or may only be applied in a weakened form.

This can be illustrated in detail from the law of contract. When the student has learnt that in English law there are positive conditions required for the existence of a valid contract, i.e. at least two *parties*, an *offer* by one, *acceptance* by the other, a *memorandum* in writing in some cases and *consideration*, his understanding of the legal concept of a contract is still incomplete, and remains so even if he has learnt the lawyers' technique for the interpretation of the technical but still vague terms, 'offer', 'acceptance', 'memorandum', 'consideration'. For these conditions, although necessary, are not always sufficient and he has still to learn what can *defeat* a claim that there is a valid contract, even though all these conditions are satisfied. That is the student has still to learn what can follow on the word 'unless', which should accompany the statement of these conditions. This characteristic of legal concepts is one for which no word exists in ordinary English. The words 'conditional' and 'negative' have the wrong implications, but the law has a word which with some hesitation I borrow and extend: this is the word '*defeasible*', used of a legal interest in property which is subject to termination or '*defeat*' in a number of different contingencies but remains intact if no such contingencies mature. In this sense, then, contract is a defeasible concept.

The list of defences with which an otherwise valid claim in contract can be met is worth a philosopher's inspection because it is here that reference to the factor that intrigues him—the mental factor—is mainly to be found. Thus the principal defences include the following:[1]

A. Defences which refer to the knowledge possessed by the defendant.
  i. Fraudulent misrepresentation.
  ii. Innocent misrepresentation.
  iii. Non-disclosure of material facts (in special cases, e.g. contracts of insurance, only).

B. Defences which refer to what may be called the will of the defendant.
  i. Duress.
  ii. Undue influence.

C. Defences which may cover both knowledge and will.
  i. Lunacy.
  ii. Intoxication.

D. Defences which refer to the general policy of the law in discouraging certain types of contract, such as
  i. Contracts made for immoral purposes.
  ii. Contracts which restrain unreasonably the freedom of trade.
  iii. Contracts tending to pervert the course of justice.

E. The defence that the contract is rendered 'impossible of performance' or 'frustrated' by a fundamental and unexpected change of circumstance, e.g. the outbreak of a war.

F. The defence that the claim is barred by lapse of time.

Most of these defences are of general application to all contracts. Some of them, e.g. those made under (D), destroy altogether the claim that there is a contract, so that it is void *ab initio*; others, e.g. those under (B) or (C), have a weaker effect,

[1] This list, of course, is only a summary reference to the more important defences, sufficient to illustrate the point that the defeasible concept of contract cannot be defined by a set of necessary and always sufficient conditions. There are important omissions from this list, e.g. the disputed topic known to lawyers as 'Mistake'. Adequate discussion and illustration of these and other defences will be found in legal textbooks on contract, e.g. Cheshire and Fifoot, *Law of Contract*, Chap. IV.

rendering it merely 'voidable' at the option of the party concerned, and till this option is exercised the contract remains valid so that rights may be acquired by third parties under it; while the lapse of time mentioned in (F) merely extinguishes the right to institute legal proceedings, but does not otherwise affect the existence of the contract. It is plain, therefore, that no adequate characterization of the legal concept of a contract could be made without reference to these extremely heterogeneous defences and the manner in which they respectively serve to defeat or weaken claims in contract. The concept is irreducibly defeasible in character and to ignore this is to misrepresent it. But, of course, it is *possible* to obscure the character of such concepts by providing a general formula which seems to meet the demand often felt by the theorist for a definition in terms of a set of necessary and sufficient conditions; and since philosophers have, I think obscured in precisely this way the defeasible character of the concept of an action, it is instructive to consider how such an obscuring general formula could be provided in the case of contract and to what it leads.

Thus the theorist bent on providing a general definition of contract could at any rate make a beginning by selecting the groups of defences (A), (B) and (C), which refer to the will and knowledge of the defendant, and by then arguing that the fact that these defences are admitted or allowed shows that the definition of contract requires as necessary conditions that the minds of the parties should be 'fully informed' and their wills 'free'. And, indeed, legal theorists and also on occasion judges do attempt to state the 'principles' of the law of contract much in this way. Thus Sir Frederick Pollock, writing[1] of the consent of the parties required for the constitution of a valid contract, says 'but we still require other conditions in order to make the consent binding on him who gives it. . . . The consent must be true, full and free'. Now, of course, this method of exposition of the law may be innocuous and indeed helpful as a summary of various types of defences which usefully stresses their universal application to all contracts, or emphasizes the similarities between

[1] *Principles of the Law of Contract*, 10th edn., p. 442. The words omitted are 'though their absence in general is not to be assumed and the party seeking to enforce a contract is not expected to give affirmative proof that they have been satisfied'.

them and so suggests analogies for the further development of the law or what can be called 'reasons' for that development. But unless most carefully qualified, such a general formula may be profoundly misleading; for the positive looking doctrine 'consent must be true, full and free' is only accurate as a statement of the law if treated as a compendious reference to the defences with which claims in contract may be weakened or met, whereas it suggests that there are certain psychological elements required by the law as necessary conditions of contract and that the defences are merely admitted as negative *evidence* of these. But the defence, e.g., that B entered into a contract with A as a result of the undue influence exerted upon him by A, is not evidence of the absence of a factor called 'true consent', but one of the multiple criteria for the use of the phrase 'no true consent'. To say that the law requires true consent is therefore, in fact, to say that defences such as undue influence or coercion, and any others which should be grouped with them, are admitted. And the practice of the law (in which general phrases such as 'true consent' are of little importance) as distinct from the theoretical statement of it by jurists (in which general terms bulk largely) makes this clear; for no party attempting to enforce a contract is required to give evidence that there was 'true, full and free consent', though in special cases where some person in a fiduciary position seeks to enforce a bargain with the person in relation to whom he occupies that position, the onus lies upon him to prove that no influence was, in fact, exerted. But, of course, even here the proof consists simply in the exclusion of those facts which ordinarily constitute the defence of undue influence, though the onus in such cases is by exception cast on the plaintiff. Of course, the theorist could make irrefutable his theory that there are psychological elements ('full and free consent') required as necessary conditions of contract, by ascribing the actual procedure of the courts to the practical difficulties of proving 'mental facts'; and it is sometimes said that it is merely a matter of practical convenience that 'objective tests' of these elements have been adopted and that the onus of proof is usually upon the defendant to prove the non-existence of these necessary elements. Such a doctrine is assisted by the ambiguity of the word 'test' as between evidence and criteria. But to insist on this as the 'real' explanation of the actual procedure of the courts in applying the defeasible concept of a contract would merely be to express obstinate loyalty to the persuasive but misleading logical ideal that all concepts must be capable of definition through a set of necessary and sufficient conditions. And, of course, even if this programme were carried through for the defences involving the 'mental' element it is difficult to see how it could be done for the other defences with which claims in contract can be met,[1] and, accordingly, the defeasible character of the concept would still remain.

The principal field where jurists have, I think, created difficulties for themselves (in part under the influence of the traditional philosophical analysis of action) by ignoring the essentially defeasible character of the concepts they seek to clarify is the Criminal Law. There is a well-known maxim, '*actus non est reus nisi mens sit rea*', which has tempted jurists (and less often judges) to offer a general theory of 'the mental element' in crime (*mens rea*) of a type which is logically inappropriate just because the concepts involved are defeasible and are distorted by this form of definition. For in the case of crime, as in contract, it is possible to compile a list of the defences or exceptions with which different criminal charges may with differing effect be met, and to show that attempts to define in general terms 'the mental conditions' of liability, like the general theory of contract suggested in the last paragraph, are only not misleading if their positive and general terms are treated merely as a restatement or summary of the fact that various heterogeneous defences or exceptions are admitted. It is true that in crime the position is more complicated than in contract, since fewer defences apply to all crimes (there being notable differences between crimes created by statute and common-law crimes) and for some crimes proof of a specific intention is required. Further, it is necessary in the case of crime to speak of defences *or exceptions* because in some cases, e.g. murder, the onus of proof may be on the Prosecution to provide evidence that circumstances are not present which would, if present, defeat the accusation. Yet, none the less, what is meant by the mental element in criminal liability (*mens rea*) is only to be understood

[1] It could, of course, be done vacuously by specifying as the necessary and sufficient condition of contract, consent and other positive conditions and the negation of the disjunction of the various defences.

by considering certain defences or exceptions, such as Mistake of Fact, Accident, Coercion, Duress, Provocation, Insanity, Infancy,[1] most of which have come to be admitted in most crimes, and in some cases exclude liability altogether, and in others merely 'reduce' it. The fact that these are admitted as defences or exceptions constitutes the cash value of the maxim '*actus non est reus nisi mens sit rea*'. But in pursuit of the will-o'-the-wisp of a general formula, legal theorists have sought to impose a spurious unity (as judges occasionally protest) upon these heterogeneous defences and exceptions, suggesting that they are admitted as merely evidence of the absence of some single element ('intention') or, in more recent theory, two elements ('foresight' and 'voluntariness') universally required as necessary conditions of criminal responsibility. And this is misleading because what the theorist misrepresents as evidence negativing the presence of necessary mental elements are, in fact, multiple criteria or grounds defeating the allegation of responsibility. But it is easy to succumb to the illusion that an accurate and satisfying 'definition' can be formulated with the aid of notions like 'voluntariness' because the logical character of words like 'voluntary' is anomalous and ill-understood. They are treated in such definitions as words having positive force, yet, as can be seen from Aristotle's discussion in Book III of the Nicomachean Ethics, the word 'voluntary' in fact serves to exclude a heterogeneous range of cases such as physical compulsion, coercion by threats, accidents, mistakes, etc., and not to designate a mental element or state; nor does 'involuntary' signify the absence of this mental element or state.[2] And so in a murder case it is a defence that the

[1] See for a detailed discussion of these and other defences or exceptions, Kenny: *Outline of Criminal Law*, Chap. IV.

[2] Thus Mr. J. W. C. Turner, in his well-known essay (in *The Modern Approach to Criminal Law. English Studies in Criminal Science*, Vol. I, p. 199) on the 'Mental Element in Crimes at Common Law' lays down two rules defining the mental element.

(First rule): 'It must be proved that the accused's conduct was voluntary.'

(Second rule): 'It must be proved that ... he must have foreseen that certain consequences were likely to follow on his acts or omissions' (p. 199). Mr. Turner's view is indeed an improvement on previous attempts to 'define' the mental element in crime so far as it insists that there is not a single condition named *mens rea* and also in his statement on page 199 that the extent to which 'foresight of consequence' must have extended differs in the case of each specific crime. But none the less this procedure is one which really obscures the concepts it is meant to clarify, for the words 'voluntary' and 'involuntary' are used as if they refer to the presence and absence, respectively, in the agent of some single condition. Thus on page 204, Mr. Turner gives the same title of 'involun-

accused pulled the trigger reasonably but mistakenly believing that the gun was unloaded; or that there was an accident because the bullet unexpectedly bounced off a tree; or that the accused was insane (within the legal definition of insanity) or an infant; and it is a partial defence 'reducing' the charge from murder to manslaughter that the accused fired the shot in the heat of the moment when he discovered his wife in adultery with the victim. It is, of course, *possible* to represent the admission of these different defences or exceptions as showing that there is a single mental element ('voluntariness') or two elements ('voluntariness' and 'foresight') required as necessary mental conditions (*mens rea*) of full criminal liability. But in order to determine what 'foresight' and 'voluntariness' are and how their presence and absence are established it is necessary to refer back to the various defences; and then these general words assume merely the status of convenient but sometimes misleading summaries expressing the absence of all the various conditions referring to the agents' knowledge or will which eliminate or reduce responsibility.

Consideration of the defeasible character of legal concepts helps to explain how statements of fact support or refute legal conclusions and thus to interpret the phrases used by lawyers for the connection between fact and law when they speak of 'the legal effect or consequences of the facts' or 'the conclusions of law drawn from the facts' or 'consequences attached to the facts'. In particular, it shows how wrong it would be to succumb to the temptation, offered by modern theories of meaning, to identify the meaning of a legal concept, say 'contract', with the statement of the conditions in which contracts are held to exist; since, owing to the defeasible character of the concept, such a statement, though it would express the necessary and sometimes sufficient conditions for the application of 'contract', could not express conditions which were always sufficient. But, of course, any such theory of the meaning of legal concepts would fail for far more fundamental reasons: for it could not convey the composite character of these concepts nor allow for the distinctive features due to the

tary conduct' to cases of acts done under hypnotic suggestion or when sleepwalking, to 'pure' accidents, and to certain cases of insanity, drunkenness, and infancy, as well as to the case where B holds a weapon and A, against B's will, seizes his hand and the weapon and therewith stabs C.

fact that the elements in the compound are of distinct logical types.

Two of these distinctive features are of special relevance to the analysis of action and arise out of the truism that what a judge does is to judge; for this has two important consequences. First, the Judge's function is, e.g.,[1] in a case of contract to say whether there is or is not a valid contract, upon the claims and defences actually made and pleaded before him and the facts brought to his attention, and not on those which might have been made or pleaded. It is not his function to give an ideally correct legal interpretation of the facts, and if a party (who is *sui juris*) through bad advice or other causes fails to make a claim or plead a defence which he might have successfully made or pleaded, the judge in deciding in such a case, upon the claims and defences actually made, that a valid contract exists has given the right decision. The decision is not merely the best the judge can do under the circumstances, and it would be a misunderstanding of the judicial process to say of such a case that the parties were merely treated *as if* there were a contract. There *is* a contract in the timeless sense of 'is' appropriate to judicial decisions. Secondly, since the judge is literally deciding that on the facts before him a contract does or does not exist, and to do this is neither to describe the facts nor to make inductive or deductive inferences from the statement of facts, what he does may be either a *right* or a *wrong* decision or a *good* or *bad* judgement and can be either *affirmed* or *reversed* and (where he has no jurisdiction to decide the question) may be *quashed* or *discharged*. What cannot be said of it is that it is either *true* or *false*, logically necessary or absurd.

There is, perhaps, not much to tempt anyone to treat a judicial decision as a descriptive statement, or the facts as related to legal conclusions as being related as statements of fact may be to some descriptive statement they justify: though I think the tendency, which I have already mentioned, to regard the exceptions or defences which can defeat claims or accusations merely as evidence of the absence of some necessary condition required by the law in the full definition of a legal concept is in fact an attempt to assimilate a judicial decision to a theoretical model of a descriptive statement; for it is the expression of the feeling that cases where

[1] Different considerations may apply in criminal cases.

contracts are held not to exist 'must' be cases where some necessary condition, required in the definition of contract, is absent. But sometimes the law is cited as an example of a deductive system at work. 'Given the existing law,' it will be said, 'the statement of facts found by the judge entails the legal conclusion.' Of course, this could only be said in the simplest possible cases where no issue is raised at the trial except what common sense would call one of fact, i.e. where the parties are agreed that if the facts go one way the case falls within some legal rule and if they go another way it does not, and no question is raised about the meaning or interpretation of the legal rule. But even here it would be quite wrong to say that the judge was making a deductive inference; for the timeless conclusion of law (Smith is guilty of murder) is not entailed by the statements of temporal fact (Smith put arsenic in his wife's coffee on May 1st, 1944) which support it; and rules of law even when embodied in statutes are not linguistic or logical rules, but to a great extent

II

If we step outside the law courts we shall find that there are many utterances in ordinary language which are similar in important respects, in spite of important differences, to the judicial blend of law and fact. But first some cases must be distinguished which are not instances of this phenomenon but are important because they help to explain why it has been overlooked.

A. First, we, of course, very often make use of legal concepts in descriptive and other sentences and the sentences in which we so use them may be statements and hence (unlike the judge's decision in which legal concepts are primarily used) they may be true or false. Examples of these are the obvious cases where we refer to persons or things by their known legal consequences, status or position. 'Who is that woman?' 'She is Robinson's wife and the adopted daughter of Smith, who inherited all his property.' 'What is that in the wastepaper basket?' 'My contract with John Smith.'

B. Secondly, we may refer to things, events and actions not by their known legal consequences, but by their intended or reputed legal consequence or position. 'What did your father do yesterday?' 'He made his will.' It should be noticed that this use may give rise to some curious difficulties if it is later found that the reputed or intended legal conclusion has not been established. What should we say of the sentence written in my diary that 'My father made his will yesterday' if it turns out that, since it was not witnessed and he was not domiciled in Scotland, the courts refuse to recognize it as a will? Is the sentence in my diary false? We should, I think, hesitate to say it is; on the other hand, we would not repeat the sentence after the court's decision is made. It should be noticed also that we may make use of our own legal system and its concepts for the purpose of describing things or persons not subject to it, as when we speak of the property of solitary persons who live on desert islands.

C. Thirdly, even outside the law courts we use the language of the law to make or reject claims. 'My father made his will yesterday' may indeed be a claim and not a pure descriptive statement, though it will, of course, carry some information with it, because with the claim is blended reference to some justifying facts. As a claim it may be later upheld or dismissed by the courts, but it is not true or false.

But in all these instances, though such sentences are uttered in ordinary life, the technical vocabulary of the law is used in them and so we are alert to the possibility that they may not function as descriptive sentences though very often they do. But consider now sentences where the words used derive their meaning from legal or social institutions, for example, from the institution of property, but are simple non-technical words. Such are the simple indicative sentences in which the possessive terms 'mine', 'yours', 'his' appear as grammatical predicates. 'This is mine', 'This is yours', 'This is his' are primarily sentences for which lawyers have coined the expression 'operative words' and Mr. J. L. Austin the word 'performatory'.[1] By the utterance of such sentences, especially in the present tense, we often do not describe but actually perform or effect a transaction; with them we *claim* proprietary rights, *confer* or *transfer* such rights when they are claimed, *recognize* such rights or *ascribe* such rights

[1] See his discussion of some cases in 'Other Minds', *Proceedings of the Aristotelian Society*, Suppl. Vol. XX, pp. 169-74.

whether claimed or not, and when these words are so used they are related to the facts that support them much in the same way as the judge's decision. But apart from this, these sentences, especially in past and future tenses, have a variety of other uses not altogether easy to disentangle from what I have called their primary use, and this may be shown by a sliding scale of increasing approximation to a pure descriptive use, as follows:

(*a*) First, the operative or performatory use. 'This is yours' said by a father handing over his gold watch to his son normally effects the transfer of the father's rights in the watch to the son; that is, makes a gift of it. But said by the elder son at the end of a dispute with his brother over the family possessions, the utterance of such a sentence constitutes a recognition of the rights of the younger son and abandons the claims of the elder. Of course, difficulties can arise in various ways over such cases analogous to the problems that confront the judge: we can ask whether the use of the words is a valid method of making gifts. If English law is the criterion, the answer is 'yes' in the example given; but it would be 'no' if what the father had pointed to was not his watch but his house, though in this case it may be that we would consider the son morally entitled to the house and the father morally bound to make it over to him. This shows that the rules which are in the background of such utterances are not necessarily legal rules. But the case to which I wish to draw attention is that where we use such sentences not to transfer or confer rights, but to ascribe or recognize them. For here, like a judge, the individual decides, *on* certain facts, that somebody else has certain rights, and his recognition is like a judgement, a blend of fact and rule if not of law.

(*b*) Secondly, sentences like 'This is mine', 'This is yours', 'This is his' can be used simply as descriptive statements to describe things by reference to their owners. Taking visitors round my estate, I say, pointing to a field, 'This is mine' or 'I own this' purely by way of information.

(*c*) Thirdly, there is the more casual ascriptive use of these sentences in daily life which is difficult to classify. Suppose as we get up to go I see you have left a pen and give it to you, saying 'This is yours', or suppose I am walking in the street and notice as the man in front takes out his handkerchief a watch falls from his pocket. I pick it up and hand it back to him with the words 'This is yours'. We might be tempted to say that we are using the sentence here simply as a descriptive statement equivalent to 'You were carrying this and you dropped it or you left it'; but that this is not at any rate clearly so can be seen from the following considerations. If after we have handed back the watch the police drive up in a car and arrest the man for theft, I shall not willingly repeat the sentence and say it was true, though if it were 'descriptive' of the physical facts why should I not? On the other hand, I will not say of what I said that it was false. The position is, of course, that a very common good reason for recognizing that a person has some rights to the possession of a thing is that he is observed physically in the possession of it; and it is, of course, correct in such circumstances to ascribe such rights with the sentence 'This is yours' in the absence of any claim or special circumstance which may defeat them. But as individuals we are not in the position of a judge; our decision is not final, and when we have notice of new circumstances or new claims we have to decide in the light of them again. But in other respects the function of sentences of this simple and non-technical sort resembles that of judicial decisions. The concepts involved are defeasible concepts like those of the law and similarly related to supporting facts. It would be possible to take the heroic course of saying that sentences like 'This is his', 'This is yours' have acquired, like the word 'give', a purely descriptive sense to signify the normal physical facts on which it is customary to ascribe rights of possession; but this would not account for the peculiarity of our usage and would commit the mistake of ignoring their defeasible character and identifying the meaning of an expression with which we make decisions or ascriptions with the factual circumstances which, in the absence of other claims, are good reasons for them. With more plausibility it may be said that there is a sense of 'mine', 'yours', 'his' which is descriptive—the sense in which my teeth (as distinct from my *false* teeth) are mine or my thought and feelings are mine. But, of course, with regard to these we do not make and challenge utterances like 'This is mine', 'This is yours', 'This is his', and it is the logical character of these with which I am concerned.

III

So much for the ascription and recognition of rights which we effect with the simple utterances 'This is yours', 'This is his' and the associated or derivative descriptive use of these sentences. I now wish to defend the similar but perhaps more controversial thesis that the concept of a human action is an ascriptive and a defeasible one, and that many philosophical difficulties come from ignoring this and searching for its necessary and sufficient conditions. The sentences 'I did it', 'you did it', 'he did it' are, I suggest, primarily utterances with which we *confess* or *admit* liability, make accusations, or *ascribe* responsibility; and the sense in which our actions are ours is very much like that in which property is ours, though the connection is not necessarily a *vinculum juris*, a responsibility under positive law. Of course, like the utterances already examined, connected with the non-descriptive concept of property, the verb 'to do' and generally speaking the verbs of action, have an important descriptive use, especially in the present and future senses, their ascriptive use being mainly in the past tense, where the verb is often both timeless and genuinely refers to the past as distinguished from the present. Indeed, the descriptive use of verbs of action is so important as to obscure even more in their case than in the case of 'this is yours', 'this is his', etc., the non-descriptive use, but the logical character of the verbs of action is, I think, betrayed by the many features which sentences containing these verbs, in the past tense, have in common with sentences in the present tense using the possessive pronouns ('this is his', etc.), and so with judicial decisions by which legal consequences are attached to facts.

I can best bring out my point by contrasting it with what I think is the mistaken, but traditional philosophical analysis of the concept of an action. 'What distinguishes the physical movement of a human body from a human action?' is a famous question in philosophy. The old-fashioned answer was that the distinction lies in the occurrence before or simultaneously with the physical movement of a mental event related (it was hoped) to the physical movement as its psychological cause, which event we call 'having the intention' or 'setting ourselves' or 'willing' or 'desiring' to do the act in question. The modern answer is that to say that X performed an action is to assert a categorical proposition about the movement of his body, *and* a general hypothetical proposition or propositions to the effect that X would have responded in various ways to various stimuli, or that his body would not have moved as it did or some physical consequence would have been avoided, had he chosen differently, etc. Both these answers seem to me to be wrong or at least inadequate in many different ways, but both make the common error of supposing that an adequate analysis can be given of the concept of a human action in any combination of descriptive sentences, categorical or hypothetical, or any sentences concerned wholly with a single individual. To see this, compare with the traditional question about action the question 'What is the difference between a piece of earth and a piece of property?' Property is not a descriptive concept, and the difference between 'this is a piece of earth' or 'Smith is holding a piece of earth' on the one hand, and 'this is someone's property' and 'Smith owns a piece of property' on the other cannot be explained without reference to the non-descriptive utterances by means of which laws are promulgated and decisions made, or at the very least without reference to those by which rights are recognized. Nor, I suggest, can the difference between 'His body moved in violent contact with another's' and 'He did it' (e.g. 'He hit her') be explained without reference to the non-descriptive use of sentences by which liabilities or responsibility are ascribed. What is fundamentally wrong in both the old and the new version of the traditional analysis of action as a combination of physical and psychological events or a combination of categorical and hypothetical descriptive sentences, is its mistake in identifying the meaning of a non-descriptive utterance ascribing responsibility in stronger or weaker form, with the factual circumstances which support or are good reasons for the ascription. In other words, though of course not all the rules in accordance with which, in our society, we ascribe responsibility are reflected in our legal code nor vice versa, yet our concept of an action, like our concept of property, is a social concept and logically dependent on accepted rules of conduct. It is fundamentally not descriptive, but ascriptive in character; and it is a defeasible concept to be defined through exceptions and not by a set of necessary and sufficient conditions whether physical or psychological. This contention is supported by the following considerations:

First, when we say after observing the physical movements of a living person in conjunction with another, 'Smith hit her', or 'Smith did it' in answer to the question 'Who hit her?' or 'Who did it?' we surely do not treat this answer as a combined assertion that a physical movement of Smith's body took place, and that some inferred mental event occurred in Smith's mind (he set himself or intended to hit her); for we would be adding something to this answer if we made any such reference to psychological occurrences. Nor do we treat this answer as a combination of categorical or hypothetical sentences descriptive of a physical movement and of Smith's disposition or what would have happened had he chosen differently. On the contrary, saying 'He hit her' in these circumstances is, like saying 'That is his', a blend. It is an ascription of liability justified by the facts; for the observed physical movements of Smith's body are the circumstances which, in the absence of some defence, support, or are good reasons for the ascriptive sentence 'He did it'. But, of course, 'He did it' differs from 'That is his' for we are ascribing responsibility not rights.

Secondly, the sentence 'Smith hit her' can be challenged in the manner characteristic of defeasible legal utterances in two distinct ways. Smith or someone else can make a flat denial of the relevant statement of the physical facts, 'No, it was Jones, not Smith'. Alternatively (but since we are not in a law court, not also cumulatively), any of a vast array of defences can be pleaded by Smith or his friends which, though they do not destroy the charge altogether, soften it, or, as lawyers say, 'reduce' it.

Thus, to 'He did it' ('He hit her') it may be pleaded:

1. 'Accidentally' (she got in his way while he was hammering in a nail).

2. 'Inadvertently' (in the course of hammering in a nail, not looking at what he was doing).

3. 'By mistake for someone else' (he thought she was May, who had hit him).

4. 'In self defence' (she was about to hit him with a hammer).

5. 'Under great provocation' (she had just thrown the ink over him).

6. 'But he was forced to by a bully' (Jones said he would thrash him).

7. 'But he is mad, poor man.'

Thirdly. It is, of course, possible to take the heroic line and say that all these defences are just so many signs of the absence in each case of a common psychological element, 'intention', 'voluntariness', 'consciousness', required in a 'full' definition of an action, i.e. as one of its necessary and sufficient conditions, and that the concept is an ordinary descriptive concept after all. But to this, many objections can be made. These positive-looking words 'intention', etc., if put forward as necessary conditions of all action only succeed in posing as this if in fact they are a comprehensive and misleadingly positive-sounding reference to the absence of one or more of the defences, and are thus only understandable when interpreted in the light of the defences, and not vice versa. Again, when we are ascribing an action to a person, the question whether a psychological 'event' occurred does not come up in this suggested positive form at all, but in the form of an inquiry as to whether any of these extenuating defences cover the case. Further, when a more specific description of the alleged common mental element is given, it usually turns out to be something quite special, and characteristic only of a special kind of action, and by no means an essential element in all actions. This is plainly true of Professor H. A. Pritchard's[1] 'setting ourselves', which well describes some grim occurrences in our lives, but is surely not an essential ingredient in all cases where we recognize an action.

Fourthly. The older psychological criterion affords no explanation of the line we draw between what we still call an action though accidental and other cases. If I aim at a post and the wind carries my bullet so that it hits a man, I am said to have shot him accidentally, but if I aim at a post, hit it, and the bullet then ricochets off and hits a man, this would not be said to be my action at all. But in neither case have I intended, set myself to do, or wished what occurred.

Fifthly. The modern formula according to which to say that an action is voluntary is to say that the agent could have avoided

[1] See *Duty and Ignorance of Fact*, pp. 24 *et seq.* [Recently reprinted as Chapter II of his *Moral Obligation*, O.U.P., 1949.—EDITOR.]

it if he had chosen differently either ignores the heterogeneous character of our criteria qualifying 'He did it' when we use words like 'accidentally', 'by mistake', 'under coercion', etc., or only avoids this by leaving the meaning of the protasis 'If he had chosen differently' intolerably vague. Yet our actual criteria for qualifying 'He did it', though multiple and heterogeneous, are capable of being stated with some precision. Thus, if the suggested general formula is used to explain our refusal to say 'He did it' without qualification when a man's hand is forcibly moved by another, it is misleading to use the same formula in the very different cases of accident, mistake, coercion by threats or provocation. For in the first case the statement 'the agent could not have acted differently if he had chosen' is true in the sense that he had no control over his body and his decision was or would have been ineffective; whereas in, e.g., the case of accident the sense in which the statement is true (if at all) is that though having full control of his body the agent did not foresee the physical consequences of its movements. And, of course, our qualification of 'He did it' in cases of coercion by threats or provocation (which have to be taken into account in any analysis of our usage of verbs of action) can only be comprehended under the suggested general formula if the protasis is used in still different senses so that its comfortable generality in the end evaporates; for there will be as many different senses as there are different types of defences, or qualifications of 'He did it'. Some seek to avoid this conclusion by saying that in cases where we qualify 'He did it', e.g. in a case of accident, there are, in fact, two elements of which one is *the genuine* action (firing the gun) and the other are its effects (the man being hit), and that our common usage whereby we say in such cases 'He shot him accidentally' is inaccurate or loose. 'Strictly', it is urged, we should say 'He fired the gun' (action in the strict sense) and 'the bullet hit the man'. But this line of thought, as well as supposing that we can say what a 'genuine' action is independently of our actual usage of verbs of action, breeds familiar but unwelcome paradoxes. If cases of accident must be analysed into a genuine action *plus* unintended effects, then, equally, normal action must be analysed into a genuine action *plus* intended effects. Firing the gun must be analysed on this view into pulling the trigger *plus*

. . . and pulling the trigger into cocking the finger *plus* . . . So that in the end the only 'genuine actions' (if any) will be the minimal movements we can make with our body where nothing 'can' go wrong. These paradoxes are results of the insistence that 'action' is a descriptive concept definable through a set of necessary and sufficient conditions.

Sixthly. When we ascribe as private individuals rights or liabilities, we are not in the position of a judge whose decision is authoritative and final, but who is required only to deal with the claims and defences actually presented to him. In private life, decisions are not final, and the individual is not relieved, as the judge often is, from the effort of inquiring what defences might be pleaded. If, therefore, on the strength of merely the physical facts which we observe we judge 'Smith hit her' and do not qualify our judgement, it can be wrong or defective in a way in which the judge's decision cannot be. For if, on investigating the facts, it appears that we should have said 'Smith hit her accidentally', our first judgement has to be qualified. But it is important to notice that it is not withdrawn as a false statement of fact or as a false inference that some essential mental event necessary for the truth of the sentence 'He did it' had occurred. Our ascription of responsibility is no longer justified in the light of the new circumstances of which we have notice. So we must judge again: not *describe* again.

Finally, I wish to say, out of what lawyers call abundant caution, that there are two theses I have not maintained. I have maintained no form of behaviourism, for although it often is correct to say 'He did it' on the strength only of the observed physical movements of another, 'He did it' never, in my view, merely describes those movements. Secondly, I wish to distinguish from my own the thesis, often now maintained as a solution or dissolution of the problem of free will, that to say that an action is voluntary *means* merely that moral blame would tend to discourage the agent blamed from repeating it, and moral praise would encourage him to do so. This seems to me to confuse the question of what we mean by saying that a man has done an action with the question of why we bother to assign responsibility for actions to people in the way we do. Certainly, there is a connection between the two questions, that is between theories of punishment and reward and attempts to elucidate the criteria we do in fact employ in assigning responsibility for actions. No doubt we have come to employ the criteria we do employ because, among other things, in the long run, and on the whole not for the wretched individual in the dock but for 'society', assigning responsibility in the way we do assign it tends to check crime and encourage virtue; and the social historian may be able to show that our criteria slowly alter with experience of the reformative or deterrent results obtained by applying them. But this is only one of the things which applying these criteria does for us. And this is only one of the factors which lead us to retain or modify them. Habit, or conservatism, the need for certainty, and the need for some system of apportioning the loss arising from conduct, are other factors, and though, of course, it is open to us to regret the intrusion of 'non-utilitarian' factors, it yet seems to me vital to distinguish the question of the history and the pragmatic value and, in one sense, the morality of the distinctions we draw, from the question what these distinctions are.

CHAPTER IX

THE LANGUAGE OF POLITICAL THEORY

By Margaret Macdonald

To read the classical texts of political philosophy, in a critical mood, is to be both fascinated and perplexed by the curious notation in which they are written. One meets here a 'contract' which one is carefully warned was never contracted; an 'organism' unknown to biology; a superior 'person' or higher 'self' with whom one can never converse; an 'association' or 'corporation', whose objects are obscure and which is not listed in any of the recognized directories. All these descriptions, analogies or pictures have been applied to the State. One or other of them can be found in the works of the most notable political philosophers from Plato and Hobbes to Laski and MacIver. Here, too, will be found elaborate discussions and disputes about whether men are or are not 'naturally' social; whether they 'really' will what they don't will; whether there is a Law of Nature or a 'natural law' not established by any known empirical methods; whether freedom or 'objective' freedom is not properly judicious coercion in the interests of order, etc.

There is a genuinely philosophic air about these strange uses of ordinary words. They seem to resemble the replies sometimes given to the haunting doubts which attack us when we reflect on other subjects. On our sensible experience, for example. Is it, perhaps, only a perpetual illusion? Or on moral actions. Can an action ever be completely disinterested? Or on other people. Do they have feelings as we do, or are they merely perfectly acting automata? How can we ever be sure? It seems, then, likely that the tales about the social contract and the unmeetable person will be related to similar puzzles. I do not, however, intend to expound in detail any of the answers in which the words I have given are key words. I shall avoid exegesis of Hobbes or of Hegel. I want rather to discuss how the uses of these words with the pictures or analogies they embody are related to the puzzles by which they were suggested and to the ordinary uses of language about social relationships and political affairs. What sort of propositions are they and how do they function? For, at first glance, they seem very peculiar. To be told you are party to a contract, of which you were unaware, and which is nothing like what anyone would ever call a contract, seems to have little to do with giving your vote at a general election, sending your child to a State school, or paying a fine for exceeding the speed limit. Nor is your depression at the Labour Exchange likely to be much relieved by being told that you 'really' willed your unemployment (you would never have thought so, unaided) or that the State is a very superior moral person, only even more anonymous and inaccessible than the Permanent Secretary to the Ministry of Labour.

One trouble in politics is to determine how far the questions are empirical and to what extent they are linguistic. Another is to discover what are the ordinary uses of the words involved. For many important words used in political discussion have a degree of vagueness which makes it even easier in political than in other branches of philosophy to disguise a linguistic elucidation or recommendation as an important factual discovery. A further problem is the causation of these puzzles. Is it merely philosophical discomfort about language that induces people to ask certain questions about their social life and accept these answers? If not, is this philosophically important?

It is sometimes said that no one can understand or criticize political theories without a thorough knowledge of history. Hobbes and Locke cannot be properly understood without knowing the history of the English Civil War, the Revolution of 1688 and their relation to these events. Rousseau cannot be detached from the conditions in France immediately before the French Revolution of 1789. Hegel is inexplicable apart from the luscious yet strenuous atmosphere of the Romantic Movement and the beginnings of German nationalism. All these theories arose in peculiar circumstances of crisis in the particular societies of which their writers formed part and cannot be discussed as though they were of general application like the propositions of mathematics. This, however, is not quite true. It is certainly true that the propositions of politics are not like those of mathematics and it does indicate that practical as well as purely philosophical dissatisfactions have frequently co-operated to move philosophers to write political philosophy. Indeed, they have usually done so with the avowed intention of influencing political affairs. Nevertheless, they never supposed themselves merely to be writing tracts for their times. Locke doubtless wished to justify the Revolution Settlement, but not merely by considering how a reasonable social life was possible in seventeenth-century England, but upon what relationship the life of the members of any community, divided into rulers and ruled, must be based if it is not to appear contemptible to rational human beings. What justifies us in forming political societies, in obeying laws, in being subjected to other persons? This is not a puzzle peculiar to any age. Moreover, so far from having died with the controversies of the seventeenth and eighteenth centuries, the 'contract theory' is now being revived.[1] But even this may be philosophically as well as historically important. For present political conditions may be somewhat similar to those in which contract theories formerly flourished. Historical circumstances, then, may be important in answering the question, 'Why have philosophers been induced to ask these questions and accept these answers?' It may be objected that this is to confuse causes and reasons. A philosopher may be moved to doubt the existence of matter because he has swallowed too much opium, but this would be completely irrelevant to any reason with which he supported his view. Why, then, should it be philosophically important that he asks certain philosophical questions because he feels oppressed by the government, or, alternatively, because, like Hobbes, he is worried by the lack of order in the country? It is because the circumstances in which they are asked and answered may work differently for different kinds of philosophical propositions in influencing their effects. And this may be connected with their philosophical 'point'. With some, e.g. those of 'pure epistemology', their importance may be negligible; with others, those of ethics, perhaps, and, even more, those of politics, they may be more important.

[1] Cf. Gough, *The Social Contract*, 1936 (Introduction and last chapter), H. D. Lewis, 'Is there a Social Contract?', *Philosophy*, January and April, 1940.

What must also be considered, then, are the practical and psychological effects of these problems and their answers. No one will deny that in political affairs philosophical nonsense may have serious effects. Is this philosophically relevant, or not? To deny that it is seems to reduce philosophizing to mere scholastic verbalism. Not for any moral reason. Not because philosophers ruin themselves and their subject by sitting in ivory towers and talking about the uses of words instead of considering how the people perish (or flourish) on nonsensical theories and slogans. But simply because, not to try to understand how this language has effects, even though it may give no information, is to miss half its philosophical point and so is bad philosophy. The philosophical 'point' of a remark (or the 'point' of a remark which is of philosophical interest) is, at least partly, connected with the cause or reason which induces people to go on making it, though it can neither be supported nor refuted by any empirical evidence. It may be false, it may, if taken literally, be meaningless, but they feel that it has some use. This does seem to be relevant to the understanding of some philosophical remarks, if not of all.

It is true that no solipsist refuses to converse with others, unless he is also suffering from incipient schizophrenia. Nor does the sceptic about the existence of material objects sit down very gingerly on every chair for fear it isn't really there. For these problems have not, usually, been suggested by any practical difficulties about communication or knowledge in ordinary life. Nor will any answer which the philosopher gives to them be likely to alter his subsequent behaviour. The problems of epistemology are mainly academic. Their practical causation and effects, therefore, are unimportant. That is, perhaps, why it is easier to see from such examples the predominantly linguistic character of philosophical problems, so emphasized recently by Wittgenstein, Wisdom and others. They can be traced, roughly, to a certain discomfort which the philosopher obscurely feels about what seem to be unjustifiable inconsistencies in our uses of certain words, e.g. those of 'know' and 'feel'. And once he can be made to realize this and that no linguistic change which he may wish to suggest will give him that super-empirical information about the world which he supposed possible, he will cease asking unanswerable questions. The whole drama might be played by two solitary sages on a desert island. But I am not convinced that Butler, e.g., was merely puzzled about the use or misuse of the word 'interest' or that he supposed that such misuse was the only mistake of his opponents. He was worried because their philosophical remark that 'All action is really selfish' was seducing many people to a disregard of their duties. And though Burke, quite rightly, thought most of what Rousseau wrote was, strictly, nonsense, he did not underestimate his influence on the French Revolution. For whereas a person would be thought slightly crazy who took seriously his doubts about the uniformity of nature and refused to eat his dinner for fear the laws of nature might have changed since yesterday and it would now poison him, many people would not think it at all *absurd* that anyone who said, 'An action is right only if by doing it the agent will promote his own advantage' should so interpret this as to neglect most of the actions that would ordinarily be called his duties. They might think he would come to a bad end, but not necessarily in Bethlem. Yet, in a sense, to ask whether all action isn't really selfish is a senseless question. And to assert that all action is 'really' selfish is to make not an empirical but a grammatical statement. It expresses either a misuse of or an intention to extend the use of 'selfish' to cover actions to which it does not ordinarily apply. But the distinctions formerly marked by the ordinary uses of 'selfish/unselfish' must reappear in the new notation if it is to fulfil all the tasks of the old. Nor does this change give us any fresh information about our duties to others. In this it resembles the epistemological puzzle about 'know'. When clearly stated, it takes the form of a linguistic recommendation. Yet it has, or may have, or perhaps only seems to have, certain effects which have been considered important. Not that it predicts any such effects. A linguistic recommendation predicts nothing about behaviour. It is empty of factual content. How, then, does it work so as to seem to need taking seriously in practical life? How does anyone 'act' on a purely grammatical statement, except in speech and writing? Yet it does seem sometimes as if they do. The connection of utilitarianism with social reform is another instance. So that completely to understand ethical problems and theories, more than linguistic considerations are required. Or rather, perhaps, different sorts of elements may be involved in linguistic considerations.

If this is true of ethics, it is even more true of politics. Consider the statement, 'The authority of the State derives from the contract or agreement by which men consented to give up certain liberties, to form a society and submit to government in order to obtain greater benefits. The interests of a State, therefore, are subordinate to the interests of its members.' The attitude thus expressed may have importantly different results from the one expressed by 'The authority of the State is absolute for it embodies the "real" will and permanent interests of its members. It does, moreover, further certain historical and/or divine purposes incapable of fulfilment by any or all of its members. The State, therefore, is a moral person of a higher type than its members who must be subordinated to it.' There may be a sense in which neither of the theories epitomized in these statements is directly verifiable by the facts. For the 'contract' and the 'real will' may correspond to nothing directly discoverable. There may be another sense in which all the facts to which both theories appeal are the same for each. There is, then, no empirical means of deciding between them. But do not two statements or theories mean the same if all their empirical consequences are identical? Yet the 'contractual' and the 'organic' views of political relations would never be ordinarily said to mean the same and they have had very different effects. If the difference is not an empirical one of finding facts which will support the one and refute the other; if it is not a difference in their truth or falsity, what sort of difference is it? How can they differ in meaning without differing in verifiable consequences? But how *do* they differ? They differ, obviously, in picturing political relationships with the help of two very different images. One represents them under the guise of a contract freely entered into between responsible agents who understand the provisions and are prepared to keep them unless infringed by the other party. Joining society in general and keeping its laws is rather like joining a Trade Union and agreeing not to blackleg or work for less than the minimum rates, so long as the Union, on its side, agrees to maintain and improve the conditions of labour. Or it is like undertaking to provide goods or services in return for certain payment. Most people have had some experience of such agreements. They know what they imply and how they feel about them. If they have accepted the terms, they do not resent being bound by them, so long as they are observed by the other contractees. And, if not, either the law will enforce the terms or they will be released from their share of the obligation. They do not regard themselves, after entering such agreements, as being any 'higher' or 'lower' than they were before. Such contracts are convenient devices to secure desired social ends. They are useful, and their obligations should be respected, but no sensible person would rhapsodize about them. If, then, people picture the relation between themselves, the State and the Government in these terms, certain consequences will tend to follow. They will tend to be affected, emotionally as well as intellectually, in some ways rather than others. They will probably tend to stress the fact of or the need for the *consent* of the governed to its governors. For no one can enter a contract without consenting to it. They will emphasize the importance of the *responsibility* of governors to the governed. No contract can be solely one-sided. Because of the reciprocal nature of contract, their attitude to rulers will be critical rather than reverential. Certainly nothing done by rulers to fulfil their part of the bargain will be accepted because proceeding from a higher moral authority than that of mere individuals. The attitude induced by the 'contract' picture might be expected to stress personal freedom and the existence on sufferance of all governments; to be, in general, liberal, democratic and unmystical. And it has, historically, tended to produce this result. It encourages the view that social arrangements of all kinds are made by men for their own ends and can be altered and even ended at their will and pleasure. This does not preclude acknowledging that some arrangements, e.g. those comprised by the State, are very important, even that they function as fundamental conditions for most others. Only that they are not sacrosanct. Nor does it follow that changes must or will be undertaken without due regard for the customs and traditions of the past and the welfare of the future as well as of the present. But only that if, in spite of all this, they are *consented* to by a majority of the present members of a society, no higher authority can be found with a *right* to prevent them. The 'contract' view can take account of every fact stressed by other views, but its own difference of emphasis alters their point or effects. In political theory, as, indeed, in philosophy generally, it is very often not what is said, but the spirit in which it is said, which makes the difference.

The other picture tells a very different story. My relation to an organism of which I form part or to my 'higher' self is not determined by free choice. 'The State', said Burke,[1] 'ought not to be considered as nothing better than a partnership agreement in a trade of pepper and coffee, calico or tobacco, or some other such low concern, to be taken up for a little temporary interest, and to be dissolved by the fancy of the parties. It is to be looked on with other reverence. . . . It is a partnership in all science, a partnership in all art, a partnership in every virtue and in all perfection . . . it is a partnership not only between those who are living, but between those who are living, those who are dead, and those who are to be born . . . linking the lower with the higher natures, connecting the visible and invisible world, according to a fixed compact sanctioned by the inviolable oath which holds all physical and all moral natures each in their appointed place.' Compared with this splendid spectacle we, who compose any society here and now, are very small fry indeed. Should we not accept with becoming gratitude the fortunate chance that permits us to abase ourselves before this embodiment of 'all virtue and all perfection'? 'Consent', 'choice', can mean only acceptance of what seems good to it, and not to our unimportant selves. This is the attitude of submission to and reverence for what is done by Authority, especially if the Authority is or represents what is old and respectable—or, now-a-days, if it commands forces of great physical power—which is induced by this language. Consent, freedom, criticism, which the contract picture emphasized, are not necessarily denied, but they are minimized or re-interpreted. I am no foe to liberty, said Burke, but it must be a liberty connected with *order*. If a man is misguided enough to resist the General Will, say Rousseau and Bosanquet, he must be forced to be free. The individual is trivial; the social organism or organization is almost sacred.

These two ways of picturing political relationships may, then,

[1] Burke, *Reflections on the Revolution in France.*

have very different practical and psychological effects which may induce people to want to go on using them, although they learn nothing much from them about political affairs. Some people like to feel part of a vast and important organization in which their chief function is to admire and obey. The picture of themselves deliberating about contracts, making decisions, criticizing representatives, is much too fatiguing. For others, any picture in which they were wholly subordinate would be intolerable. A similar situation sometimes occurs in science. It is true, I believe, that all the planetary motions could, with suitable complications, be described as well by the Ptolemaic as by the Copernican system. In one sense, therefore, they mean the same. But that in another they do not is shown by the fierce resistance met by Copernicus and his followers. It had very little connection with the scientific value of their theory. The Ptolemaic theory included the picture of man and his world at the centre of the universe with the heavens revolving round them in cosy circles. The alternative Copernican picture terrified people. They felt lost, insecure, unimportant. Something had gone for ever. Yet nothing had gone, for the facts were precisely the same for each. But the *point* of the two notations, with their accompanying pictures, used to describe the facts was very different. In their psychological effects they were very different theories.

It may be objected that this use of the words 'picture' and 'image' is itself a misuse, or, at least, an extension of the ordinary use of these words.[1] This is true. I cannot draw the social organism as I can a rat, nor paint a portrait of the 'higher' self. And though I can imagine the scene when King John signed Magna Carta, I cannot similarly imagine that when Hobbes' pre-social beings contracted to form society. I can have an image of signing a building contract but not of signing the social contract. But, it may be urged, when it is said that the State resembles an organism or is based on contract, no particular organism or contract is meant. What is thus asserted is a general resemblance between political relationships and those between the parts of *any* organism or *any* contractees. But this seems very peculiar. I cannot have an image or paint a picture of a general resemblance. The words 'image' and 'picture' appear to be used

[1] I owe this point to Mr. G. Ryle.

for something which cannot be imaged or pictured at all, in the ordinary senses of these words. But this peculiar usage can be recommended. It emphasizes the fact that philosophical remarks resemble poetic imagery rather than scientific analogy.[1] There is a pictorial or analogical element in most theories, scientific as well as philosophical. In poetry there are metaphors and images, but no theories. And philosophical theories have always seemed slightly odd, if not bogus. The use of 'analogy' suggests 'argument by analogy', i.e. the deduction of new verifiable facts from a suggested resemblance which increases our knowledge about the world. Philosophical theories have no such application. Nevertheless, in common with the scientific analogies they have other, psychological and semi-logical effects. Compare, e.g., the different effects of the planetary theories already mentioned or of the 'mechanistic' and 'purposive' hypotheses in biology. Philosophical remarks about social contracts and higher selves work chiefly in these ways. Perhaps to look for a contract or a new biological entity after reading Locke and Hegel on the State is only slightly less absurd than to look for flaming tigers after reading Blake or to ask how Wordsworth knew 'at a glance' that he saw ten thousand daffodils. The theories of the scientist give new information about empirical facts; they also induce certain emotional and intellectual attitudes. The language of the poet is predominantly emotive; that of the philosopher less so, but both also have some relation to certain facts, though not that involved in the application of a scientific analogy. They do, however, partly by the use of certain images and metaphors express or call attention in a very vivid way to facts and experiences of whose existence we all know but which, for some reason, it seems important to emphasize.[2] I do not wish to say that philosophy *is* (inferior) poetry and not (pseudo) science, for it is neither, but philosophy. But it is sometimes useful when considering philosophical theories, and particularly political theories, to realize how unlike scientific theories they are, in some respects, and how much, in others, they resemble the works of the poets. Rousseau is far more like Shelley than he is like Lavoisier. The use of the

[1] Cf. Wisdom, 'Other Minds', *Mind*, Vols. 49 and 50.

[2] I think this is true of some poetry, at least, but I do not wish to dogmatize about the function of poetry.

words 'picture' and 'image' stresses this resemblance and avoids the scientific associations of the word 'analogy'. This gives some justification for the extended use of these words.

But, according to their authors, political theories profess to explain certain puzzles about social life which must now be examined.

The surprising fact about political life, according to Hume, is the ease with which the many are governed by the few. Why should people thus submit to the jurisdiction of others of their own kind? Obviously, it is not solely because of the constant exercise or threat of physical force to compel conformity. The ruled, as Hume said, are always more numerous and therefore more powerful than the rulers. Not even Hitler can literally turn the whole of Germany into a concentration camp. For if he did, one result would be, presumably, that production would cease, and power would soon be useless. Nor is force any explanation. For it is conceivable that someone should prefer, and many people have preferred to die rather than obey rulers of whom they disapproved. Nevertheless, most people most of the time do obey laws and accept the control of governments. It must then be either because they want to, or because they believe they ought to do so. But they do not always want to, and sometimes when they do want to they think they ought not to. The fundamental puzzle of political philosophy, then, is to find a valid reason for political obligation. Why should men be obliged to obey laws and be penalized if they do not? This leads to consideration of the nature of that which appears to command and enforce laws, viz., the State. And there is, perhaps, an even more 'fundamental' puzzle. Why should man live with others of his own kind at all? The laws which political obligation acknowledges are the rules of societies. But is it necessary to form political societies? Is man 'naturally' social or only by convention? If the second, why was this convention adopted, and how? We all know how individuals join a trade union, a church, a club. These are particular societies. But how and why did we all join society in general? What sort of process was this?

These questions have the familiar tone. Philosophers do not ask whether Zulus or Dodos exist, but whether *any* material objects exist: not whether I can climb Mount Everest, if I choose, but whether I can do *any* action, however carefully I choose. So the political question is not 'Why should I pay income tax?' or 'Why should I support the present British Government?' but 'Why should I obey *any* law, support *any* Government, acknowledge the authority of *any* State?' Why, indeed, should I be a member of *any* civil society?

I cannot consider all the answers which have been suggested to all these questions. Two have already been mentioned. If I have contracted with others to form a society and obey certain rules then my justification for keeping the laws will be that I formerly promised to do so, at least as long as they were generally observed by the other parties to the contract. But this theory leads to no original in the facts. When did I sign this agreement and with whom? One answer is, you did not sign it, but your ancestors did, only so long ago that all trace of it has been lost. The original Magna Carta of society has vanished. Can it really be on account of this undiscoverable transaction that we keep the laws of England in 1941? For suppose, after incredible labour, archaeologists found the lost document, should we feel happier about observing the Education Acts? Ah, that settles it. Now we know why we should send Johnny to school at five instead of into the fields to mind the sheep. Absurd, of course. And what are the provisions of the contract? Am I bound by it to observe laws yet to be made, of which I know nothing, just because they are laws of the contracted society and government? That would be a very peculiar contract to sign. No, the existence of a contract of the kind required cannot be verified. And no contract which could be discovered would answer our question. This is always admitted by political philosophers. 'The social contract theory is really an attempt at analysing the logical presuppositions rather than the historical antecedents of the State',[1] says Mr. Gough. The answer it gives to the question of political obligation is that our only justification for obeying laws and governments is that we have consented to do so and that political obligation is not an asymmetrical relationship between rulers and ruled. Hence the use of the contract picture in supporting the claims of individuals and groups against despotic governments.

The word 'contract', then, is admittedly not used in its ordinary

[1] *The Social Contract*, p. 4.

legal sense of the State and the basis of political obligation. It is only 'as if' we had signed a contract. The contract theory points not to a contract but to the fact that what we mean by saying that we ought to obey a law is that we have consented to it. But, as Hume said, unless habit, indolence and indifference are to be taken as consent, very few laws would be obeyed at all on this criterion. To how many do we individually consent, and how do we do so? However important, this cannot be the whole story.

What, then, of the view that the laws of the State ought to be obeyed because they are the edicts of some higher being with which each of us is for the time being identified, or because they represent what we ourselves 'really' will in our best moments? According to Rousseau, by the act of social union a moral and collective person, endowed with the general will, is thereby brought into existence and thereafter known as the State or Sovereign. Nor, he is careful to add, must this person be regarded as fictitious because not a man.[1] For Bosanquet, the State and its system of law and order represents my 'higher' self, and its actions, even those which I explicitly reject, ought to be accepted because they are willed by the General Will which is my 'real' will as opposed to my selfish and trivial actual will. The earlier quotation from Burke expresses a similar view. The essential point of this view is that the State or Society (no distinction is usually made between them) is something of far greater value than any or all of the individuals at any one time who compose it. What it ordains, therefore, and expresses as law must be good and must, therefore, be what I should also will if I were as wise as it is. In fact, it is what my higher self wills though I do not. Therefore, I 'really' will it and I ought to do what I 'really' want to do although I actually don't want to do it. I do not intend to examine all the linguistic shifts and ambiguities of this theory; the use of 'self' and 'will', e.g., and the tendentious use of 'higher' and 'lower' where difference of value should be proved and not merely asserted. In fact, the extremely perverse use of language by these philosophers often blinds one to the undoubted facts which they emphasize and which are neglected by alternative theories. The State is not identified with any one or with the

[1] *The Social Contract*, Chapters 6 and 7.

whole collection of its members but is something over and above them. That is to say, propositions can be made about the State which would be nonsense if made about any or all of its members. E.g., 'The English State has been established for at least four hundred years'. The State is a moral person. That is to say, it is sensible to say of actions which we ascribe to the State that they are right—or wrong. The sense in which these words are used is different from that for individuals but it is not nonsense to say 'I think the State acts rightly in providing Old Age pensions', though the analysis of this statement would be very complicated. The State is greater and more permanent than the individual. That is true. The generations pass, but English state power remains. It is, therefore, likely that laws made according to the Constitution will be such as may reasonably be accepted. There is a presumption in their favour. Nor will responsible citizens wish rashly to destroy an established power and order which has served the past and serves the present moderately well and may be valued by future generations. The State serves more important purposes than the individual. Without accepting a mystical march of history, this also may be admitted. The actions of few individuals, e.g., are likely to affect so many people for so long a time as do most State actions. The State has international functions, relations to colonies, to other States which may have lastingly bad or good effects. No individuals, in their private capacity, could perform such functions. None of these facts about the difference between the State and the individual need be denied. Indeed, they are important criteria for the use of 'political obligation'. But they are *differences* merely. It does not follow from them that the State is either morally better or worse than any individual. Nor are any or all of them a sufficient basis for political obligation. I do not mean by saying that 'I ought to obey this law', that I was born, without my choice, a member of English society from which I received education, culture, the means of livelihood and the general system of law and order without which these would be impossible. Even though it may be true that all that one is and can do, is due to the facilities provided by the State and the social order, it does not follow that all State action is right and that all laws should be obeyed. For it is not self-contradictory to say 'This is an English law but it is a bad law and ought not to be kept'. Moreover, this view leads to the absurd conclusion that the laws of any community are equally good. The Nuremberg laws, therefore, are good for the Germans though they are bad for everyone else. But if they are bad, they are bad also for the Germans, though they may not recognize this.

Then is it, perhaps, because of their social effects that laws ought to be obeyed? Do we mean by the State, the dispenser of social benefits on the largest possible scale? This is the Utilitarian or realist view of the State. The State, like any other institution, is ustified by its works. It does not depend on mythical contracts or mystical organisms but on a pragmatic sanction. 'The State is an organization for enabling the mass of men to realize social good on the largest possible scale' and social good 'consists in the unity our nature attains when the working of our impulses results in a satisfied activity'.[1] I am justified in obeying the laws only if I am tolerably satisfied with my life in the community. And anyone's life will, or ought to be, tolerably satisfactory if his 'impulses' are being satisfied. But what is the criterion that they are? I can know whether I am satisfied with my life, but even if I am, what follows? Does it follow that I am justified in obeying the laws because the State does or will provide the conditions of such satisfaction? Or that I am entitled to rebel if my impulses are not satisfied? Could I not be satisfied as the result of a bad law and dissatisfied as the result of a good? But Laski would say, it will be urged, that the good must be social. State action should be approved only if it promotes this desirable unity for all or most people. But what exactly *is* this desirable state and how do we know whether it has been achieved for everyone? Without an adequate criterion of this, how do we know what laws to obey and what governments to approve? The conditions of personal satisfaction are numerous and many could not be provided by the most benevolent State. I do not wish to suggest that Laski, or any other philosopher, supposes that all the conditions of a happy life can be provided by the State. But it is not easy to see from his remarks on the social good why any should be excluded. The utilitarian criterion, which seems so practical, is not one of the easiest to apply, or even to state clearly.

[1] Laski, *Grammar of Politics*, pp. 24, 25. London, 1925.

Bentham's criterion is at least clear, if impossible to accept. Once this is discarded what *is* the 'social good' or the 'general welfare' whose promotion is the purpose of the State and the criterion of the goodness or badness of its actions and laws? Only the vaguest statements ever seem to be offered. This may be condemned as pedantic. To say that the State is justified by its works is to say, and this is known by all but the perverse, that it should be judged by the way in which it makes possible for all citizens the material and cultural conditions of good living. The laws of a State should be chiefly directed to securing for all its members, employment, a reasonable income, health, education, good houses, etc. Certainly not all the conditions can be provided communally, but a great many can and should, and the more a State provides the more it should be approved. In fact, only if it tends to maximize certain obvious benefits should any law be obeyed. No laws ought to be partial. That is, I think, the point of the theory, which is generally favoured by social reformers. Far be it from me to minimize its importance. But again, I think, it is not and cannot be the whole story. For is it not conceivable that all these desirable objects might be promoted by what everyone would call a bad, e.g. a completely tyrannous State? The government of such a State might be exceedingly efficient in promoting social welfare to obtain popular support and the majority of its citizens might be thoroughly satisfied that all their impulses were satisfactorily fulfilled. Ought one then to support such a government and respect its laws? The usual reply is, 'Ah, but there must always be some important impulses left unsatisfied by such a Government; no bad governments could possibly promote the general good'. But now, is this an empirical statement? Suppose people no longer feel these important impulses, why should they bother about their satisfaction? Does this remove the difficulty? If people no longer resent actions which would normally be called tyrannical, do they cease to be tyrannical? Is contented slavery not repulsive? Utilitarian philosophers would probably not agree. They would say, as most people would, that such actions *ought* to be resented, and that they are not does not make them good. But then the utilitarian view can surely be expressed in the tautology, 'Only the governments which we ought to support are those which we ought to support because they promote general social good'. This is not very enlightening.

The utilitarian view, then, which pictures the State as an institution or association for promoting the interests of its members is not adequate. The picture likens the State to any other association with a specific purpose, e.g. a trade union, a college, a commercial company or a church. But the difference is that the objects of these associations can all be fairly clearly stated and, indeed, must be before they are given legal status. The object of the State itself cannot be thus stated. High wages and good working conditions might conceivably be achieved by other means than combining in trade unions: a copper mine might be discovered and worked without floating a commercial company, but there is no describable purpose or object of social life as such any more than of human life as such, which could be obtained by some alternative means. This picture, then, remains as inapplicable as the others. But it, too, points to important criteria for our use of 'political obligation'. That some laws promote desirable social improvements in the general conditions of living for the majority of people, is a good reason for accepting them. But it is not the sole justification for accepting any and every law.

What, then, is the answer to the original puzzle, 'Why should I obey *any* law or acknowledge the authority of *any* State or Government?' to solve which these pictures were invented? The discussion of the three most prominent types of answer seems to show that even discounting nonsense or picturesque terminology, none of them alone is sufficient. May it not also suggest that no such general answer is either possible or necessary? This would not be surprising. A general proof of the existence of material objects seems impossible, and to ask for it, absurd. No general criterion of all right actions can be supplied. Similarly, the answer to 'Why should I obey *any* law, acknowledge the authority of *any* State or support *any* Government?' is that this is a senseless question. Therefore, any attempted reply to it is bound to be senseless, though it may perform certain other useful or harmful functions. It makes sense to ask 'Why should I obey the Conscription Act?' or 'Why should I oppose the present German Government?' because by considering the particular circumstances and the characteristics of all concerned, it is possible to decide for or against obedience and support. We all know the kind of criteria according to which we should decide these two issues. But although it looks harmless and even very philosophical to generalize from these instances to 'Why should I obey *any* law or support *any* government?' the significance of the question then evaporates. For the general question suggests an equally general answer and this is what every political philosopher has tried to give. But no general criterion applies to every instance. To ask why I should obey *any* laws is to ask whether there might be a political society without political obligations, which is absurd. For we mean by political society, groups of people organized according to rules enforced by some of their number. A state of anarchy is just not a state of political society and to ask whether, since laws are not obeyed in the first state they ought to be obeyed in the second is to ask a nonsensical question. But neither does it follow, as some idealists seem to suppose, that all laws should be equally accepted because commanded by a political authority. For this is, in fact, only another attempt to find a general criterion for political obligation. But it is not that which we always apply when considering political action. The political theorists want an answer which is always and infallibly right, just as the epistemologists want a guarantee that there are material objects or that generalization to the unexamined must be valid. But these are all equally senseless requests, for they result from stretching language beyond the bounds of significance. I know how to determine on any particular occasion whether or not I am suffering from an optical illusion. Therefore, it is sensible to ask 'Is this line really crooked or does it only seem to be?' But to ask whether, after applying all the relevant tests unsuccessfully, I am still and always deluded, is senseless. For the word 'deluded' has now lost all significance since however hard and carefully I look I can never find a veridical perception with which to compare my delusions. The word 'delusion' no longer significantly opposed to 'veridical' becomes meaningless. Similarly, I can determine whether or not I ought to observe the Education Acts or the Income Tax law. Obviously, I think I ought partly because they were passed by a freely elected Parliament, according to all the usual procedure, so that in some complicated and indirect sense I have consented to them. Then, too, they promote useful social ends and there may be other criteria for rightly obeying them. One or two of these criteria might be absent and I should not think it right to resist, if too many of them were I might get restive but not yet rebellious. A trade unionist, e.g., might rightly think that the Trade Union Disputes Act passed after the general strike was harsh and unfair but not sufficient in itself to risk civil war about, especially since a new government which trade unionists could help to elect might repeal the Act. But if too many acts are passed in suspicious circumstances and with dubious objects, the duty to resist tyranny will over-rule the duty to obey law. When or how cannot be stated in advance. Nor can the criteria for accepting a law be precisely stated. Consent, tradition, objects promoted, all the criteria emphasized by the political theorists are important, but not all are equally important on every occasion, though if one or more were persistently absent over a long period we should, rightly, object. The manner in which they (and probably others) are blended is indefinitely various and no precise definition could describe our usage. Nevertheless, it does not in the least follow that we do not very often know that a law should be obeyed and a government supported and sometimes that both should be resisted. Just as we know very well that the pillar box is red and that Jane Austen was not vulgar, although both 'red' and 'vulgar' are used vaguely.

This may seem a disappointing conclusion and not likely to have the stirring effects of the homeric stories of the social contract and the 'higher' self or even of Burke's rhapsodies on the British Constitution. But I think it has some practical value. The general, metaphysical theories are really very simple. They seek to reduce all political obligation to the application of an almost magical formula. All laws which should be obeyed result from the social contract, or the general will, or promote the greatest happiness of the greatest number, so in order to know your political duties look for the trade mark and leave the rest to government. They do imply that we can know once and for all almost by learning a single sentence, how and when politial obedience is justified. But if there is no general criterion, but an indefinite set of vaguely shifting criteria, differing for different times and circumstances, then it may often, if not nearly always, be necessary to scrutinize our political relations to see whether we are on this particular occasion justified in giving or withholding our support to a measure or a government. The value of the political theorists, however, is not in the general information they give about the basis of political obligation but in their skill in emphasizing at a critical moment a criterion which is tending to be overlooked or denied. The common sense of Locke and the eloquence of Rousseau reinforced and guided the revolt against dogmatic authority by vividly isolating and underlining with the contract metaphor the fact that no one is obliged to obey laws concerning none of which he has had a chance to express consent or dissent. It does not follow that this is the sole criterion of political obedience, still less that having derived all political obligations from a social contract or a general will we can accept them all happily and go to sleep. As rational and responsible citizens we can never hope to know once and for all what our political duties are. And so we can never go to sleep.

CHAPTER X

GODS

By John Wisdom

1. *The existence of God is not an experimental issue in the way it was.* An atheist or agnostic might say to a theist 'You still think there are spirits in the trees, nymphs in the streams, a God of the world.' He might say this because he noticed the theist in time of drought pray for rain and make a sacrifice and in the morning look for rain. But disagreement about whether there are gods is now less of this experimental or betting sort than it used to be. This is due in part, if not wholly, to our better knowledge of why things happen as they do.

It is true that even in these days it is seldom that one who believes in God has no hopes or fears which an atheist has not. Few believers now expect prayer to still the waves, but some think it makes a difference to people and not merely in ways the atheist would admit. Of course with people, as opposed to waves and machines, one never knows what they won't do next, so that expecting prayer to make a difference to them is not so definite a thing as believing in its mechanical efficacy. Still, just as primitive people pray in a business-like way for rain so some people still pray for others with a real feeling of doing something to help. However, in spite of this persistence of an experimental element in some theistic belief, it remains true that Elijah's method on Mount Carmel of settling the matter of what god or gods exist would be far less appropriate to-day than it was then.

2. *Belief in gods is not merely a matter of expectation of a world to come.* Someone may say 'The fact that a theist no more than an atheist expects prayer to bring down fire from heaven or cure the sick does not mean that there is no difference between them as to the facts, it does not mean that the theist has no expectations different from the atheist's. For very often those who believe in God believe in another world and believe that God is there and that we shall go to that world when we die.'

This is true, but I do not want to consider here expectations as to what one will see and feel after death nor what sort of reasons these logically unique expectations could have. So I want to consider those theists who do not believe in a future life, or rather, I want to consider the differences between atheists and theists in so far as these differences are not a matter of belief in a future life.

3. *What are these differences? And is it that theists are superstitious or that atheists are blind?* A child may wish to sit a while with his father and he may, when he has done what his father dislikes, fear punishment and feel distress at causing vexation, and while his father is alive he may feel sure of help when danger threatens and feel that there is sympathy for him when disaster has come. When his father is dead he will no longer expect punishment or help. Maybe for a moment an old fear will come or a cry for help escape him, but he will at once remember that this is no good now. He may feel that his father is no more until perhaps someone says to him that his father is still alive though he lives now in another world and one so far away that there is no hope of seeing him or hearing his voice again. The child may be told that nevertheless his father can see him and hear all he says. When he has been told this the child will still fear no punishment nor expect any sign of his father, but now, even more than he did when his father was alive, he will feel that his father sees him all the time and will dread distressing him and when he has done something wrong he will feel separated from his father until he has felt sorry for what he has done. Maybe when he himself comes to die he will be like a man who expects to find a friend in the strange country where he is going, but even when this is so, it is by no means all of what makes the difference between a child who believes that his father lives still in another world and one who does not.

Likewise one who believes in God may face death differently from one who does not, but there is another difference between them besides this. This other difference may still be described as belief in another world, only this belief is not a matter of expecting one thing rather than another here or hereafter, it is not a matter of a world to come but of a world that now is, though beyond our senses.

We are at once reminded of those other unseen worlds which some philosophers 'believe in' and others 'deny', while non-philosophers unconsciously 'accept' them by using them as models with which to 'get the hang of' the patterns in the flux of experience. We recall the timeless entities whose changeless connections we seek to represent in symbols, and the values which stand firm[1] amidst our flickering satisfaction and remorse, and the physical things which, though not beyond the corruption of moth and rust, are yet more permanent than the shadows they throw upon the screen before our minds. We recall, too, our talk of souls and of what lies in their depths and is manifested to us partially and intermittently in our own feelings and the behaviour of others. The hypothesis of mind, of other human minds and of animal minds, is reasonable because it explains for each of us why certain things behave so cunningly all by themselves unlike even the most ingenious machines. Is the hypothesis of minds in flowers and trees reasonable for like reasons? Is the hypothesis of a world mind reasonable for like reasons—someone who adjusts the blossom to the bees, someone whose presence may at times be felt—in a garden in high summer, in the hills when clouds are gathering, but not, perhaps, in a cholera epidemic?

4. *The question 'Is belief in gods reasonable?' has more than one source.* It is clear now that in order to grasp fully the logic of belief in divine minds we need to examine the logic of belief in animal and human minds. But we cannot do that here and so for the purposes of this discussion about divine minds let us acknowledge the reasonableness of our belief in human minds without troubling ourselves about its logic. The question of the reasonableness of belief in divine minds then becomes a matter of whether there are facts in nature which support claims about divine minds in the way facts in nature support our claims about human minds.

In this way we resolve the force behind the problem of the existence of gods into two components, one metaphysical and the same which prompts the question 'Is there *ever any* behaviour which gives reason to believe in *any* sort of mind?' and one which finds expression in 'Are there other mind-patterns in

[1] In another world, Dr. Joad says in the *New Statesman* recently.

nature beside the human and animal patterns which we can all easily detect, and are these other mind-patterns super-human?'

Such over-determination of a question syndrome is common. Thus, the puzzling questions 'Do dogs think?', 'Do animals feel?' are partly metaphysical puzzles and partly scientific questions. They are not purely metaphysical; for the reports of scientists about the poor performances of cats in cages and old ladies' stories about the remarkable performances of their pets are not irrelevant. But nor are these questions purely scientific; for the stories never settle them and therefore they have other sources. One other source is the metaphysical source we have already noticed, namely, the difficulty about getting behind an animal's behaviour to its mind, whether it is a non-human animal or a human one.

But there's a third component in the force behind these questions, these disputes have a third source, and it is one which is important in the dispute which finds expression in the words 'I believe in God', 'I do not'. This source comes out well if we consider the question 'Do flowers feel?' Like the questions about dogs and animals this question about flowers comes partly from the difficulty we sometimes feel over inference from *any* behaviour to thought or feeling and partly from ignorance as to what behaviour is to be found. But these questions, as opposed to a like question about human beings, come also from hesitation as to whether the behaviour in question is *enough* mind-like, that is, is it enough similar to or superior to human behaviour to be called 'mind-proving'? Likewise, even when we are satisfied that human behaviour shows mind and even when we have learned whatever mind-suggesting things there are in nature which are not explained by human and animal minds, we may still ask 'But are these things sufficiently striking to be called a mind-pattern? Can we fairly call them manifestations of a divine being?'

'The question', someone may say, 'has then become merely a matter of the application of a name. And "What's in a name?"'

5. *But the line between a question of fact and a question or decision as to the application of a name is not so simple as this way of putting things suggests.* The question 'What's in a name?' is engaging because we are inclined to answer both 'Nothing' and 'Very much'. And this 'Very much' has more than one source. We might have tried to comfort Heloise by saying 'It isn't that

Abelard no longer loves you, for this man isn't Abelard'; we might have said to poor Mr. Tebrick in Mr. Garnet's *Lady into Fox* 'But this is no longer Silvia'. But if Mr. Tebrick replied 'Ah, but it is!' this might come not at all from observing facts about the fox which we have not observed, but from noticing facts about the fox which we had missed, although we had in a sense observed all that Mr. Tebrick had observed. It is possible to have before one's eyes all the items of a pattern and still to miss the pattern. Consider the following conversation:

' "And I think Kay and I are pretty happy. We've always been happy."

'Bill lifted up his glass and put it down without drinking.

' "Would you mind saying that again?" ' he asked.

' "I don't see what's so queer about it. Taken all in all, Kay and I have really been happy."

' "All right," Bill said gently, "Just tell me how you and Kay have been happy."

'Bill had a way of being amused by things which I could not understand.

' "It's a little hard to explain," I said. "It's like taking a lot of numbers that don't look alike and that don't mean anything until you add them all together."

'I stopped, because I hadn't meant to talk to him about Kay and me.

' "Go ahead," Bill said. "What about the numbers." And he began to smile.

' "I don't know why you think it's so funny," I said. "All the things that two people do together, two people like Kay and me, add up to something. There are the kids and the house and the dog and all the people we have known and all the times we've been out to dinner. Of course, Kay and I do quarrel sometimes but when you add it all together, all of it isn't as bad as the parts of it seem. I mean, maybe that's all there is to anybody's life."

'Bill poured himself another drink. He seemed about to say something and checked himself. He kept looking at me.'[1]

Or again, suppose two people are speaking of two characters in a story which both have read[2] or of two friends which both

[1] *H. M. Pulham, Esq.*, p. 320, by John P. Marquand.

[2] e.g. Havelock Ellis's autobiography.

have known, and one says 'Really she hated him', and the other says 'She didn't, she loved him'. Then the first may have noticed what the other has not although he knows no incident in the lives of the people they are talking about which the other doesn't know too, and the second speaker may say 'She didn't, she loved him' because he hasn't noticed what the first noticed, although he can remember every incident the first can remember. But then again he may say 'She didn't, she loved him' not because he hasn't noticed the patterns in time which the first has noticed but because though he has noticed them he doesn't feel he still needs to emphasize them with 'Really she hated him'. The line between using a name because of how we feel and because of what we have noticed isn't sharp. 'A difference as to the facts', 'a discovery', 'a revelation', these phrases cover many things. Discoveries have been made not only by Christopher Columbus and Pasteur, but also by Tolstoy and Dostoievsky and Freud. Things are revealed to us not only by the scientists with microscopes, but also by the poets, the prophets, and the painters. What is so isn't merely a matter of 'the facts'. For sometimes when there is agreement as to the facts there is still argument as to whether defendant did or did not 'exercise reasonable care', was or was not 'negligent'.

And though we shall need to emphasize how much 'There is a God' evinces an attitude to the familiar[1] we shall find in the end that it also evinces some recognition of patterns in time easily missed and that, therefore, difference as to there being any gods is in part a difference as to what is so and therefore as to the facts, though not in the simple ways which first occurred to us.

6. *Let us now approach these same points by a different road.*

6.1. *How it is that an explanatory hypothesis, such as the existence of God, may start by being experimental and gradually become something quite different can be seen from the following story:*

Two people return to their long neglected garden and find among the weeds a few of the old plants surprisingly vigorous. One says to the other 'It must be that a gardener has been coming and doing something about these plants'. Upon inquiry they find that no neighbour has ever seen anyone at work in their garden.

[1] 'Persuasive Definitions', *Mind*, July, 1938, by Charles Leslie Stevenson, should be read here. It is very good. [Also in his *Ethics and Language*, Yale, 1945.—EDITOR.]

The first man says to the other 'He must have worked while people slept'. The other says 'No, someone would have heard him and besides, anybody who cared about the plants would have kept down these weeds'. The first man says 'Look at the way these are arranged. There is purpose and a feeling for beauty here. I believe that someone comes, someone invisible to mortal eyes. I believe that the more carefully we look the more we shall find confirmation of this.' They examine the garden ever so carefully and sometimes they come on new things suggesting that a gardener comes and sometimes they come on new things suggesting the contrary and even that a malicious person has been at work. Besides examining the garden carefully they also study what happens to gardens left without attention. Each learns all the other learns about this and about the garden. Consequently, when after all this, one says 'I still believe a gardener comes' while the other says 'I don't' their different words now reflect no difference as to what they have found in the garden, no difference as to what they would find in the garden if they looked further and no difference about how fast untended gardens fall into disorder. At this stage, in this context, the gardener hypothesis has ceased to be experimental, the difference between one who accepts and one who rejects it is now not a matter of the one expecting something the other does not expect. What is the difference between them? The one says 'A gardener comes unseen and unheard. He is manifested only in his works with which we are all familiar', the other says 'There is no gardener' and with this difference in what they say about the gardener goes a difference in how they feel towards the garden, in spite of the fact that neither expects anything of it which the other does not expect.

But is this the whole difference between them—that the one calls the garden by one name and feels one way towards it, while the other calls it by another name and feels in another way towards it? And if this is what the difference has become then is it any longer appropriate to ask 'Which is right?' or 'Which is reasonable?'

And yet surely such questions *are* appropriate when one person says to another 'You still think the world's a garden and not a wilderness, and that the gardener has not forsaken it' or 'You still think there are nymphs of the streams, a presence in the hills, a spirit of the world'. Perhaps when a man sings 'God's in His heaven' we need not take this as more than an expression of how he feels. But when Bishop Gore or Dr. Joad write about belief in God and young men read them in order to settle their religious doubts the impression is not simply that of persons choosing exclamations with which to face nature and the 'changes and chances of this mortal life'. The disputants speak as if they are concerned with a matter of scientific fact, or of trans-sensual, trans-scientific and metaphysical fact, but still of fact and still a matter about which reasons for and against may be offered, although no scientific reasons in the sense of field surveys for fossils or experiments on delinquents are to the point.

6.2. *Now can an interjection have a logic?* Can the manifestation of an attitude in the utterance of a word, in the application of a name, have a logic? When all the facts are known how can there still be a question of fact? How can there still be a question? Surely as Hume says '. . . after every circumstance, every relation is known, the understanding has no further room to operate'?[1]

6.3. When the madness of these questions leaves us for a moment *we can all easily recollect disputes which though they cannot be settled by experiment are yet disputes in which one party may be right and the other wrong* and in which both parties may offer reasons and the one better reasons than the other. *This may happen in pure and applied mathematics and logic.* Two accountants or two engineers provided with the same data may reach different results and this difference is resolved not by collecting further data but by going over the calculations again. Such differences indeed share with differences as to what will win a race, the honour of being among the most 'settlable' disputes in the language.

6.4. *But it won't do to describe the theistic issue as one settlable by such calculation*, or as one about what can be deduced in this *vertical* fashion from the facts we know. No doubt dispute about God has sometimes, perhaps especially in mediaeval times, been carried on in this fashion. But nowadays it is not and we must look for some other analogy, some other case in which a dispute is settled but not by experiment.

[1] Hume, *An Enquiry concerning the Principles of Morals.* Appendix I.

6.5. *In courts of law* it sometimes happens that opposing counsel are agreed as to the facts and are not trying to settle a question of further fact, are not trying to settle whether the man who admittedly had quarrelled with the deceased did or did not murder him, but are concerned with whether Mr. A who admittedly handed his long-trusted clerk signed blank cheques did or did not exercise reasonable care, whether a ledger is or is not a document,[1] whether a certain body was or was not a public authority.

In such cases we notice that the process of argument is not a *chain* of demonstrative reasoning. It is a presenting and re-presenting of those features of the case which *severally co-operate* in favour of the conclusion, in favour of saying what the reasoner wishes said, in favour of calling the situation by the name by which he wishes to call it. The reasons are like the legs of a chair, not the links of a chain. Consequently although the discussion is *a priori* and the steps are not a matter of experience, the procedure resembles scientific argument in that the reasoning is not *vertically* extensive but *horizontally* extensive—it is a matter of the cumulative effect of several independent premises, not of the repeated transformation of one or two. And because the premises are severally inconclusive the process of deciding the issue becomes a matter of weighing the cumulative effect of one group of severally inconclusive items against the cumulative effect of another group of severally inconclusive items, and thus lends itself to description in terms of conflicting 'probabilities'. This encourages the feeling that the issue is one of fact—that it is a matter of guessing from the premises at a further fact, at what is to come. But this is a muddle. *The dispute does not cease to be* a priori *because it is a matter of the cumulative effect of severally inconclusive premises.* The logic of the dispute is not that of a chain of deductive reasoning as in a mathematic calculation. But nor is it a matter of collecting from several inconclusive items of

[1] *The Times*, March 2nd, 1945. Also in *The Times* of June 13th, 1945, contrast the case of Hannah v. Peel with that of the cruiser cut in two by a liner. In the latter case there is not agreement as to the facts. See also the excellent articles by Dr. Glanville L. Williams in the *Law Quarterly Review*, 'Language and the Law', January, and April 1945, and 'The Doctrine of Repugnancy', October, 1943, January, 1944, and April, 1944. The author, having set out how arbitrary are many legal decisions, needs now to set out how far from arbitrary they are—if his readers are ready for the next phase in the dialectic process.

information an expectation as to something further, as when a doctor from a patient's symptoms guesses at what is wrong, or a detective from many clues guesses the criminal. It has its own sort of logic and its own sort of end—the solution of the question at issue is a decision, a ruling by the judge. But it is not an arbitrary decision though the rational connections are neither quite like those in vertical deductions nor like those in inductions in which from many signs we guess at what is to come; and though the decision manifests itself in the application of a name it is no more merely the application of a name than is the pinning on of a medal merely the pinning on of a bit of metal. Whether a lion with stripes is a tiger or a lion is, if you like, merely a matter of the application of a name. Whether Mr. So-and-So of whose conduct we have so complete a record did or did not exercise reasonable care is not merely a matter of the application of a name or, if we choose to say it is, then we must remember that with this name a game is lost and won and a game with very heavy stakes. With the judges' choice of a name for the facts goes an attitude, and the declaration, the ruling, is an exclamation evincing that attitude. But *it is an exclamation which not only has a purpose but also has a logic*, a logic surprisingly like that of 'futile', 'deplorable', 'graceful', 'grand', 'divine'.

6.6. *Suppose two people are looking at a picture or natural scene.* One says 'Excellent' or 'Beautiful' or 'Divine'; the other says 'I don't see it'. He means he doesn't see the beauty. And this reminds us of how we felt the theist accuse the atheist of blindness and the atheist accuse the theist of seeing what isn't there. And yet surely each sees what the other sees. It isn't that one can see part of the picture which the other can't see. So the difference is in a sense not one as to the facts. And so it cannot be removed by the one disputant discovering to the other what so far he hasn't seen. It isn't that the one sees the picture in a different light and so, as we might say, sees a different picture. Consequently the difference between them cannot be resolved by putting the picture in a different light. And yet surely this is just what can be done in such a case—not by moving the picture but by talk perhaps. To settle a dispute as to whether a piece of music is good or better than another we listen again, with a picture we look again. Someone perhaps points to emphasize certain features and we see it in a different light. Shall we call this 'field work' and 'the last of observation' or shall we call it 'reviewing the premises' and 'the beginning of deduction (horizontal)'?

If in spite of all this we choose to say that a difference as to whether a thing is beautiful is not a factual difference we must be careful to remember that there is a procedure for settling these differences and that this consists not only in reasoning and redescription as in the legal case, but also in a more literal re-setting-before with re-looking or re-listening.

6.7. *And if we say as we did at the beginning that when a difference as to the existence of a God is not one as to future happenings then it is not experimental and therefore not as to the facts, we must not forthwith assume that there is no right and wrong about it*, no rationality or irrationality, no appropriateness or inappropriateness, no procedure which tends to settle it, *nor even that this procedure is in no sense a discovery of new facts*. After all even in science this is not so. Our two gardeners even when they had reached the stage when neither expected any experimental result which the other did not, might yet have continued the dispute, each presenting and re-presenting the features of the garden favouring his hypothesis, that is, fitting his model for describing the accepted fact; each emphasizing the pattern he wishes to emphasize. True, in science, there is seldom or never a pure instance of this sort of dispute, for nearly always with difference of hypothesis goes some difference of expectation as to the facts. But scientists argue about rival hypotheses with a vigour which is not exactly proportioned to difference in expectations of experimental results.

The difference as to whether a God exists involves our feelings more than most scientific disputes and in this respect is more like a difference as to whether there is beauty in a thing.

7. *The Connecting Technique*. Let us consider again the technique used in revealing or proving beauty, in removing a blindness, in inducing an attitude which is lacking, in reducing a reaction that is inappropriate. Besides running over in a special way the features of the picture, tracing the rhythms, making sure that this and that are not only seen but noticed, and their relation to each other—besides all this—there are other things we can do

to justify our attitude and alter that of the man who cannot see. For features of the picture may be brought out by setting beside it other pictures; just as the merits of an argument may be brought out, proved, by setting beside it other arguments, in which striking but irrelevant features of the original are changed and relevant features emphasized; just as the merits and demerits of a line of action may be brought out by setting beside it other actions. To use Susan Stebbing's example: Nathan brought out for David certain features of what David had done in the matter of Uriah the Hittite by telling him a story about two sheep-owners. This is the kind of thing we very often do when someone is 'inconsistent' or 'unreasonable'. This is what we do in referring to other cases in law. The paths we need to trace from other cases to the case in question are often numerous and difficult to detect and the person with whom we are discussing the matter may well draw attention to connections which, while not incompatible with those we have tried to emphasize, are of an opposite inclination. A may have noticed in B subtle and hidden likenesses to an angel and reveal these to C, while C has noticed in B subtle and hidden likenesses to a devil which he reveals to A.

Imagine that a man picks up some flowers that lie half withered on a table and gently puts them in water. Another man says to him 'You believe flowers feel'. He says this although he knows that the man who helps the flowers doesn't expect anything of them which he himself doesn't expect; for he himself expects the flowers to be 'refreshed' and to be easily hurt, injured, I mean, by rough handling, while the man who puts them in water does not expect them to whisper 'Thank you'. The Sceptic says 'You believe flowers feel' because something about the way the other man lifts the flowers and puts them in water suggests an attitude to the flowers which he feels inappropriate although perhaps he would not feel it inappropriate to butterflies. He feels that this attitude to flowers is somewhat crazy *just as it is sometimes felt that a lover's attitude is somewhat crazy even when this is not a matter of his having false hopes about how the person he is in love with will act.* It is often said in such cases that reasoning is useless. But the very person who says this feels that the lover's attitude is crazy, is inappropriate like some dreads and hatreds, such as some horrors of enclosed places. And often one who says 'It is useless to reason proceeds at once to reason with the lover, nor is this reasoning always quite without effect. We may draw the lover's attention to certain things done by her he is in love with and trace for him a path to these from things done by others at other times[1] which have disgusted and infuriated him. And by this means we may weaken his admiration and confidence, make him feel it unjustified and arouse his suspicion and contempt and make him feel our suspicion and contempt reasonable. It is possible, of course, that he has already noticed the analogies, the connections, we point out and that he has accepted them—that is, he has not denied them nor passed them off. He has recognized them and they have altered his attitude, altered his love, but he still loves. We then feel that perhaps it is we who are blind and cannot see what he can see.

8. *Connecting and Disconnecting.* But before we confess ourselves thus inadequate there are other fires his admiration must pass through. For when a man has an attitude which it seems to us he should not have or lacks one which it seems to us he should have then, not only do we suspect that he is not influenced by connections which we feel should influence him and draw his attention to these, but also we suspect he is influenced by connections which should not influence him and draw his attention to these. It may, for a moment, seem strange that we should draw his attention to connections which we feel should not influence him, and which, since they do influence him, he has in a sense already noticed. But we do—such is our confidence in 'the light of reason'.

Sometimes the power of these connections comes mainly from a man's mismanagement of the language he is using. This is what happens in the Monte Carlo fallacy, where by mismanaging the laws of chance a man passes from noticing that a certain colour or number has not turned up for a long while to an improper confidence that now it soon will turn up. In such cases our showing up of the false connections is a process we call 'explaining a fallacy in reasoning'. To remove fallacies in reasoning we urge a man to call a spade a spade, ask him what he means by 'the

[1] Thus, like the scientist, the critic is concerned to show up the irrelevance of time and space.

State' and having pointed out ambiguities and vaguenesses ask him to reconsider the steps in his argument.

9. *Unspoken Connections. Usually, however, wrongheadedness or wrongheartedness in a situation, blindness to what is there or seeing what is not, does not arise merely from mismanagement of language but is more due to connections which are not mishandled in language, for the reason that they are not put into language at all.* And often these misconnections too, weaken in the light of reason, if only we can guess where they lie and turn it on them. In so far as these connections are not presented in language the process of removing their power is not a process of correcting the mismanagement of language. But it is still akin to such a process; for though it is not a process of setting out fairly what has been set out unfairly, it is a process of setting out fairly what has not been set out at all. And we must remember that the line between connections ill-presented or half-presented in language and connections operative but not presented in language, or only hinted at, is not a sharp one.

Whether or not we call the process of showing up these connections 'reasoning to remove bad unconscious reasoning' or not, it is certain that in order to settle in ourselves what weight we shall attach to someone's confidence or attitude we not only ask him for his reasons but also look for unconscious reasons both good and bad; that is, for reasons which he can't put into words, isn't explicitly aware of, is hardly aware of, isn't aware of at all—perhaps it's long experience which he *doesn't* recall which lets him know a squall is coming, perhaps it's old experience which he *can't* recall which makes the cake in the tea mean so much and makes Odette so fascinating.[1]

I am well aware of the distinction between the question 'What reasons are there for the belief that S is P?' and the question 'What are the sources of beliefs that S is P?' There are cases where investigation of the rationality of a claim which certain persons make is done with very little inquiry into why they say what they do, into the causes of their beliefs. This is so when we have very definite ideas about what is really logically relevant to their claim and what is not. Offered a mathematical theorem we ask for the proof; offered the generalization that parental

[1] Proust: *Swann's Way*, Vol. I, p. 58, Vol. II. Phoenix Edition.

discord causes crime we ask for the correlation co-efficients. But even in this last case, if we fancy that only the figures are reasons we underestimate the complexity of the logic of our conclusion; and yet it is difficult to describe the other features of the evidence which have weight and there is apt to be disagreement about the weight they should have. In criticizing other conclusions and especially conclusions which are largely the expression of an attitude, we have not only to ascertain what reasons there are for them but also to decide what things are reasons and how much. This latter process of sifting reasons from causes is part of the critical process for every belief, but in some spheres it has been done pretty fully already. In these spheres we don't need to examine the actual processes to belief and distil from them a logic. But in other spheres this remains to be done. Even in science or on the stock exchange or in ordinary life we sometimes hesitate to condemn a belief or a hunch[1] merely because those who believe it cannot offer the sort of reasons we had hoped for. And now suppose Miss Gertrude Stein finds excellent the work of a new artist while we see nothing in it. We nervously recall, perhaps, how pictures by Picasso, which Miss Stein admired and others rejected, later came to be admired by many who gave attention to them, and we wonder whether the case is not a new instance of her perspicacity and our blindness. But if, upon giving all our attention to the work in question, we still do not respond to it, and we notice that the subject matter of the new picture is perhaps birds in wild places and learn that Miss Stein is a bird-watcher, then we begin to trouble ourselves less about her admiration.

It must not be forgotten that our attempt to show up mis-connections in Miss Stein may have an opposite result and reveal to us connections we had missed. Thinking to remove the spell exercised upon his patient by the old stories of the Greeks, the psycho-analyst may himself fall under that spell and find in them what his patient has found and, incidentally, what made the Greeks tell those tales.

10. *Now what happens, what should happen, when we inquire in this way into the reasonableness, the propriety of belief in gods?* The

[1] Here I think of Mr. Stace's interesting reflections in *Mind*, January, 1945, 'The Problems of Unreasoned Beliefs'.

answer is: A double and opposite-phased change. Wordsworth writes:

> '. . . And I have felt
> A presence that disturbs me with the joy
> Of elevated thoughts; a sense sublime
> Of something far more deeply interfused,
> Whose dwelling is the light of setting suns,
> And the round ocean and the living air,
> And the blue sky, and in the mind of man:
> A motion and a spirit, that impels
> All thinking things, all objects of all thought,
> And rolls through all things . . .'[1]

We most of us know this feeling. But is it well placed like the feeling that here is first-rate work, which we sometimes rightly have even before we have fully grasped the picture we are looking at or the book we are reading? Or is it misplaced like the feeling in a house that has long been empty that someone secretly lives there still. Wordsworth's feeling *is* the feeling that the world is haunted, that something watches in the hills and manages the stars. The child feels that the stone tripped him when he stumbled, that the bough struck him when it flew back in his face. He has to learn that the wind isn't buffeting him, that there is not a devil in it, that he was wrong, that his attitude was inappropriate. And as he learns that the wind wasn't hindering him so he also learns it wasn't helping him. But we know how, though he learns, his attitude lingers. It is plain that Wordsworth's feeling is of this family.

Belief in gods, it is true, is often very different from belief that stones are spiteful, the sun kindly. For the gods appear in human form and from the waves and control these things and by so doing reward and punish us. But varied as are the stories of the gods they have a family likeness and we have only to recall them to feel sure of the other main sources which co-operate with animism to produce them.

What are the stories of the gods? What are our feelings when we believe in God? They are feelings of awe before power, dread of the thunderbolts of Zeus, confidence in the everlasting

[1] *Tintern Abbey.*

arms, unease beneath the all-seeing eye. They are feelings of guilt and inescapable vengeance, of smothered hate and of a security we can hardly do without. We have only to remind ourselves of these feelings and the stories of the gods and goddesses and heroes in which these feelings find expression, to be reminded of how we felt as children to our parents and the big people of our childhood. Writing of a first telephone call from his grandmother, Proust says: '... it was rather that this isolation of the voice was like a symbol, a presentation, a direct consequence of another isolation, that of my grandmother, separated for the first time in my life, from myself. The orders or prohibitions which she addressed to me at every moment in the ordinary course of my life, the tedium of obedience or the fire of rebellion which neutralized the affection that I felt for her were at this moment eliminated.... "Granny!" I cried to her ... but I had beside me only that voice, a phantom, as unpalpable as that which would come to revisit me when my grandmother was dead. "Speak to me!" but then it happened that, left more solitary still, I ceased to catch the sound of her voice. My grandmother could no longer hear me ... I continued to call her, sounding the empty night, in which I felt that her appeals also must be straying. I was shaken by the same anguish which, in the distant past, I had felt once before, one day when, a little child, in a crowd, I had lost her.'

Giorgio de Chirico, writing of Courbet, says: 'The word yesterday envelops us with its yearning echo, just as, on waking, when the sense of time and the logic of things remain a while confused, the memory of a happy hour we spent the day before may sometimes linger reverberating within us. At times we think of Courbet and his work as we do of our own father's youth.'

When a man's father fails him by death or weakness how much he needs another father, one in the heavens with whom is 'no variableness nor shadow of turning'.

We understood Mr. Kenneth Graham when he wrote of the Golden Age we feel we have lived in under the Olympians. Freud says: 'The ordinary man cannot imagine this Providence in any other form but that of a greatly exalted father, for only such a one could understand the needs of the sons of men, or be softened by their prayers and be placated by the signs of their remorse. The whole thing is so patently infantile, so incongruous with reality. . . .' 'So incongruous with reality'! It cannot be denied.

But here a new aspect of the matter may strike us.[1] For the very facts which make us feel that now we can recognize systems of superhuman, sub-human, elusive, beings for what they are—the persistent projections of infantile phantasies—include facts which make these systems less fantastic. What are these facts? They are patterns in human reactions which are well described by saying that we are as if there were hidden within us powers, persons, not ourselves and stronger than ourselves. That this is so may perhaps be said to have been common knowledge yielded by ordinary observation of people,[2] but we did not know the degree in which this is so until recent study of extraordinary cases in extraordinary conditions had revealed it. I refer, of course, to the study of multiple personalities and the wider studies of psycho-analysts. Even when the results of this work are reported to us that is not the same as tracing the patterns in the details of the cases on which the results are based; and even that is not the same as taking part in the studies oneself. One thing not sufficiently realized is that some of the things shut within us are not bad but good.

Now the gods, good and evil and mixed, have always been mysterious powers outside us rather than within. But they have also been within. It is not a modern theory but an old saying that in each of us a devil sleeps. Eve said: 'The serpent beguiled me.' Helen says to Menelaus:

> '. . . And yet how strange it is!
> I ask not thee; I ask my own sad thought,
> What was there in my heart, that I forgot
> My home and land and all I loved, to fly
> With a strange man? Surely it was not I,
> But Cypris there!'[3]

[1] I owe to the late Dr. Susan Isaacs the thought of this different aspect of the matter, of this connection between the heavenly Father and 'the good father' spoken of in psycho-analysis.

[2] Consider Tolstoy and Dostoievsky—I do not mean, of course, that their observation was ordinary.

[3] Euripides: *The Trojan Women*, Gilbert Murray's Translation. Roger Hinks in *Myth and Allegory in Ancient Art* writes (p. 108): 'Personifications made their appearance very

Elijah found that God was not in the wind, nor in the thunder, but in a still small voice. The kingdom of Heaven is within us, Christ insisted, though usually about the size of a grain of mustard seed, and he prayed that we should become one with the Father in Heaven.

New knowledge made it necessary either to give up saying 'The sun is sinking' or to give the words a new meaning. In many contexts we preferred to stick to the old words and give them a new meaning which was not entirely new but, on the contrary, *practically* the same as the old. The Greeks did not speak of the dangers of repressing instincts but they did speak of the dangers of thwarting Dionysos, of neglecting Cypris for Diana, of forgetting Poseidon for Athena. We have eaten of the fruit of a garden we can't forget though we were never there, a garden we still look for though we can never find it. Maybe we look for too simple a likeness to what we dreamed. Maybe we are not as free as we fancy from the old idea that Heaven is a happy hunting ground, or a city with streets of gold. Lately Mr. Aldous Huxley has recommended our seeking not somewhere beyond the sky or late in time but a timeless state not made of the stuff of this world, which he rejects, picking it into worthless pieces. But this sounds to me still too much a looking for another place, not indeed one filled with sweets but instead so empty that some of us would rather remain in the Lamb or the Elephant, where, as we know, they stop whimpering with another bitter and so far from sneering at all things, hang pictures of winners at Kempton and stars of the 'nineties. Something good we have for each other is freed there, and in some degree and for a while the miasma of time is rolled back without obliging us to deny the present.

The artists who do most for us don't tell us only of fairylands.

early in Greek poetry.... It is out of the question to call these terrible beings "abstractions".... They are real daemons to be worshipped and propitiated.... These beings we observe correspond to states of mind. The experience of man teaches him that from time to time his composure is invaded and overturned by some power from outside, panic, intoxication, sexual desire.'

'What use to shoot off guns at unicorns?
Where one horn's hit another fierce horn grows.
These beasts are fabulous, and none were born
Of woman who could lay a fable low.'—

The Glass Tower, Nicholas Moore, p. 100.

Proust, Manet, Breughel, even Botticelli and Vermeer show us reality. And yet they give us for a moment exhilaration without anxiety, peace without boredom. And those who, like Freud, work in a different way against that which too often comes over us and forces us into deadness or despair,[1] also deserve critical, patient and courageous attention. For they, too, work to release us from human bondage into human freedom.

Many have tried to find ways of salvation. The reports they bring back are always incomplete and apt to mislead even when they are not in words but in music or paint. But they are by no means useless; and not the worst of them are those which speak of oneness with God. But in so far as we become one with Him He becomes one with us. St. John says he is in us as we love one another.

This love, I suppose, is not benevolence but something that comes of the oneness with one another of which Christ spoke.[2] Sometimes it momentarily gains strength.[3] Hate and the Devil do too. And what is oneness without otherness?

[1] Matthew Arnold: *Summer Night.*
[2] St. John xvi. 21.
[3] 'The Harvesters' in *The Golden Age*, Kenneth Graham.